The Act of Imagination

"This is a book on psychosynthesis with a difference, emphasizing the individual's lived experience and, in this sense, takes the reader on a remarkable journey. It elucidates several highly held values in psychosynthesis—that it is empirical and to be validated according to how it fits one's experience, rather than a doctrine or dogma to be swallowed. It also provides a context for psychosynthesis, the ground it stands on and a container for which to approach psychosynthesis theory. Allan is thinking outside the box with this writing, inviting the reader to contemplate how they know what is true for them and how they make sense of their life's journey. It requires us to read with a confluence of our head and our heart, providing a refreshing approach to learning. *The Act of Imagination* demonstrates a deep and profound insight into the true depths of psychosynthesis, and of the meaning of synthesis, especially in terms of presenting it as an eco-system, which I know Assagioli would have loved."

—Diana Whitmore,
author of *Psychosynthesis Counselling in Action*

"Allan Frater's *The Act of Imagination* is a contemporary, original description of psychosynthesis, with a wealth of examples and useful explanations, and a lucid view of its apparent contradictions, its secret gifts and promises. It evidently comes from an insider's knowledge of the material. Allan is not only a capable therapist but also a fine writer. I learned quite a bit from this book."

—Piero Ferrucci,
author of *The Art and Science of Psychotherapy*
and *The Power of Kindness*

"*The Act of Imagination* is an original, refreshing, and revitalizing read. Allan Frater offers us a meticulous and incisive exposition of the essential context and dynamics of psychosynthesis. Weaving together the experiential with the conceptual, the foundational process of "synthesis" is illuminated as the motive force at the heart of all psychological life. The book does well to avoid the linguistic abstraction that sometimes clouds the rigour and precision of Assagioli's conception. Indeed, it both honours and develops Assagioli's articulation of psychosynthesis, drawing upon parallels with contemporary ecological principles and systems theory. Put simply, it is the clearest exposition of psychosynthesis I have read in my 20 years of practice as a psychotherapist. A must-read for students and practitioners alike."

—Susan Holliday,
author of *Hidden Wonders of the Human Heart*

"*The Act of Imagination* is an extremely thoughtful contribution to the evolving literature of psychosynthesis. Its central argument is disarmingly simple yet philosophically ambitious: psychosynthesis is not a doctrine but an *experience* defined by synthesis — by bringing together diverse aspects of the human psyche into an organic whole. This is a book written by a practitioner who has wrestled with psychosynthesis from the inside — its brilliance, its contradictions, and its living history. A rich, intellectually honest, and forward-looking text that can deepen our understanding of Psychosynthesis while refusing to domesticate it. It will be especially valuable to practitioners who want not just to *learn* Psychosynthesis, but to *think about* it, question it, and most importantly — experience it.

—Phillip Carr-Gomm,
author of *The Gift of the Night*

"Assagioli said that psychosynthesis takes us to the doorway of the Mystery; the rest is up to us. Allan Frater charts how, as we approach the doorway, inevitably we find it shifting deeper into endless mystery. If it is acts of will that keep us moving, he suggests, it is acts of imagination that keep us oriented and inspired. This milestone in the literature will bring practitioners and newcomers alike to a profound reassessment and appreciation of the depth and vitality of psychosynthesis, and how essential the creativity of imagination is for these liminal times.

—Mark Skelding,
Chair of *The Association for the Advancement of Psychosynthesis*

"*The Act of Imagination* is a clear and profound work that invites the reader to explore psychosynthesis—not as a closed system of theories or techniques but as a living experience, an open and dynamic process, an inner adventure that is constantly renewing itself. Rather than attempting to determine what the "correct" presentation of psychosynthesis should be, Allan Frater is more immediately and realistically concerned with showing us that "placing limits upon psychosynthesis is not possible or even desirable", and with giving meaning to all the diversity and difference that characterize it. It is an approach that captures the very essence of the psychosynthetic teaching, and in this particular historical moment renews its incredible relevance. Congratulations to the author for this fine work!"

—Petra Guggisberg Nocelli,
author of *Know, Love, Transform Yourself*
and *The Way of Psychosynthesis*

The Act of Imagination

Psychosynthesis Psychotherapy in Experiential Context

Allan Frater

TransPersonal Press

TransPersonal Press
(a Kaminn Media imprint)
Clyde Offices
48 West George Street
Glasgow G2 1BP
Scotland
transpersonalpress.com

A CIP record for this title is available from the British Library.

ISBN 978-1-912698-14-1 (print)
ISBN 978-1-912698-15-8 (ebook)

Cover Illustration: "Portrait of a young woman, 1727" by Madeleine Françoise Basseporte, Rijksmuseum, Amsterdam

Edited by Nicky Leach
Text layout and cover design by Thierry Bogliolo
This book was typeset in Calluna.

Printed, bound and distributed by Ingram Spark

Contents

with gratitude to

my students and teachers

past, present, and future

"Our Game is neither philosophy nor religion;
it is a discipline of its own, in character most akin to art.
It is an art sui generis."

—Hermann Hesse

Foreword

by Molly Young Brown

Psychosynthesis has been foundational to my professional and personal life since I encountered the field in my late 20s. My husband, Jim, and I studied with Dr. Roberto Assagioli when I was 31 (in 1973). At that time he emphasized that he wanted psychosynthesis to evolve and urged me (and I suspect nearly everyone who studied with him) to carry psychosynthesis forward in whatever ways I could.

So I began teaching psychosynthesis and offering one-on-one sessions as a psychosynthesis guide. Eventually, I published two major books in the field: *Unfolding Self: The Practice of Psychosynthesis* (Allworth 2004) and *Growing Whole: Self-Realization for the Great Turning* (Psychosynthesis Press 2009)

Although, for the last 35 years, I have focused my teaching and writing on the Work That Reconnects, I never left psychosynthesis. Moreover, I have come to realize that many people working for the "Great Turning" towards a life-affirming and just world could benefit greatly from psychosynthesis (or similar psycho-spiritual modalities).

Psychosynthesis can help people attune to an inner source of clarity and strength that is so needed in today's chaotic world, as well as transform old unconscious patterns that can compromise the effectiveness in their activism. I believe that psychosynthesis can support, and even help shape, the desperately needed radical changes to our societies, economies, and political structures.

So I welcome *The Act of Imagination* as a major contribution to the evolution of psychosynthesis in today's world.

Ambiguities and Contradictions

Through all these years, I have continued to heed Assagioli's call to help psychosynthesis evolve. Along with close colleagues, I have questioned some of the ambiguities and contradictions within psychosynthesis theory and practice, and often formulated my own revisions and/or adopted other psychosynthesists' proposed adaptations.

In many cases, I've just let the contradictions slide, knowing that all human knowledge is provisional and subject to change.

So I have been thoroughly delighted that, in this book, Allan Frater directly addresses these contradictions, explaining how they occurred and making room for conflicting perspectives as the difference between an analytical-empirical approach and an experiential-synthesis approach.

He explains that Assagioli wanted to make psychosynthesis acceptable in a culture dominated at that time by analytical-empirical (I might add "reductionist") science. Nevertheless, I am certain that if he had to choose between them, Assagioli would come down solidly on the experiential-synthesis side—and Frater supports that with several quotations.

Assagioli often said and wrote that psychosynthesis (with a lower case p) is a natural process available to all humans, given adequate support and nurture. In other words, he was trying to describe and uplift common human *experience*, not trying to create a new belief system, theory, or dogma. He also urged practitioners especially to *experience* a practice themselves, so that they would know what it feels like and what effects it might have before suggesting the practice to a client.

Frater also suggests that many of the specific concepts, structures, and exercises that Assagioli proposed are meant to be metaphorical rather than ultimate pronouncements about Reality (for example, the oval diagram, the star diagram, or the Disidentification Exercise). Reading this, I realize that I have often approached and used most of Assagioli's teachings in just this way—trying them on for size, as it were, seeing what effect they have on my behaviour and consciousness, and asking myself if they really work for me. If they do, great! If they don't, forget about it!

Systems Thinking and Psychosynthesis

When I began to study systems thinking in the 1990s, I recognized that psychosynthesis is a systems psychology, and I even wrote a paper on that theme! So I am excited that Frater explicitly shows how Assagioli was a systems thinker, way before "systems thinking" was widely known.

Indeed, I could say that Assagioli was an early ecological thinker. I acknowledge that most Indigenous cultures and many Eastern religious traditions (which Assagioli studied) were originally based in a deep ecological understanding of living systems, long before Western scientists and thinkers developed systems thinking or systems theory, or even the field of ecology.

Frater illustrates how growth and change through psychosynthesis occur in the same way that all living systems function in interaction with the larger ecosystems of which they are a part. So, rather than trying to direct a client's process or imposing preconceived outcomes, Frater urges psychosynthesis practitioners to *facilitate, support, and trust* their client's ongoing process as a living system. He not only urges this but also gives very practical guidance on how to do it.

Frater describes how synthesis is actually how healthy systems function (providing me with another "aha!"). Synthesis is the goal of psychosynthesis, of course. But true to essential systems thinking, synthesis is understood as dynamic, ecological, and ever changing in response to an ever changing world. We never arrive at a final state of being.

Imagination in Psychosynthesis

Anyone who has studied psychosynthesis knows about the importance of imagination; specifically as one of six personality functions illustrated in the "star diagram". And many psychosynthesis practitioners use a lot of "guided imagery" and "inner dialogue" in their work with individuals and groups.

Frater goes beyond this, however, explaining just how critical and basic imagination is to psychosynthesis guiding/counseling/

coaching/therapy. Psychosynthesis can help us become aware of imagination's role in our everyday lives, in the stories we unconsciously live out in our lives, in the images and interpretations we project onto others and the larger world, in who we think we are.

As we become aware of how imagination shapes our thoughts, feelings, and behaviour, we can discover how to work with the transformative possibilities of this imagining in order to create healthier and more empowered stories for ourselves and our world. Frater guides the reader through how that works, especially in therapy, with case studies from his own practice.

Although Frater focuses primarily on one-to-one psychosynthesis therapy and counseling, I see implications far beyond the therapist's office. Like Assagioli, I have believed from the start that psychosynthesis can and should be shared in a variety of educational settings in order to give people tools and perspectives they can apply to their own lives.

I look forward to exploring how understanding "the act of imagination" can help us all live more fulfilling and creative lives and together transform our societies, economies, and political structures to serve and sustain all of life, human and more-than-human, on this pearl of a planet.

Molly Brown
Mount Shasta, California
9 December 2025

Prologue

This Is Not the Truth

I assumed the teacher was joking when she wrote THIS IS NOT THE TRUTH across the top of the whiteboard.

"The following seminar," she went on to explain, "will not be the truth."

This was just too weird to get my head around.

It was the first day of my training to be a psychosynthesis psychotherapist. I'd arrived full of enthusiasm, expecting to have all the best, most efficacious theories and therapeutic methods spelt out clearly and precisely. To be told how things were; to be told the truth.

But as the training went on, whenever I grabbed hold of one truth it was quickly eclipsed by another—both coming under the heading of psychosynthesis, and also not.

The importance of finding something called an "observer position" was emphasized by some teachers and critiqued as dangerously alienating by others; for some, we were "not our feelings", while others suggested we were "more than our feelings". Some teachers offered "harmony" and "unity" as desirable goals, but this seemed to clash with the acceptance of tensions and differences favoured by others.

I wanted to know what made psychosynthesis particular. It was all well and good learning about a broad swathe of teachings and techniques, but as time went by, a clear outline of something that could reasonably be called psychosynthesis seemed ever harder to recognize.

Why were all these seemingly well-meaning teachers being so deliberately eclectic? Was this mystical NOT THE TRUTH stuff really necessary? Couldn't they just agree among themselves on the best version of psychosynthesis and then give me a coherent training?

My wish for a more easily understood psychosynthesis might have been granted in an alternative history. In my imagined scenario, Roberto Assagioli (1888–1974), founder of psychosynthesis, would have taught his psychology to a small cohort of students in an isolated Italian town tucked away at the end of a dusty mountain path and then those same students would have faithfully passed on the teachings intact to successive generations—all of whom continued to live cut off from the rest of the world. Within such a hermetic society it might have been possible to write up a distinct set of teachings and practices, a book that we could hold up and say, "This is psychosynthesis."

But of course, this is just a silly fantasy. Psychosynthesis has long since stepped down into the world.

Assagioli was no hermit. He travelled widely, speaking at conferences, giving interviews, and meeting and corresponding with many of the leading intellectuals of his day. His was a lifetime of discussion and reflection that he poured into published works across many decades; a written legacy that, far from offering a simplistic and standardized presentation, is, in fact, a complex body of work, with many subtle tensions and beguiling inconsistencies. But we need not stop there.

There is no orthodoxy in psychosynthesis.[1] Assagioli never saw his teaching as the final word on psychosynthesis and encouraged others to build upon the beginnings he had made.[2,3]

In training schools around the world, the next generation of teachers and writers has now shaped psychosynthesis into a multitude of presentations, some more similar than others, but nevertheless, with significant differences emerging between them.

These teachers and writers are moving psychosynthesis ever further away from an easily recognizable and distinct set of teachings and practices. And yet, despite their differences, there is a commonality in all these presentations, something that determines what is and is not psychosynthesis that can be traced back to the original presentation by Assagioli.

The problem is that establishing what constitutes this original presentation is not entirely straightforward. While there are many brilliant teachers and writers who studied directly with Assagioli and can tell us all about his psychosynthesis, their teaching will not be exactly the same as the primary source but an interpretation of the original.

In the same way that a contemporary performance of *Romeo and Juliet*, even if we try to make it "authentic", will be seen very differently to how it was received in Shakespeare's time, so too how we read, understand, and practise the original teachings of psychosynthesis will be different from how they were originally conceived and communicated in Assagioli's time.

Psychosynthesis today happens in a very different world to the one in which Assagioli first presented it.[4] Post-Assagioli teachers and writers will have inevitably drawn upon personal, cultural, and intellectual influences unavailable to Assagioli, all of which will have shaped how the wealth of material produced across Assagioli's lifetime is presented, with some aspects being emphasized and elaborated upon, while other aspects are critiqued, downplayed, or quietly ignored.

In this way, the practice of psychosynthesis moves on, incorporating new developments. This means that, rather than trying to figure out which is the correct presentation, a perhaps more immediate or realistic concern is how to make sense of all this diversity and difference.

A first quotation from Assagioli shares his thinking on this matter:

> Since each can only be a partial expression of what we call "psychosynthesis", it is well to gain experience of psychosynthesis through the methods and personalities of various psychosynthesists.[5]

Assagioli acknowledges in this statement how each book, article, essay, video, or training seminar on psychosynthesis will only ever be "a partial expression". Each source will provide a more or less different emphasis or perspective on what we call "psychosynthesis", but no singular account will express the whole truth. Assagioli therefore recommends gaining experience from "various psychosynthesists", attending to a multiplicity of sources, as if gathering the pieces of a jigsaw in order to establish as full a picture as possible; hence, the eclecticism in my psychotherapy training.

The protean multiplicity of teaching perspectives was entirely intentional, as was the reluctance to pin down psychosynthesis to any one system or framework. On offer was a smorgasbord of partial expressions, from which students were encouraged to critically allow their own understanding of psychosynthesis to evolve—and then become yet another partial expression.

As a beginning student, I found this seemingly limitless openness somewhat overwhelming. I felt confused as to what, if anything, was holding it all together. I did not understand where to begin.

My problem lay in assuming psychosynthesis is something it is not: a set of ideas and techniques written down on whiteboards and found in books. But this is not really what it is. What we call psychosynthesis, writes Assagioli, "should not be looked upon as a particular psychological doctrine, nor as a single technical procedure".[6]

And yet, to conclude from this that it has no coherence would be to go too far.

Psychosynthesis does have a recognizable shape and expression, which this book now sets out to explore. Psychosynthesis counsellors, coaches, and psychotherapists will most obviously find this of interest. However, what follows has also been written with the general interest reader in mind and requires no prior knowledge of psychosynthesis. It is both an introduction and a new presentation of psychosynthesis, one that emphasizes its creative and imaginative aspects in experiential context.

Introduction

What Is Psychosynthesis?

Before describing what psychosynthesis is, it is important to first make clear what it is not.

Psychosynthesis is not the theoretical frameworks used to think about it. In the same way that a book about oil painting—filled with ideas on composition, brushstroke technique, and colour theory—is clearly not to be confused with the actual experience of painting a picture on a canvas, so too theories about psychosynthesis are not the actual experience of psychosynthesis. This is a distinction that Assagioli pointed towards when he wrote, "Experience is one thing, doctrine another."[7]

Of course, this is not to suggest that the theories are false or wrong. The literature on psychosynthesis is a rich source of practically useful psychological knowledge, revealing patterns of meaning that would otherwise remain hidden, such as when one uses a map to navigate unfamiliar terrain. If we are lost in a psychological storm, buffeted by the winds of anxiety and depression, such theoretical maps can be incredibly helpful; however, as the saying goes, "The map is not the territory."[8]

There is always a radical gap between theory and lived experience. Books contain ideas and examples, but actual attempts to put them into experiential practice will always bring up lots of questions not answered by the text.

No matter how effective or beneficial the theory, it will never completely mirror the complexity of lived experience; therefore, instead of getting caught up in searching for psychosynthesis in the literature, appreciating this experiential gap allows us to turn our attention towards what it is really about. This is why the first teaching on my psychosynthesis training was THIS IS NOT THE TRUTH.

When the teacher wrote this phrase across the top of the whiteboard, she was effectively saying, "What follows in this seminar is a collection of ideas about the truth, but don't mistake them for that truth." The theoretical presentation was intended heuristically; that is, something to help us notice and engage the experiential wellspring of psychosynthesis but not itself to be mistaken for it.

This is indicated by another aphorism from psychosynthesis training:

> When we take the principles and methods of psychosynthesis as "working hypotheses", life is an adventure. But if we take the principles and methods as "the truth", life becomes a tragedy.[9]

As a "working hypothesis", psychosynthesis theory requires additional research—in the sense of trying it out in practice to see if the teachings and techniques do indeed describe and shape experience as promised.

Certainly, for me, as a trainee therapist, the working hypothesis more than delivered on its promises. It gave me a language that seemed to have an almost magical explanatory power, bringing previously vague and overlooked feelings and thoughts into sharp and enlivening focus; such that, instead of muddling along on autopilot, there were moments when I responded more creatively to difficult people and situations.

It was not that my problems all suddenly went away, but there were glimpses of new possibility creeping into my life, as if someone had opened a gate to a beautiful garden and said, "This is all for you. Go explore."

This begs the question: How can such an adventure turn to tragedy?

Tragedy ensues when we mistake effectiveness for truth, and despite occasional reminders of THIS IS NOT THE TRUTH, much of the training and literature on psychosynthesis fails to distinguish between ideas about the psyche and psychological life itself. Bold assertions such as "The lower unconscious is where . . ." and "Childhood wounding is the source of . . ." can seem to imply at least a degree of certitude.

For example, rather than being understood as just a helpful way of thinking about experience, the idea of "the unconscious" becomes mistaken for a personal psychological interiority, and instead of being appreciated as just one of many possible ways of thinking about the causes of psychological suffering, the idea of "childhood wounding" becomes the only explanation.

In this way, the gap between theory and experience collapses and psychosynthesis becomes a tragedy by quickly explaining away experiences.

To maintain psychosynthesis as an adventure, this book will be presenting a "principial" perspective. The word "principial", meaning "related to or based on principles", is an adjective that connects well to the above aphorism, where "life is an adventure" when we approach "the principles . . . of psychosynthesis as 'working hypotheses'". Assagioli explicitly made this same point when he wrote, "What is important are the principles and the basic purpose of the entire endeavour."[10]

A shared principial basis will be shown to be what connects the diversity of teachings and techniques on psychosynthesis, and also what makes them recognizable as something called 'psychosynthesis', like the taste of salt running through all the oceans and seas. It is therefore important to begin by clarifying these principles.

The first principle has already been established.

> [Psychosynthesis] is proven by its direct experience; it is one of those primary experiences which are the evidences of themselves. Just as colour, a sense of beauty . . . need no explanation.[11]

The first guiding principle of psychosynthesis is *experience*. Just as eating, sleeping, and walking are naturally occurring experiences, so too is psychosynthesis. It is therefore not so much explained or taught or proven by ideas or theories as discovered by an experiential engagement.

It is an engagement that can be seen across all psychosynthesis teachings and techniques—the various theoretical "partial expressions" involving many different ways to notice and think about the experience of psychosynthesis, and the numerous techniques and applications involving many different ways to actively participate and engage with this same experiential ground.

However, this first principle alone is not sufficient, as it does not tell us what type of experience is particular to psychosynthesis, so we now turn to a description of a related twin principle.

Synthesis not Analysis

The second guiding principle of psychosynthesis begins with its name, which can be traced to the title of Assagioli's doctoral thesis *"La Psicosintesi" (Psychosynthesis)*, submitted to the University of Florence in 1910.

While Assagioli was not the first to use the term "psychosynthesis", he was the first to base a whole psychology around a comprehensive application of it.[12,13] At least in part, this application can be seen to have emerged as a result of his involvement in the psychoanalytic group that formed around Freud during the early 1900s.

Assagioli did not reject this early influence upon his thinking but in writing his doctoral thesis took the opportunity to critique what he considered "to be some of the limitations of Freud's views".[14] Within this context, the inclusion of the word "synthesis" offers a significant clue as to the second guiding principle of psychosynthesis, because synthesis is the opposite of analysis.

Freud conceived of analysis as a method to rationally explain the psychological life of his patients. His insight was that it is easier to understand the complexity of a whole life by analyzing its parts (analysis meaning "the separation of a whole into its component parts").

Breaking down psychological difficulties and relationships into constituent parts—feelings, thoughts, obsessional behaviours, traumatic memories, and so on—can certainly be a helpful way of making experiences comprehensible.

And yet, there are downsides to an analytical treatment of psychological life. So before considering the advantages Assagioli saw in synthesis, it will be important to first understand the limitations—not of the rich field of psychoanalysis as a whole, but more specifically the idea and method of analysis, per se.

Let's explore this idea by using the analogy of a lion in a zoo.

To study a lion in a zoo is not the same as studying a lion in the savannah. A dusty and bored lion viewed through the bars of a cage in a western zoo is not a sleek and alert lion wandering free beneath the African sun. Of course, the animal in the cage is technically the same as the savannah lion, but only in a narrow physical sense, as an object. Without the network of relations needed to support its full expression—the environment, the lion community, the prey it hunts, and so on—what lies in the corner of the cage is a mere shadow of the lion in its natural context.

The savannah lion is not just surrounded by this network of relations but is actually created and sustained by them. Broadly speaking, the savannah lion effectively is this web of relations, such that, on transportation to the zoo, separated from the other relationships or parts that make up the whole, the savannah lion no longer really exists.

As with lions separated from the savannah, this is also the case with aspects of psychological life separated from experiential context. The limitation of analysis on psychological life is therefore a radical simplification of complex experience.

Consider my own feelings of anxiety, for example. Analysis takes my anxious life—a complex amalgam of confused thoughts, sleeplessness, a sickness in my gut, and endless doom scrolling on my phone—and turns it into a psychological "part". In this way, my being an anxious whole person has been changed by analysis into only part of me being anxious.

It is a subtle but significant shift in emphasis, turning the complexity of my overall anxious experience into the simplicity of an inner psychological object; such that, I can now think about my anxiety from a safe distance, like peering at a lion through the bars of a cage. In the short term, this can give a welcome sense of perspective, as now what matters is not so much that I'm anxious but how I think about this anxiety.

This might appear to be a good thing, right? Well, yes and no.

The problem comes when attempts to change one part happens without any consideration of the network of relationships that constitute my anxiety. This is a familiar scenario to any psychotherapist, as clients often begin therapy wanting to change a particular behaviour or symptom, as if it is somehow completely separate from the rest of their lives.

Of course, it is reasonable to want therapeutic help with anxiety, and if a therapist then analyzes my anxiety as part of me, this can also reasonably lead to the assumption that changing this anxious part will be what helps.

However, this anxious part does not exist in isolation, like a lion in the zoo; rather, it is created and sustained by an intricate web of relationships, not just within me but also with other people and the surrounding world.

So if the therapy continues to ignore the perpetuation of my anxiety within this wider experiential context, then at best only superficial change will be possible, and at worst, what might have been a perfectly appropriate anxious response to a difficult real-world situation (economic insecurity, political instability, ecological collapse) is signposted as a personal psychological failure, resulting in an internalized shame that drains the vitality and spontaneity out of my life.

Analysis is a way of thinking about the human psyche as if it were a machine that can be broken down into component parts and simply repaired. However, the rather obvious but much overlooked limitation of this metaphor is that human beings are not machines. Psychological life can be analyzed as if it is a machine with parts, but we need to remember that it is not actually a mechanism with clear dividing lines between the parts.

Psychological parts only exist as abstractions, as simplified ideas about experiences that are quite unlike the drive shafts, fan belts and spark plugs that make up machines. For example, when we pay close attention to personal experience, we do not find a clear point of separation where feeling ends and thought begins, nor where a bodily sensation becomes an intuition or a memory.

Not all theories are of equal value. While there will always be a gap between theory and lived experience, the more valuable theories will be those that close the gap by more closely aligning conceptual understanding with experiential practice.[15]

As we have seen, the idea of analysis unwittingly alters what it seeks to explain by assuming it to be a simplistic mechanism of discrete parts. But this does not help us notice and engage with the experiential complexity of psychological life, where everything is connected to everything else with no clear separation between the parts. What is needed then is a better idea that does.

Assagioli chose to employ the word "synthesis" precisely because it describes the relational complexity of psychological life. Instead of dividing up the whole into its parts, synthesis is the process and outcome of bringing the parts together, having a two-fold dictionary definition as both "the process of combining objects or ideas into a complex whole" and "the combination or whole produced by such a process".[16] The choice of the term "psychosynthesis" underscores the importance Assagioli attributed to an experiential appreciation of psychological life, not as a machine but as an ecosystem, in what he calls a "bio-synthesis":

> Psychosynthesis is essentially . . . a bringing together in an organic whole, diverse and sometimes conflicting elements, but in an organic whole in which each element preserves its own individuality and function in operation with all the others, and the faithful human body is the perfect example of bio-synthesis; that is, each cell, each organ, each apparatus concurs to the general health, the vitality of the whole organism, but each completes its own function more or less independently, up to a certain point, but in unison, by that I mean organic unity.[17]

Just as a body is made up of a network of cells and organs, psychosynthesis combines diverse psychological elements into an "organic whole". In the view of psychosynthesis, psychological suffering is not due to a faulty part, as analysis would have it, but to restricted synthesis and the resulting isolation or identification of psychological life with only a part of the whole, in the same way that a blocked artery causes a heart attack or an unwatered houseplant withers and dies.

Psychosynthesis seeks to improve the relationships among all the various parts of the psyche, facilitating what Assagioli suggested to be a natural evolutionary tendency towards increasingly complex levels of synthesis.

During the early 20th century, a time when mechanistic analysis dominated psychology, the development of psychosynthesis involved a prescient vision, one that anticipated a now almost taken-for-granted contemporary recognition of a synthetic perspective across multiple disciplines. This involves a perspective where the health of any one part—whether an individual human or a humpback whale, a rainforest, or a nation state—feeds back and affects the health of the system as a whole; a world view no longer dominated by separation but learning to appreciate a holistic understanding.

A Psychology of Wholeness

With the recognition of synthesis as a second guiding principle, a beginning description of psychosynthesis could then be a "psychology of wholeness that synthesizes all the parts".

The teachings of psychosynthesis are those ideas and concepts that help us better notice and think about the process of synthesis in psychological life, and the techniques are ways to cooperate experientially with this in clinical practice. The outcome, or aim, of this process is the healing of the suffering created by a fragmented part-life cut off from the wider possibilities of the psyche as a whole.

In other words: The psychosynthesis method is one of facilitating the process of synthesis, and its goal is the outcome of this synthesis process, an understanding that can be seen in the following brief descriptions:

> In its most basic sense, psychosynthesis is a name for the conscious attempt to cooperate with the natural process

> of growth—the tendency in each of us and in our world to harmonize and synthesize various aspects at ever higher levels of organization.[18]
>
> Psychosynthesis . . . can be indicated above all as an attitude and a slow conquest towards integration and synthesis in every field . . . . It could be called a movement, a trend, a destination.[19]

Psychosynthesis is not static; it is "a movement, a trend" cooperating with a "natural process of growth" by "bringing together in an organic whole" the various aspects of psychological life at "ever higher levels of organization"; in other words, a process and outcome of synthesis evident on many levels.

Synthesis is most obviously seen in the way introductory texts distinguish psychosynthesis by emphasizing its holistic inclusion of the full spectrum of human experience, bringing together psychological symptoms, such as depression and anxiety, with aesthetic, spiritual, and heightened non-ordinary states of consciousness.

Synthesis is also evident in the way that all psychological functions—feeling, thinking, sensation, imagination, intuition—are considered equally and together as a synthesis, with no single function being prioritized in isolation over any other.

Furthermore, synthesis is not only applied on the level of the individual personality but also within relationships as an "interindividual" synthesis and throughout culture, society, and ecology as a "cosmic synthesis".[20]

The particular method of any given psychosynthesis therapy session will also itself be a synthesis of theories, techniques, and influences incorporating a variety of approaches from within psychosynthesis itself, alongside contributions from other psychological orientations, including psychoanalysis, cognitive-behavioural, existential-humanistic, and many others.

However, as we have already seen, this eclecticism can make it difficult to appreciate what is distinctive about psychosynthesis.[21] Assagioli acknowledged this in an interview towards the end of his life:

> The limit of psychosynthesis is that it has no limits. It is too extensive, too comprehensive. Its weakness is that it accepts too much. It sees too many sides at the same time, and that is a drawback.[22]

Since this interview, attempts have been made to resolve this "weakness" and "drawback", which I will be discussing in the next three chapters.

One influential contribution suggests an overarching framework of "core concepts" that determine what constitutes a genuine psychosynthesis, which I will discuss in chapter 1.

Other contributions have tended to emphasize psychosynthesis as a particular set of techniques or methods, which I will discuss in chapter 2.

Other theorists have done the historical detective work of tracing the roots of psychosynthesis to the original influences Assagioli drew upon in the formation of his psychology. They use this as a basis for determining what to accept as psychosynthesis, which I will discuss in chapter 3.

While these attempts to provide a limiting framework to psychosynthesis bring a wealth of interesting and useful discussion, this book will show that placing limits upon psychosynthesis is not possible or even desirable. As we have seen, the identification of psychosynthesis with discrete concepts, techniques, and influences is to mistake it for a particular *theoretical* formulation, and therefore in danger of simplifying, if not obscuring, the *experiential* process of psychosynthesis.

By adding further presentations to the too many sides that cause the lack of limits in the first place, such frameworks only exacerbate the apparent weakness they seek to resolve. This might seem to be a somewhat circular argument, akin to a snake eating its own tail, as if there is no escape from the ineluctable slipperiness of psychosynthesis; however, if not an escape, certainly a more interesting possibility emerges when we approach the openness of "no limits"—not as a problem to be solved but rather, as the whole point of psychosynthesis.

If the point of psychosynthesis is to gather in synthesis ever more elements in the creation of an ever greater whole, this will include not just personal-experiential elements, such as feelings and thoughts, but also theoretical paradigms and ideas, as well as methodological approaches and techniques.

With ongoing research and experimentation, there will always be a growing number of elements to include, as we can see from Assagioli writing: "Psychosynthesis is an open system: There is no end to it but only temporary halting places."[23,24] "An open system" is one with porous boundaries; therefore, psychosynthesis will always be incorporating further elements, in a journey of adventure with only "temporary halting places".

If we stop travelling and imagine that we have finally arrived at the truth of psychosynthesis, this is when we are perhaps farthest from understanding. As Assagioli puts it, "Belief in having understood all indicates lack of understanding. It is a question of a gradual process."[25] But there is no final, definitive, limited presentation of psychosynthesis to be found.

The openness and lack of limits in psychosynthesis is only a weakness or drawback if we are expecting or assuming it to arrive at a destination called "the truth", a point of arrival where it finally stops continually shape shifting in understanding, practice, and expression.

Once we get past this assumption and come to appreciate psychosynthesis as being in a constant state of becoming, as a journey that never ends, then the idea of "no limits" is transformed from a weakness into a defining strength. However, this is not to suggest that all presentations are equally valid and nothing can be done to further clarify the distinctiveness of psychosynthesis.

Synthesis Turned Back on Psychosynthesis

By now it should be clear that the intention of this book is not to offer a definitive or "correct" theoretical presentation of psychosynthesis. My argument is that this possibility has never existed, and never will.

Even so, every book offers a perspective, and it would be disingenuous to claim otherwise here. In what follows, the perspective will be principial; that is, as noted earlier, derived from first principles.

Thus, instead of analyzing the various teachings, techniques, and influences as discrete ideas and methods, I will contextualize them with respect to each other, and seek the whole in the sum of the parts by turning the twin principles of "experiential synthesis" back upon psychosynthesis itself.

An account of psychosynthesis as an experiential synthesis is a novel approach, with no direct mention in the literature, but I will show it to exist as an implicit modus operandi; that is, an assumed culture that will become obvious when we examine the relationships among theoretical ideas, techniques, and influences and how they are applied experientially in relationships between teachers and students and therapists and clients.

In describing this network of relationships, I will reveal the distinctive pattern of psychosynthesis as a whole rather than focusing on the parts in isolation.

The following pages offer fresh explanations and appreciative critiques of the teachings of Assagioli. The simple preservation of concepts and methods from the past misses what makes psychosynthesis an adventure.[26] Indeed, to approach each client in the same way, with a procedural application of predetermined techniques, regardless of the unique factors at play in any given therapeutic moment, is to fail to understand that psychosynthesis psychotherapy is a creative process.

My hope is to offer a book-length reflective space and conversation that provides the space to gently question, wonder, and re-vision the richness of psychosynthesis.

Chapters 1, 2, and 3 are full of ideas, stories, clinical examples, and practical techniques that address Assagioli's psychosynthesis in its experiential context. Chapter 4 offers a new partial expression of psychosynthesis as an "act of imagination" that, though differing in style, maintains the principial spirit of the original presentation by Assagioli.

Note: In order to provide a recognizable basis for critical discussion, as well as a comprehensive introduction to the topic, this book focuses on the original English-language presentation of psychosynthesis by Assagioli. Post-Assagioli literature is considered, but these secondary sources are mostly referenced in the book's extensive end notes so as not to distract from the primary-source discussion.

Chapter 1

Teachings

Early in my psychosynthesis teaching career, I remember joking with students that despite presenting seemingly disparate topics, each of my seminars was more or less teaching the same thing, just from a slightly different viewpoint or emphasis.

For a long time, that's all it was—a joke. I did not at first recognize the importance of this interconnectedness, not least because I assumed it was my job to help students clearly distinguish the teachings, rather than cause unnecessary confusion by blurring the lines among them.

Of course, the links between teachings were mentioned. It was impossible not to do so. But I made sure to focus upon the parts in relationship, not the relationships themselves. I downplayed and tried to ignore the quiet voice of intuition, whispering in my ear: *It's all connected. A synthesis! Don't you see?*

This intuition is what this chapter now describes by turning the twin principles of experiential-synthesis back upon the teachings of psychosynthesis as a connected whole.

THE CORE CONCEPTS

Shortly before his death, Assagioli dictated a short paper called "Training" focusing on 12 points he considered essential for any training in psychosynthesis.[27]

This paper showcases a mature Assagioli looking back upon a lifelong practice of psychosynthesis; therefore, it is a useful place to begin searching for an experiential synthesis of his teachings—a usefulness evident in it being used as the basis for the most significant post-Assagioli attempt to establish a fundamental structure for psychosynthesis in what is called the "core concepts" framework.

Initially conceived by Firman and Gila,[28] there is also a version by Kenneth Sørensen.[29] Both focus upon the second of Assagioli's 12 points, in which his main teachings are listed:

1. Disidentification
2. The personal self
3. The will: good, strong, skilful
4. The ideal model
5. Synthesis
6. The superconscious
7. The transpersonal Self

The description of this list by Assagioli as "the sine qua non of psychosynthetic training" is the rationale given by Firman and Gila for proposing the core concepts framework as unequivocally the essence of psychosynthesis.[30]

As you can imagine, when I read this, it was a great relief to me. Finally, published writers were grappling with the questions that had troubled me throughout my training: What makes for a coherent psychosynthesis, and how do we recognize it? And they are not just being mysterious and saying what psychosynthesis is not, but providing an answer as to what it is; that is, any psychosynthesis presentation or practice may be recognized as bona-fide, depending on how well it relates to the seven core concepts. If all the core concepts are evident, at least to some extent, then it is psychosynthesis; if any are absent, it's probably not.[31,32]

Problem solved, then. Well, not quite.

While there is much value in the core concepts framework, with regard to clarifying Assagioli's main teachings, it nevertheless falls short of delivering a principial understanding of psychosynthesis teachings as a whole.

This is because the basis of the framework lies in a narrow interpretation of just one of the 12 points within the "Training" paper, resulting in an oversimplification. Moreover, Assagioli does not use the term "core concept", and instead of referring to the above-listed teachings as "concepts", "theories", or "ideas" calls them "experiences".[33]

CONCEPTS AND EXPERIENCES

While the core concepts framework provides a theoretical coherency on the page, it can be difficult to detect experientially in practice. Eavesdropping on a psychosynthesis therapist at work, one might never hear any of the seven core concepts mentioned. A whole session might pass by without any direct reference to "disidentification" or "the personal self".

To take this absence as evidence that psychosynthesis is not being practised would be to go too far, however, as even if they are not being mentioned this does not mean core concepts are not being applied.

A large part of a therapist's work takes place in a private incommunicado of non-verbalized reflection. While some therapists will decide to share some of this reflection with the client, perhaps mentioning core concept terminology, such as "the will" or "the ideal model", others will keep these concepts to themselves, using them to better understand and decide how to help the client but choosing to translate their meaning and purpose into simple everyday language.

This begs the question: If psychosynthesis therapy cannot be noticed by its usage of language, how do we decide, according to the core concepts framework, whether or not therapy is recognizably psychosynthesis?

One could perhaps interview therapists and simply ask them what theoretical position they are adopting and then judge whether this aligns with the core concepts framework. But this would again be to go too far, because therapeutic practice is not entirely informed by conscious intentions. Just as therapists may not use conceptual terminology with clients, they may not even share these concepts with themselves.

Conscious reflection is not the totality of what guides psychotherapists. Alongside explicit strategizing will also be an implicit process rooted in spontaneous sensory, emotional, and imaginal intuitions guiding the therapist from the edges of awareness.

Perhaps especially for seasoned psychosynthesis therapists who have internalized the teachings over many years, this process will be informed by core concepts. But whether this is the case is unlikely to surface during an interview, since it is operating outside of the awareness of the therapist as an implicit modus operandi.

Even if it were possible to make this implicit process explicit and the presence of the core concepts confirmed, a further question emerges: How do we decide which understanding of the core concepts is the correct one?

While the core concepts framework does offer descriptions of each core concept, the two published versions offer somewhat contrasting views, and as mentioned in the Prologue, given that training schools and individual practitioners apply these teachings in diverse ways, the question then becomes, not just whether the core concepts are being applied but what particular understanding is being applied and on what basis do we decide which understanding is recognizably psychosynthesis?

The core concepts framework fails to consider this question, because concepts are not experiences.

The core concepts framework falls short of bridging the gap between theoretical appraisal and experiential application. As I established in the Introduction, psychosynthesis is primarily an experience that the various teachings and techniques offer ways to notice, validate, and enhance.

Theoretical conceptualizations will always be a simplification of the multilayered complexity of real-world experiences. The inevitable result of presenting psychosynthesis teachings as a list of concepts is therefore that it remains on a somewhat abstract level, separated from questions of how to recognize and apply it in practice.[34]

Assagioli's choice of the word "experience" rather than the word "concept" offers a bridge between theory and practice.[35] Experiences are not divided into conceptual categories; instead, they come to us whole, as a synthesis of thinking, feeling, and bodily sensations; memories and future imaginings; intuitions; perceptions; and actions and behaviours. Therefore, because it allows for this complexity, the term "experiences" is much more closely aligned with the entanglements of life than the simplifications of a conceptual treatment.

This is not to suggest that Assagioli intended psychosynthesis as an unquestioning embrace of inchoate experience. While experiences are not reducible to concepts, they nevertheless include thought, and the conceptual elaboration of experiential understanding is an important aspect of psychosynthesis.

By way of introduction to the list of teaching "experiences" in the "Training" paper, Assagioli writes:

> Certain fundamental facts exist, and their relative conceptual elaboration, deep experience, and understanding are central, and constitute the sine qua non of psychosynthetic training. These experiences are:
>
> 1. Disidentification
> 2. The personal self
> 3. The will: good, strong, skilful
> 4. The ideal model
> 5. Synthesis (in its various aspects)
> 6. The superconscious
> 7. The transpersonal Self[36]

Assagioli steers students of psychosynthesis away from the dangers of a one-sided abstract-conceptual approach by inviting them to cultivate a "conceptual elaboration" alongside a "deep experience and understanding" of what he calls "fundamental facts".

But if these "facts" are pointing towards something experientially recognizable, how do we recognize them? What is the experiential ground that all the various formulations of psychosynthesis are pointing towards?

Once again, the "Training" paper points the way:

> Different levels of meaning are associated with each of these experiences, none of which will ever be definite and complete. Continuance of one's training, however, will

> always reveal new and more interesting aspects, which link the experiences together. That is to say, each experience will be seen to be not isolated, but to imply others.[37]

Perhaps first encountered in books and seminars as discrete teachings, this is only a beginning understanding. The "continuance of one's training" will gradually come to reveal "new and more interesting aspects, which link the experiences together"; such that, each teaching comes to be recognized as "not isolated" but rather, containing an implication of all the others.

The guiding principle of synthesis can therefore be seen to be directing attention *away* from parts in isolation and *towards* the networking of teachings as an experiential whole.[38] In the same way that learning to drive initially involves a series of steps that results in a stilted, self-conscious driving action (engage clutch, put into gear, check mirror, and so forth), so also is the case when learning psychosynthesis. But if we want to progress towards a more fluid and joined-up understanding and application, we would do well to avoid spending too long in a step-by-step approach to teachings.

TEACHINGS IN CONTEXT

Attention to teachings in context, and how they link together across "different levels of meaning", will reveal the underlying experiential whole of psychosynthesis.

This chapter will now chart this contextualization by describing each of the seven teaching "experiences" listed in the "Training" paper in more detail, and offer these as a basis to discuss the network of relationships that link them. A simple glossary of terms, however, will not be sufficient.

While a summary definition of each "experience" in a single paragraph might offer a convenient shorthand, it would be a gross simplification and anathema to Assagioli's original presentation. Assagioli explicitly avoided definitions, writing, "I do not use the word 'define,' because all definitions are limited and limiting."[39]

Definitions are "limited and limiting" because they only offer a theoretical simplification; therefore, they are poorly equipped to address the richness of psychosynthesis in experiential context. And yet, any discussion of the meaning of psychosynthesis teachings inevitably requires some form of shared understanding and terminology, but if not definitions, how else to proceed? To better align theoretical discussion with experiential complexity, we will be following the approach proposed by Assagioli:

> As is true of any experience, it cannot be fully communicated by words, but the paths leading to it and the conditions favouring it can be indicated.[40]

Assagioli provides indications instead of limiting definitions. The meaning of his teachings is allowed to emerge from the context of a number of indicative statements, which combine simple descriptive language, illustrative metaphors, and abstract-conceptual terminology, alongside connections with other teachings.

In this way, the "paths leading" to and the "conditions favouring" the teaching "experiences" of psychosynthesis are communicated, with the active language of "paths" and "conditions" showing once again how psychosynthesis is not a static abstract theory but instead, a dynamic experiential process and practice.

Although this avoids pinning down psychosynthesis, an indication approach creates problems of its own, however. The absence of simple definitions allows for a considerable range of interpretation, and given the variety of indicative statements, it is entirely possible, by careful selection of what are really only partial descriptions, to arrive at a number of different perspectives about the same teaching "experience".

This is certainly true of the post-Assagioli literature, but even within the original presentation (which we will be discussing), there is often more than one usage applied to the same experience.

The "experience" of "synthesis", for example, is sometimes used, with the meaning attributed to it so far in this book as "a process and outcome of bringing together elements into a greater whole". It is also used with a second meaning, as a "synthesis of opposites", whereby two opposing elements, "thesis" and "antithesis", are seen to create a "synthesis".

In the first usage, the elements combined in synthesis are understood to preserve "individuality and function, in operation with all the others."[41] In the second usage, however, the two opposing elements become fused and absorbed into a "higher synthesis."[42]

In this way, synthesis as well as many other teaching "experiences" (as we will soon discover) are sometimes applied in one sense and then subsequently or even simultaneously applied in quite another sense.

Given that each perspective on a teaching will be "not the truth", this need not be a problem. Indeed, a multiplicity of meanings is perhaps what we might expect from a psychology that avoids identifying any single perspective as a settled truism. In practice, though, this multiplicity of meanings does become problematic due to seldom being acknowledged or discussed.

The elusive nature of psychosynthesis is due in large part to it mistakenly being presented as a coherent and unified meaning system. As discussed in the Introduction, there is no orthodoxy, only a variety of partial expressions, but psychosynthesis is often presented as if it were an established singular system of thought and practice, when this is far from the case.

Dating all the way back to Assagioli's original presentation, there have always been (and arguably always will be) diverse understandings and applications of psychosynthesis, resulting in a number of tensions and contradictions amongst the teachings of psychosynthesis, which is partly what makes searching for a distinctiveness on the level of these teachings alone an elusive endeavour.

What is needed is an enquiry that gets beneath the surface-level presentation of the teachings to the underlying principles that connect them, so the principial enquiry that follows will consider multiple statements from Assagioli on each of the seven "experiences".

By bringing together a number of significant statements, rather than cherry-picking one or two quotations, the discussion of the various tensions and contradictions will reveal two groups that are distinguished by the type of language they employ.

The first group of statements, which use simple descriptive language, will be shown to most clearly align with the twin principles of experiential-synthesis and a context of usage that demonstrates links among the seven "experiences". The more abstract-conceptual terminology of the second group of statements will be shown to be where psychosynthesis strays from a principial understanding and application.

The personal self

In beginning a detailed discussion of the seven teaching "experiences", it will be important to first appreciate how the psychosynthesis literature tends to have several different names for the same teaching, when just one would be sufficient and a lot less confusing.

An example of this is "the personal self" as being synonymous with "the self", "I", and "observer":

> In my opinion, the direct experience of the self ["I"], of pure self awareness . . . is a true, "phenomenological" experience, an inner reality which can be empirically verified and deliberately produced through appropriate techniques.[43]

> The "self," that is to say, the point of pure self-awareness, is often confused with the conscious personality . . . but in reality it is quite different from it. This can be ascertained by the use of careful introspection. The changing contents of our consciousness (the sensations, thoughts, feelings, etc.) are one thing, while the "I," the self, the centre of our consciousness is another.[44]

The terminology of a "centre" that is "pure" prompts the following questions: Where is my centre? How do I find it? What makes it pure? How is it purified?

These questions will be explored further when we discuss the "experience" of "disidentification"; for now, it will be helpful to simply make a note of "centre" and "pure" as abstract-conceptual terminology that Assagioli is employing to assist in thinking about the personal self.

As a starting point for an experiential understanding of the personal self, a good place to begin is with the idea of "contents of consciousness", a term that will become familiar as a result of future discussions.

Put simply, "contents" are the feelings, thoughts, sensations, fantasies, memories, and so forth that make up experience at any given moment. These changing contents are one thing, but the personal self is another. In other words, it is important not to confuse the personal self with the changing contents of our consciousness.

To say that the personal self is not these changing contents is another example of psychosynthesis saying what it is not. This makes it a tricky thing to notice and describe, because it is not any particular feeling, thought, or sensation content. It is not simply a matter of finding, for example, a particular "calm and collected" or "centred" experience, as this would be an act of separation from all other possible "contents", which would go against the guiding principle of synthesis—separation being the opposite of synthesis.

So, if the "personal self" is not any "content" of experience, what is it?

Put simply, the personal self is the experiencer rather than the experiences; that is, an awareness of awareness, rather than what we are aware of. Experiences or contents come and go. We sometimes feel anxious, other times sad or angry, but the personal self, as an awareness of being aware, or "self-awareness", is seen to continue whatever the "psychological contents and activities".[45,46]

Assagioli wrote of how this can be "ascertained" by a sustained "careful introspection" of the passing "contents" of consciousness.[47]

By observing feelings, thoughts, and sensations, we come to recognize that we are not these contents of consciousness but are, in fact, "the observer", a popular synonym for the personal self. For this reason, the personal self is sometimes presented exclusively with regard to the self-awareness, insight, and understanding of this observer position. However, this is only a partial understanding, as neither self-awareness nor observation alone constitute the personal self. Instead, Assagioli writes of:

> . . . the self, who is not only an observer but also a will-er, a directing agent of the play of the various functions and energies.[48]

The personal self includes self-awareness as well as the ability to act upon that self-awareness with the will. The synonym of "observer" should therefore not be taken to imply a merely passive and receptive experience. To the extent we only have self-awareness without the will, and vice versa, then to that extent the personal self is not experienced.

For instance, to be aware of feeling sad but unable to act upon it by expressing or modifying this sadness in some way would constitute an absence of the "I", or personal self. Only to the extent that awareness is matched by a corresponding range of actions does it fully characterize what is meant by the "personal self".

This gives us the first recognition of the seven "experiences" being linked, in that the "personal self" and "the will" are inseparable aspects of the same experience.

The will: strong, skilful, good

To indicate the "will" firstly requires distinguishing it from the commonly received usage of a forced "willpower". To the extent that will-power involves overriding or repressing experience, it will be a separating action.[49]

The twin principles of experiential-synthesis, which bring together ever more elements into a greater whole, will never be characterized by any such separation. And yet, nor will they be characterized by turning away from the will and emphasizing a merely passive awareness.

As seen above, with respect to the personal self, the experience of psychosynthesis includes both awareness and the ability to act upon that awareness with the will, but not in a forced manner. This is why Assagioli set about reclaiming the will from its popular usage:

> The will is not something hard, rigid, imperative, and excluding.[50]

> The true function of the will is not to act against the personality drives to force the accomplishment of one's purposes. The will has a directive and regulatory function; it balances and constructively utilizes all the other activities and energies of the human being without repressing any of them.[51]

The will is not something "rigid" or "excluding". It does not "act against the personality" or "force" accomplishments but rather, acts as a "directive and regulatory function".

For example, upon noticing it is time to go to bed, the will allows us to direct or guide experience towards turning off the television and getting up from the couch. With insufficient will, we may not just stay up too late watching TV but become prone to all manner of compulsive behaviours and addictions.

However, the will is not always an overt action. A choice not to act—for example, abstaining from voting in an election—is still an act of will.

As the topic of Assagioli's second book, *The Act of Will*, many further statements on the will could be given here. Still, it is noteworthy that despite the wealth of material available to him on the topic, in the "Training" paper Assagioli chooses the most straightforward experiential description of the will by focusing on its three aspects: strong, skilful, and good.

The most recognizable of these, given how close it is to the commonly received understanding, is that of "strong will":

> In the strength of will lies its power, its impetus, its energy.[52]

Any act of will requires a degree of strength, an energy and determination without which we become blown about by the will of others and/or lost in the frustrations of inaction. However, an isolated strong will is in danger of remaining a merely forced will. What stops this happening is its synthesis with the other two aspects, as becomes apparent in the description of "skilful will" as:

> . . . the ability to develop that strategy which is most effective and which entails the greatest economy of effort, rather than the strategy that is most direct and obvious.[53]

A "skilful will" works smarter not harder, allowing for a more creative action, one that considers a variety of options and refines its expression over time, rather than pushing through unreflectively and repetitively with brute strength. In this way, the dangers of forced will are ameliorated.

And yet, the ability to skilfully direct the will can also become misused when it becomes directed towards manipulation and exploitation, as for example happens when charismatic politicians and advertising agencies coerce people into acting against their best interests.

Again, this would be a divisive act of separation not synthesis. Psychosynthesis needs to include the system as a whole—both within the individual and across an "inter-individual and cosmic synthesis" between individuals, groups, and nations;[54] hence, the need for the third aspect of "good will" to highlight the ability to enact:

> "such aims as are consistent with the welfare of others and the common good of humanity".[55]

By including "the welfare of others", good will directs awareness towards those actions that best support "the common good"—not that finding such an action is necessarily obvious or straightforward; there are always tensions between competing needs and motivations, whether within individuals, between persons, or across society.

Nevertheless, the task of good will is to find a direction towards this common good. It's a task that is not one of good will alone but, as we shall soon see, also carried across all of the seven teaching "experiences".

Disidentification

The "experience" of "disidentification" is discussed throughout both of Assagioli's major works, especially with regard to the "Exercise in Dis-Identification," which we will be examining in detail.[56]

A good place to begin is by noting that disidentification is a naturally occurring life process. Assagioli writes of its inevitability in those turning points that are "implicit in human consciousness",[57] such as the midlife crisis, when a habitual way of being can no longer continue and is replaced with a new identity. While naturally occurring, such a transformation can nevertheless require therapeutic assistance, as prior to the new identity becoming fully established, "the individual feels himself or herself lost."[58,59]

This is a transitional period of helplessness described by Assagioli as:

> . . . a period of transition; a passing out of the old condition, without having firmly reached the new, an intermediate stage, in which . . . one is like a caterpillar undergoing the process of transformation into the winged butterfly. The insect must pass through the stage of the chrysalis, a condition of disintegration and helplessness.[60]

The processes and outcomes of disidentification align with this delicate work of self-transformation. And in typical fashion, this "experience" is often introduced with reference to what it is not: a state of being "identified".

Assagioli wrote that, "We are dominated by everything with which our self becomes identified",[61] such as might happen, for example, when a person who habitually feels calm feelings, thinks calm thoughts, and generally behaves in a calm manner becomes identified with being a calm person. In other words, they assume that their "calm" way of being is who they really are.

This might seem to be a reasonable conclusion (as indeed might a caterpillar reasonably presume that they are and always will be a caterpillar); however, because identification functions by excluding contents of consciousness that do not align with it, this calm person will seldom feel excited or angry. In this way, identification maintains the personal self within a restricted range of experience.

In an echo of the earlier description of recognizing the personal self by "careful introspection", disidentification simply involves directing attention towards "the world of psychological facts, of psychological events"; that is, physical sensations, feelings, and thoughts.[62] This gradually expands awareness and will beyond habitual limitations and allows for novel experiential opportunities previously excluded by identification.

When the previously calm-identified person disidentifies, they might notice the following: *If I can be calm but also angry, then I can't just be a calm person; maybe who I am isn't about being calm or angry or any other set way of being; perhaps it's something else.*

The search for "something else" then leads to a growing experience of the personal self as not just the feeling of calm, or the thinking of calm thoughts, or any particular set of experiences. The previous limited contents—feeling calm, thinking calm—will remain an option within a now expanded experiential repertoire and allow the possibility of feeling angry or excited as well as sometimes (but not always) feeling calm.

The enhanced "I", or personal self created by disidentification, is therefore additive, gathering ever more contents and engaging more experiences not less. In this way, we participate more fully within a whole "world of psychological facts, of psychological events", such that we are less dominated by and more able to influence in various degrees the flow of experiential life.

Instead of conflating "identity" with "experience" (assuming that we are what we sense/feel/think), there is now a growing distinction between the two, providing yet another link between the experiences. Assagioli writes of disidentification as a process of actively discriminating between the "personal self" or identity with the "contents of consciousness".[63]

Thus far, the basic premise of disidentification can clearly be seen to align with a principial understanding of psychosynthesis—as the process and outcome of gathering a synthesis of ever more experiential elements. However, the above-described understanding is given by Assagioli only as an introduction to the "Exercise in Dis-Identification" as a particular method to release "the personal self" from the limitations of "identification". This exercise is not really a teaching "experience" but rather, a technique; nevertheless, it has had a considerable influence upon not just how disidentification is practised but how it is understood, and will therefore now provide an important framework for further discussion.

The Exercise in Disidentification

The "Exercise in Dis-Identification" will be familiar to all psychosynthesis therapists and students. It is taught early on and frequently returned to throughout any training course.[64]

In other words, it is something of a "bread-and-butter" technique, and while various versions have been developed, the following abbreviated original version by Assagioli will be a recognizable basis for discussion.[65]

The exercise begins by finding a "comfortable and relaxed position" and then saying a series of affirmations that are repeated "slowly and thoughtfully" so as to realize them "as an experienced fact in your consciousness":[66]

> My body may find itself in different conditions of health or sickness; it may be rested or tired, but that has nothing to do with myself, my real "I". My body is my precious instrument of experience and of action in the outer world, but it is only an instrument. I treat it well . . . but it is not myself. I have a body, but I am not my body.
>
> I have emotions, but I am not my emotions. These emotions are countless, contradictory, changing, and yet I know that I always remain "I", myself . . . . Since I can observe, understand, and judge my emotions, and then increasingly dominate, direct, and utilize them, it is evident that they are not myself. I have emotions, but I am not my emotions.
>
> I have an intellect, but I am not my intellect. It is more or less developed and active; it is undisciplined but teachable . . . but it is not myself.
>
> I recognize and affirm that I am a Centre of pure self-consciousness. I am a Centre of Will, capable of mastering, directing, and using all my psychological processes and my physical body.[67]

Given the salience of the "Exercise in Dis-Identification" within psychosynthesis training, it may come as something of a surprise that it now introduces the first significant divergence from a principial understanding and practice.

The primary reason for this is the relationship between psychosynthesis theory and experience established throughout this book being actively reversed by the methodology of affirmations. By first affirming the truth of the theory in order to recognize it experientially, the tentativeness of theory as a "working hypothesis" is replaced with faith, belief, and conviction:

> Effective affirmation involves several factors: the first is faith—not simply "belief" but a living dynamic faith,

> even more, an assured conviction. If this is lacking, affirmation can yet be made on the basis of a willingness or decision to "attempt," to take risks, in a spirit of courageous adventure.[68]

While "courageous adventure" might suggest a spirit of open-ended enquiry, the method of affirmations is all about realizing an expected outcome.

Put simply, there are no surprises with affirmations. Instead of theory being applied, as discussed in the Introduction, as a rough approximation, or something to guide an unpredictable exploration of experiential life, the methodology of affirmations directs attention towards the discovery of pre-established truisms. In this way, the exercise collapses the theory/experience gap by proclaiming its particular theoretical phrasing as *a direct experiential truth*.

From a principial basis, the result can be seen to create a series of misunderstandings and misapplications of disidentification, which we will now discuss across four related "separations": outcome, control, centre, and cognitive.

Outcome Separation

A significant problem with affirmations is confirmation bias. The exercise instruction to recognize and affirm sets up the likely confirmation of indeed recognizing and affirming the indicated experience.

Given Assagioli's premise that "a Centre of pure self-consciousness" is provable by direct experience, this might not seem to be an issue; however, as a method of cultivating disidentification, the *outcome* focus of the affirmation methodology is in danger of neglecting the *process* by which this outcome is achieved.

Recollect the two-fold meaning of synthesis as a process of gathering disparate elements *and also* the outcome of this process. A psychosynthesis technique like the "Exercise in Dis-Identification" will therefore, on a principial basis, need to have both: a desired outcome or result to be created and a method or process by which to effect this outcome. However much we might want to instantaneously conjure an outcome, we cannot simply bypass the process needed to get there.

The earlier described introductory remarks given by Assagioli emphasized the *process* of disidentification.[69] The temporal language of "patiently observing" across a series of "successive disidentifications" connotes a process unfolding over a period of time. All that is indicated is an "indirect" and general direction of travel with results that will arise "naturally" and "spontaneously" as a sequence of ever fuller disidentifications. There is no mention of a particular outcome or destination.

In the "Exercise in Dis-Identification," this *process* emphasis is replaced with an *outcome* emphasis. The understanding of disidentification is now presented as a recognizable result: "a Centre of pure self-consciousness" capable of mastering, directing, and using all "psychological processes" and the "physical body".

The pros and cons of this description of disidentification will be discussed below, but for now, let's focus upon the instantaneous theory of change offered by the affirmation methodology and how by simply recognizing and affirming that we are already "a Centre of pure self-consciousness", somehow an experiential equivalent is realized.

At times, such sudden realizations can happen, but this is certainly not always the case. Even when it does occur, it is usually the result of efforts over time, as suggested by the earlier analogy to a chrysalis stage, where the strange new experiences borne from disidentifying emerge only after a period of incubation.

The "Exercise in Dis-Identification" provides no indication of any need for such time to pass by. It promises a sudden transition from identified to disidentified, an invitation to leap into the air as if a fully formed butterfly, with no need for a mushy in-between chrysalis stage.

In seeking to recognize and affirm experiences of butterfly-like freedom and mastery, the exercise is liable to direct attention away from noticing those more vulnerable, confused, and inchoate experiences that are an important aspect of the process of disidentification. To the extent these process experiences are neglected, a separation rather than a synthesis is produced—what we will be calling "outcome separation."[70]

Control Separation

A considerable amount of experience is beyond conscious control. Other people and events are seldom completely controllable; someone pulling a gun on me, for example, will not be something I have chosen. And neither will the tumultuous vulnerability that results upon a gun being pointed at my head be an experience I have chosen.

While such immediate events and experiences arrive without any effort or choice, active possibilities emerge in how we respond. Depending on the extent to which we are identified, responses will be conditioned by the momentum of past behaviours and reactive; for example, freezing with fear in response to the threatening behaviour of the gunman.

But to the extent that disidentification has resulted in an expanded awareness and will, a perspective or "gap" opens up between initial experience and response, allowing a degree of creative choice to be made. Disidentification allows me, for example, to feel into the anxious vulnerability of being threatened by the gunman so as to create the consciousness and will to first imagine possibilities of how to respond and then act upon those possibilities.

Disidentification is additive, not a concern about whether vulnerability or any other content is present. If there is any control, it will be with respect to how we direct responses towards whatever experiences arise. A principial understanding of "disidentification" is therefore not so much about *what* the contents of consciousness are, per se, but *how* we direct responses towards whatever experiences arise.

Disidentification may move away from this principial basis when it becomes mistaken for a complete control over all experience. This is an understandable mistake, given the terminology employed by Assagioli in the exercise to "dominate, direct, and utilize . . . mastering, directing, and using", and also in many other similar statements on disidentification throughout his writings, such as:

> One can then—at will, and at any moment—disidentify from any overpowering emotion, annoying thought, inappropriate role, etc., and from the vantage point of the detached observer gain a clearer understanding of the situation, its meaning, its causes, and the most effective way to deal with it.[71]

This is one of many statements by Assagioli extoling the benefits of disidentification as an idealized state of self-mastery.[72,73]

But a freedom at "any moment" to disidentify "at will" from any "overpowering emotion", while perhaps describing the *outcome of disidentification*, is clearly in danger, once again, of directing attention away from the *process of disidentification*. As the individual releases themselves from a previous identification, this will often involve a period of vulnerable uncertainty prior to the establishment of a new identity. During such times, they will experience periods of decidedly not feeling able to direct experience, let alone feel able to dominate, master, and control.

Far from including the possibly vulnerable process of disidentification, the description of the body in the exercise as an "instrument of experience" casts the personal self in the role of a technician or engineer, pulling the levers of bodily control, which Assagioli elsewhere elaborates to also include feelings and mental abilities:

> . . . the body, the feelings, and the mind are *instruments* of experience, perception, and action—instruments that are changeable and impermanent, but which can be dominated, disciplined, deliberately used by the "*I*".[original italics][74]
>
> In other words, one becomes a self who uses the body, the feeling apparatus, and the mental abilities as tools,

> as instruments, in the same way as a car is the extension of a driver.[75]

> We must realize that the mind is in reality an "instrument", an inner tool from which we must disidentify ourselves if we are to make use of it at will. While we are wholly identified with the mind, we cannot control it.[76]

These statements employ a metaphorical usage of "instrument" to allow the somewhat intangible experience of disidentification to be imagined in terms of something familiar and every day. In the same way an instrument can be controlled and used as a tool to effect change, so too with disidentification.

But metaphorical usage needs to be appreciated as only a comparison, not an equivalence. While the metaphor of an instrument or tool does reveal something of the outcomes of disidentification, it also conceals something of the process of disidentification. In other words, the truth of mastery and control is, once again, "not the whole truth".

Disidentification is much more complex and mysterious than a mechanical process capable of being turned on and off at will. If taken literally, a metaphorical framing of disidentification as "control" over the "instrument" of experience is in danger of not just implying but creating an experiential *separation* rather than *synthesis*.

This is what we call "control separation", which structures a relationship of controller and controlled whereby the personal self is now somehow on the outside, separated from the fray of experiential process;[77] the result of which can be the distortion of disidentification into a power-based manipulation of self, others, and events.[78]

A principial understanding of disidentification requires a relationship of synthesis not separation. As we have seen, disidentification is the result of directing attention towards "the world of psychological facts, of psychological events", which requires an intimate and up-close engagement with feelings, thoughts, and sensations.

The direction of attention is therefore a relational participation, which, with increasing awareness and will, will be ever more able to guide and direct experiences beyond the limitations of habitual responses.

This is indeed the qualification Assagioli gives in his own usage of "control", writing:

> Control does not mean repression or suppression . . . . Right control, however, means the regulation of expression, aiming at a guided, constructive utilization of the biological and psychological energies. Thus, in practice, wise control is often quite the opposite of repression and suppression. The same can be said of inhibition. Here again, the antagonism aroused by this word is due to a misunderstanding of its real meaning and function. Inhibition is not suppression; it is a temporary check of reflex actions.[79]

The "control" of disidentification allows experiences to be "guided", allowing for "regulation of expression" rather than "repression or suppression".

This is very similar to the earlier description of the will and provides yet another link between the seven teaching "experiences", as quite clearly, the language of "control" and "domination" is in danger of mistakenly suggesting "disidentification" as the brute force and "power over" that Assagioli is at pains to distinguish from his understanding of the will when he writes: "The true function of the will is not . . . to *force* the accomplishment of one's purposes" but instead, to be a "directive" function.[80]

Given that the outcome of disidentification creates an expanded range of awareness and will, it makes sense that both these "experiences" coincide on a principial level, as neither a total "control-over" experience or a simplistic going-with-the-flow spontaneity but rather, the ability to guide and regulate experience.

Centre Separation

At the heart of disidentification is a mysterious paradox: As we become ever more disidentified, we simultaneously become ever more identified.

According to Assagioli the outcome of disidentification is "self-identification", which is why the "Exercise in Dis-Identification" is also known as the "Self-Identification Exercise".[81]

The two names describe different ends of the same process, whereby, as we disidentify from the various "contents of consciousness", what remains is the discovery of "self-identification":

> What remains after discarding from my self-identity the physical, emotional, and mental contents of my personality, my ego? It is the essence of myself—a centre of pure self-consciousness and self-realization. It is the permanent factor in the ever-varying flow of my personal life. It is that which gives me the sense of being, of permanence, of inner security.[82]

> The self is there all the time, what is lacking is a direct awareness of its presence.[83]

> The "I" is simple, unchanging, constant.[84]

The contents of consciousness are changeable and passing but the personal self or self that experiences them is seen to *already exist* as a constant and unchanging "essence," or "centre".[85] Through the removal of successive identifications, we come to recognize "the experience of "I", the deep sense of *self-identification*, of knowing who we are".[86] This "self-identification", or who we really are, is not the passing contents of sensations, feelings, thoughts, and actions but a "centre of pure self-consciousness".

The mysterious paradox of disidentification is due to the term "identification" being used to describe two entirely different experiences: First, as the familiar sense of identification with a content of consciousness (a particular amalgam of feeling/thinking/sensing) that becomes a limitation to the extent that it excludes the possibility of other potential "contents"; and second, in another sense, where it is no longer an identification with any particular content but rather, a self-identification with the centre of consciousness and will, from which we recognize and experience all contents, a condition of freedom not restriction.

In summary, we are *identified* with feelings, thoughts, and sensations, but we are *self-identified* with a centre of consciousness and will. Assagioli indicates this distinction with a cinematic metaphor:

> The changing contents of our consciousness (the sensations, thoughts, feelings, etc.) are one thing, while the "I", the self, the centre of our consciousness is another. From a certain point of view this difference can be compared to that existing between the white lighted area on a screen and the various pictures which are projected upon it.[87]

Notice how the words "from a certain point of view" signpost the metaphorical usage. The experience of the self is being indicated as if it were a blank screen upon which the contents of feelings, thoughts, and sensations are projected. While the contents of consciousness are an ever-changing procession—sometimes it's a romantic comedy, other times an action or horror movie—the screen, or self, remains forever unchanged.

This self-identification therefore distinguishes who we are (the self) from these contents of consciousness; whereas, to be identified is to forget this distinction, which is indeed literally what is happening when we become absorbed in a good film, forgetting it is all just a trick of lights and getting caught up in the story as if it were really happening, hence the metaphorical comparison. To the extent that we fail to distinguish who we really are, the self, from the cinematic roles of hero or lover or peacemaker, or whatever identification is adopted, we get caught up in the story-making activity of everyday life.

The comparison to the cinema screen is not total, however. In the same way that identification limits possibilities, so also do the metaphors employed to describe disidentification. Metaphor only ever provides a similarity to experiential life, never an exact equivalence, as discussed above with regard to "instrument" and "tool".

A more comprehensive understanding of the self can therefore be clarified by discussing how it also differs from a cinema screen.

Most obviously, a cinema screen is a physical object, something we can point towards and upon which we can indeed distinguish a centre point. This is not at all the case with the self. While the use of definite articles and pronouns, such as "the self", "the will", and my "I", suggests actual objects of awareness, this is only a metaphorical framing, a transfer of experiencing simple objects in the world into an imagined psychological world filled with psychological objects revolving around a permanent and static "centre".[88]

As a complex system consisting of a network of relationships, psychological life need not be considered to have a centre at all, in the same way as, for example, a flock of starlings has no single centre of control, no "controller bird" with a megaphone telling the stragglers to keep in formation. Rather, it has a consciousness and will distributed throughout the flock, with each individual bird performing subtle micro-movements that synthesize to create swirling mass synchronized movements, or murmurations, across the dusk sky.

While there are many such ecological metaphors that could be used to theorize the possibilities of a dynamic and de-centred understanding of the self, as will be further developed in chapter 4, for now, the point is to recognize the possible misunderstanding created when the metaphor indication of the self as a centre becomes mistaken for an accurate experiential description of self-identification, as the following commentary upon the "Self-Identification Exercise" by Assagioli shows:

> Focus your attention on the central realization: "I am a centre of pure self-consciousness and of will." Attempt, as much as you can, to realize this as an experienced fact in your awareness, as the purpose of the exercise is to achieve a specific state of consciousness . . . [89]

The above statement of a "specific state of consciousness" comes very close to contradicting the principial understanding given earlier of self-identification as not the changing contents of our consciousness.

Assagioli provides no explicit clarification of the difference between "state" and "content"; therefore, the exercise is sometimes read as promoting an idealized specific content. This can be seen from many characterizations of self-identification in the literature as "being centred"; that is, solid, confident, and focused, rather than exhibiting an "off-centre" confusion and vulnerability; or involving a discovery of a true "essence" that allows for healthy decisions and behaviours rather than destructive impulses and emotions.[90]

The misunderstanding of self-identification as a particular "centred" content of consciousness creates a tension with "de-centred" experiences. If a "centred" experience is characterized as being one that exhibits a confident sense of control, then we might think about "de-centred" experiences as the opposite: vulnerable states of impotence and anxiety.

While in principal both these contents of experience, the centred and de-centred, can be encompassed by self-identification, when it is mistaken for only an experience of so-called "centred" contents, this will result in the avoidance and rejection of "de-centred" experiences; that is, a separation, rather than an act of synthesis, what we can call a "centre separation", which, far from being a disidentification process and outcome, is ironically an identification with feeling calm and acting in a confident and controlled manner.[91,92]

Cognitive Separation

"Cognitive separation", whereby thinking about psychosynthesis becomes mistaken for its actual experience, has already been implied in the above discussion.

Due to the repetition of affirmations, which are really only theoretical ideas about disidentification, the "Exercise in Dis-Identification" can tend towards focusing upon a conceptual or cognitive understanding of outcomes, while moving away or separating from the vulnerable process experiences of disidentification.

Not yet mentioned in this discussion is a further contribution to "cognitive separation": the treatment within the exercise of the body, emotions, and intellect as separate psychological functions.

Experiential life is not separable into component parts. For example, only in the abstract can we think about a feeling in isolation from thoughts and sensations. The experiential world of psychological facts is always going to be a complex mix of shifting elements, such that it is impossible to tell where feeling ends, and a thought or sensation begins. As Assagioli writes:

> There is, as a matter of fact, a constant interplay between sensation, emotion, and mental activity—and the distinction we have made is only a question of emphasis, of focusing the attention of the observer.[93]

Despite Assagioli's qualification here, the exercise directs attention towards one function at a time and requires a separation from the experiential whole; for example, to focus on an experience in just "the body" requires separation from experiences of emotion and intellect.

Furthermore, while it might seem reasonable to assume the body, emotion, and intellect are straightforward experiences, this is not the case. Our actual experience involves not just a singular entity called "the body" but a synthesis of passing aches and tensions, itches and shivers and digestive rumbles, in-breaths and out-breaths; not a single entity called "emotions", but a multilayered mix of feeling and shifting moods; and never a singular entity called "the intellect" but rather, a constant flux of ideas, beliefs, and questions.

In summary, "the body" and "emotions" and "intellect" are simplified abstract concepts that are not found on an experiential level. This means that, instead of a deepening experiential engagement, the "Exercise in Dis-Identification" can unwittingly turn attention towards an abstract mental analysis. This can happen to such a degree that we end up thinking about abstract concepts of "the body", "emotions", and "the intellect" as somehow not being the personal self, which, far from being a state of disidentification is a further cause of cognitive separation—in effect a deepening identification with an idea about disidentification.[94,95,96,97]

Understood principially, "disidentification" is the process and outcome of a holistic synthesis among sensations, feelings, and thoughts. This natural tendency can be helped along by allowing awareness to gently recognize hitherto previously neglected or unnoticed aspects of experience. The result is an increasing range of awareness and will, cultivating freedom from identifications with any particular contents of consciousness.

However, a more abstract-conceptual treatment can arise when the outcome of disidentification is prematurely prioritized over this gradual process, resulting in the outcome, control, centre, and cognitive separations. Given the importance of disidentification within psychosynthesis theory and practice, the further implications of these separations will be discussed throughout the book.

The ideal model

The "experience" of the "ideal model" needs to be distinguished from its frequent application in the "Technique of Ideal Models".[98] This section will therefore focus upon the general "ideal model" principle and how it informs the experience of psychosynthesis as a whole. The technique will be discussed in the next chapter.

Once again, a good place to begin is by noting that the "ideal model" is a way to describe a naturally occurring life process. Put simply, ideal models are found in those persons or role models we look up to and aspire to emulate. According to Assagioli, this could be anyone "who represents what is considered as desirable or who arouses admiration or represents an ideal".[99] Perhaps it is a parent or teacher, a famous novelist or actor, a historical person, or a mythical figure or fictional character.

No matter who captures our imagination in this way, "ideal models imply vital relationships with the outer world and other human beings."[100] It is within these relationships, for better and for worse, that the personality is shaped and influenced.

The "ideal model" provides a theory to consciously recognize and work with the direction of this naturally occurring transformational process. A necessary first step is to recognize and begin to let go of previous ideal models that have shaped the personal self into its current identification. This will involve exploring messages received from significant role models in the family of origin and surrounding culture, the making conscious of which is the beginning of a "disidentification" process.

Once these previously limiting ideal models become apparent as choices rather than inevitabilities, scripts or roles rather than fixed truths, the expanded possibilities of new ideal models can then be imagined, just as when the caterpillar, never having looked up towards the sky, begins to imagine the forms and movements of a butterfly.

The ideal model is thus not only a vision of a future outcome but also the process of how we get there. In this respect, the connotations of an idealized or final state of perfection, which sometimes arise upon mention of an ideal model, are an unfortunate distraction from the incremental nature of engaging in a "disidentification" process.

As Assagioli makes clear:

> This picture should be realistic and "authentic"; that is, in line with the natural development of the given individual and therefore capable—at least in some measure—of realization, and should not be a neurotic, unreal "idealized" image.[101]

> . . . be careful to avoid making their "ideal picture" too rigid; they should be ready to modify or enlarge it—and even to change it altogether as later experiences, fresh outlooks, or new clarifications indicate and demand this change.[102]

The "ideal model" will be an attainable next step forward. It will be something proximate, able to be imagined as a realistic possibility, which is not too rigid but open to modification as the process continues, thereby avoiding the pitfalls of reaching for an ideal model in an idealized sense.

For example, asking a client, "Who would you like to be in five years' time?" may seem to align with the principle of the "ideal model", but if they are unable to imagine tomorrow being any different from today—never mind next month or five years from now—instead of opening up new possibilities, the unwitting request for an idealized model will have the opposite effect. The client may collapse into frustration and shame at not being able to offer an answer, or perhaps, in covering up this response, offer the therapist a fantastical ideal model, in the shape of a "neurotic, unreal "idealized" image."

The superconscious

Psychosynthesis very much includes "existential religious or spiritual experience" as an important aspect of psychological life.[103] Assagioli's interest in the revelations and insights from spiritual seekers and mystics was an important influence in the formation of his psychology.

Psychosynthesis was among the first psychologies to move from only studying psychopathology to include an enquiry into the creative, aesthetic, and spiritual experiences of healthy human potential. The term used to describe this aspect of psychosynthesis is the "superconscious":

> . . . the elements and functions, coming from the superconscious, such as aesthetic, ethical, religious experiences, intuition, inspiration, states of mystical consciousness, are factual, are real in the pragmatic sense . . . because they are effective, producing changes both in the inner and the outer world.[104]

The inclusion of the superconscious was another bold break by Assagioli from the psychology of Freud. Psychoanalysis at that time regarded such experiences as a regressive return to pre-egoic oneness.[105] In other words, far from being indicative of a developmental step forward, spiritual "peak experiences" and states of mystical consciousness were seen to point backwards towards personal-biographical experiences, either childhood naivety or some form of developmental trauma.

In contrast, for Assagioli, the eruption of "superconscious" experiences:

> . . . arrives—so to speak—almost ready made, and has very little connection with previous experiences. It is not something which arises in the usual way . . . as the result of now released but previously repressed experiential contents; it is something new and . . . sometimes has little relationship to precedent personal experiences of the individual.[106]

The personal-biographical insights of psychoanalysis were combined by Assagioli with an understanding of "superconscious" experiences as the emergence of fresh possibilities and potential, which is to say indicative of psychological growth not regression.[107]

This is all well and good, but how do we notice these superconscious experiences when they happen? What is it that makes them superconscious? In what way are intuitive, aesthetic, religious, and mystical experiences similar? And how do they link with the other teaching "experiences" to further describe a principial understanding of psychosynthesis?

The following discussion sets out to answer these questions by considering multiple statements from Assagioli. What we shall find, as with the discussion of disidentification, is a tension within the literature.

The "experience" of the superconscious is sometimes applied in one sense and then subsequently in quite another sense, without any explicit clarification of the considerable differences between them. Once again, these two opposing understandings are distinguishable by the type of language employed: one experiential-descriptive and another abstract-conceptual.

The following first sample of statements showcases an experiential-descriptive understanding of the "superconscious":

> What has been called by various people or thinkers "spiritual" corresponds in great part to what can empirically be called "superconscious" or "those functions generally not active in average man".[108]

> . . . experience of facts or of functions which are generally superconscious . . . generally do not enter spontaneously into the field of consciousness, but which in some cases make a spontaneous, unexpected, sometimes unwanted irruption into the field of consciousness.[109]

> The opening of the channel between the conscious and the superconscious levels . . . and the flood of light, joy, and energy which follows, often produce a wonderful release. The preceding conflicts and sufferings, with the psychological and physical symptoms which they generated, vanish sometimes with amazing suddenness . . . But in some cases, not infrequent, the personality is inadequate in one or more respects and therefore unable to rightly assimilate the inflow of light and strength . . . when the inrush of spiritual energy is overwhelming in its suddenness and intensity.[110]

> The bursting in of superconscious elements, particularly if they are sudden and very intense, can disturb the former balance . . . of the ordinary personality, producing various reactions, overexcitement, or a sense of disorientation.[111]

> Man's spiritual development is a long and arduous journey . . . full of surprises, difficulties and even dangers. It involves a drastic transmutation of the "normal" elements

> of the personality, an awakening of potentialities hitherto dormant . . . . We should not be surprised, therefore, to find that so great a change, so fundamental a transformation, is marked by several critical stages, which are not infrequently accompanied by various nervous, emotional, and mental troubles.[112]

These statements showcase the "superconscious" as a dynamically transformative *experience*. It arrives "unexpected" and "full of surprises" as an altered state "generally not active in the average man". The familiar and commonplace disappear via a spontaneous "irruption", "inrush", "flood", and "inflow" of "light and strength", such that "hitherto dormant" potentialities are awakened, producing a "fundamental" transformation of the personality. In other words, it is a significant disidentification process.

The effects of this "superconscious" irruption can be noticed across an experiential spectrum. At one end of the spectrum, the sudden "inrush" of expanded consciousness can result in psychological symptoms being removed "sometimes with amazing suddenness".

Assagioli writes of this producing "a sense of *renewal* or *regeneration* . . . accompanied by a sense of *joy* or *happiness* which may result in a state of bliss" and a heightened sense of connection and participation with "a far greater consciousness".[113] However, this connective renewal is not always a welcome one.

Towards the other end of the superconscious experiential spectrum are what Assagioli described as "crises caused by the spiritual awakening".[114] Due to the personality being insufficiently prepared and "unable to rightly assimilate the inflow of light and strength", especially if this "inflow" is sudden and intense, a state of overwhelm, "over-excitement or a sense of disorientation" and "nervous, emotional, and mental troubles" can be the result.

These psychological disturbances or symptoms can be seen to provide another link between the superconscious and the earlier description of the disidentification process, where "the individual feels himself or herself lost".[115]

Because the "superconscious" is found within both states of euphoric joy and disoriented overwhelm, it cannot be recognized through any particular state or fixed quality of experience. What characterizes the superconscious is not content, per se, but its "non-ordinary" nature beyond the habitual range of identification and the transformational process that is happening through this non-ordinary "content".

It is in noticing, valuing, and working across the full spectrum of non-ordinary superconscious experiences that we align with the innate movement of the psyche towards synthesis. In this way, all psychological experiences are granted a place within the greater whole. Nothing is excluded or eliminated.[116]

This experiential understanding of the superconscious provides several links to the other teaching "experiences", including the personal self, disidentification, and synthesis. These interrelationships offer an understanding that allows the at-times startling nature of superconscious experiences to be noticed, valued, and worked with, rather than seen as a problematic regression.

However, it is important to clarify that this experiential understanding is often conflated and confused with a more abstract-conceptual treatment of the superconscious, as seen in the following second sample of statements:

> Strictly speaking, "superconscious" is just a term to designate the higher, spiritual, or transpersonal region of the psyche.[117]

> The superconscious constitutes the higher section or aspect of the person of which the ego or self . . . is not normally aware.[118]

> From this region [of the superconscious] we receive our higher intuitions and inspirations—artistic, philosophical, or scientific, ethical "imperatives" and urges to humanitarian and heroic action. It is the source of the higher feelings, such as altruistic love, of genius and of the states of contemplation, illumination, and ecstasy. In this realm

> are latent the higher psychic functions and spiritual energies.[119]
>
> . . . viewed in terms of energy, we may consider the contents of the superconscious as energies having a higher frequency than some of the contents of the lower unconscious.[120]
>
> We are using the word "spiritual" in its broader connotation, which includes, therefore, not only specific religious experience but all the states of awareness, all the functions and activities which have as common denominator the possessing of values higher than the average, values such as the ethical, the aesthetic, the heroic, the humanitarian, and the altruistic . . . all experiences connected with awareness of the contents of the superconscious.[121]

This second sample of statements conceptualizes the superconscious as a section of "the general unconscious".[122] In psychosynthesis theory, the superconscious is conceived as the top-most region of the unconscious, also known as the "higher unconscious", and distinct from two other regions: the "middle unconscious" and the "lower unconscious".

While the lower unconscious is characterized by "fundamental drives and primitive urges", and the middle unconscious by "easily accessible" memories and functions required for normal "waking consciousness", the higher region of the "superconscious" is that described by Assagioli as of "superior quality" to the "lower levels of the unconscious."[123]

The rationale for this superiority is that it is the "higher" levels of the unconscious alone that offer new experiences, whereas those of the lower unconscious are merely the emergence of previously repressed experiences.[124]

However, in pursuit of a principial understanding, this mapping of higher/new/superior and lower/old/inferior is best appreciated not as an experiential description but as an abstract conceptualization.

The description of the superconscious as a level of the unconscious is metaphorical. As mentioned earlier, in the section on disidentification, a metaphor is a way to imagine an experience that is difficult to describe—in this case, the superconscious—as similar to a familiar and easily described experience, such as climbing from the lower to higher levels on a ladder.

The metaphor of "higher" conveys something of the importance of the superconscious over lower unconscious or middle unconscious experiences, just as it is conventionally assumed to be an improvement to ascend through the grades to reach the top of the class during our schooling. However, it's important to note that the division between "higher" and "lower" is an abstraction—just as a national boundary is often just a line on a map and not at all recognizable on the ground.

Be that as it may, reference to the unconscious is frequently made in psychosynthesis theory. That's because it is an incredibly powerful explanatory idea capable of transforming the elusiveness of psychological life into neatly explained categories and structures. Bewildering and inchoate symptoms, such as addictions, depressions, and anxieties, come into sharp focus when conceived as unconscious parts, internalizations, regions, levels, conflicts, forces, drives, repressions, and resistances.

However, in the same way that a two-dimensional photograph should not be mistaken as an accurate picture of the three-dimensional world, so too ideas about "the unconscious" need to be appreciated simply as a way to orientate therapeutic practice by creating a provisional "working hypothesis", not as an accurate description of experience.

And yet, as a result of familiarity and overuse, the explanatory power of the unconscious can become mistaken for an actual description of psychological experience. This results in a lot of time and energy being put into thinking about various unconscious aspects and regions and parts, unwittingly explaining away experiences by turning them into ideas and then mistaking those ideas for experiences.

When we get past the abstract simplifications and attend to the joined-up complexity of experience it is not necessarily possible, or even desirable, to characterize the superconscious as a distinct and static "higher" category separate from a "middle" and "lower" unconscious.[125]

While superconscious experiences may at times be characterized as a heightened state of wonder and awe, as the first sample of statements indicates, they can also be characterized by a so-called "lower" state of overwhelm and anxiety, or indeed an amalgam of both "higher" and "lower" states arising together; for example, in bittersweet moments of both joy and sadness, when the beauty of a sunset is mixed with a sense of overwhelm or grief.

To be a psychosynthesis teaching, the superconscious needs, on a principial level, to reflect the processes and outcomes of bringing together all aspects of psychological life into an ever greater whole. Any prioritizing of a higher "region" or "level" will be an act of separation *not* synthesis, turning attention away from noticing and working with the full spectrum of psychological experience.[126]

This is sometimes referred to as "spiritual bypassing", whereby identification with "higher" content is used to avoid the vulnerability of transformation; that is, the sense of feeling lost prior to a new identity becoming fully established, as described above in the disidentification section.[127]

The importance that Assagioli clearly granted to the superconscious is perhaps best understood as one of the ways in which he sought to distinguish his psychology from Freudian psychoanalysis.[128] He saw the superconscious as having been "neglected by the science of psychology", which had until then solely focused upon the lower unconscious as "extensively studied by Freud and his followers".[129]

The introduction of the superconscious offered a new, higher direction for psychology, one that allows psychological disturbances to be embraced as positive indicators of future-oriented transformation. However, the need to distinguish his fledgling psychology from that of Freud can arguably be seen to have forced Assagioli to overstate his case with regard to the superconscious, resulting in the above-described divergence from the guiding twin principles of experiential-synthesis.

The transpersonal Self

The "transpersonal Self" is another psychosynthesis "experience" with multiple names, referred to synonymously as "the Self", "Higher Self", "Higher Power", "Spiritual Self", "True Self", and also sometimes just "Self". It is also another teaching that Assagioli avoids defining directly.

As we have seen, this is not particularly unusual, but what is unusual is this definitional avoidance being made explicit:

> At the present stage of psychological investigation little is definitely known concerning the Self, but the importance of this synthesizing centre well warrants further research.[130]

> *Interviewer:*
> What is the nature of the transpersonal Self? Are you talking about an entity separate from the self we experience directly in self-awareness?
> *Assagioli:*
> My dear friend, I cannot tell you what the transpersonal Self is like . . . Language is always inadequate to speak about transpersonal or spiritual experiences.[131]

Not only is little "definitely known" about transpersonal Self, what we do know is difficult to communicate given the inadequacies of language. But the same situation, as we have seen, applies to all the other seven "experiences". Experiences are not simply objects to be measured objectively in a laboratory and straightforwardly described in words; therefore, there will always be a gap between the complexities of psychological experiences and how they are simplified in theoretical language.

Acknowledging this difficulty does not mean that we stop trying to find words to more adequately describe "transpersonal Self." As Assagioli says, "further research" is needed.

To leave transpersonal Self, or indeed any of the seven teaching "experiences", as a complete mystery, a theoretical blank page, is no guarantee of a fulsome experiential understanding. There will always be assumptions, operating in the background of awareness, shaping the possibilities of experiential life. Without "further research", the limitations of these assumptions will not be exposed, nor will they be replaced with an improved understanding—one that notices and enhances the process and outcome of psychosynthesis.

The important question is then not whether a theoretical description can be found but whether this is left to the vagaries of unexamined assumptions.

Assagioli takes up this question about transpersonal Self when he states: "It is good to have some theoretical knowledge of its characteristics and the experience of its guidance."[132]

This encouragement towards "theoretical knowledge" might be read as contradicting the earlier statement that "language is always inadequate". But the principle of synthesis, which describes the bringing together and holding of tensions among disparate elements, allows both positions to coexist: Experiences are ultimately not communicable in words *and* "some theoretical knowledge" is helpful.

Assagioli can therefore be understood to be working within the theory/experience gap, opening up a provisional language usage with an awareness of its limitations as a "working hypothesis". This is why, despite hesitation in giving definitions, there can be found within psychosynthesis literature many statements that offer a good indication of how to approach the "experience" of "transpersonal Self".

Transpersonal Context

A good place to begin is with the opening question by Assagioli's interviewer asking whether transpersonal Self is "separate from the personal self".

That there is a personal self *and* a transpersonal Self does seem to suggest two discrete selves but are they actually separate from each other? Given that the guiding principle of synthesis is the opposite of separation, it is perhaps not surprising to find an interconnectedness between the two "experiences":

> . . . the personal conscious self or "I" . . . should be considered merely as the reflection of the spiritual Self, its projection, in the field of the personality.[133]

> There are not really two selves, two independent and separate entities. The Self is one; it manifests in different degrees of awareness and self-realization. The reflection appears to be self-existent but has, in reality, no autonomous substantiality. It is, in other words, not a new and different light but a projection of its luminous source.[134]

To speak of a personal self and a transpersonal Self as "separate entities" is a misunderstanding; instead of two selves, there is really just one. This is paradoxical and may seem more confusing than helpful, even deliberately obtuse. However, there is an important principial understanding being communicated in these statements.

When Assagioli writes of the personal self having "no autonomous substantiality" apart from transpersonal Self, this aligns well with the principle of synthesis, which directs attention towards the context of elements coming together in a network of relationships, rather than being separated, per analysis, into isolated parts or discrete "contents" .

In this sense, transpersonal Self is not separate from the personal self, but can be understood to be the psychological context within which the personal self exists, a contextualization that we will now discuss through analogy to a tree in a forest.[135,136,137,138]

To understand an individual tree requires appreciating its forest context. While there are many trees to be found standing alone in the middle of fields, to study an isolated specimen set apart from its natural forest environment would only result in a partial understanding of trees.

A fuller appreciation results from recognizing the capacity of individual trees to be interconnected—not just to other trees but to the whole forest ecosystem, via root, mycelial, and airborne exchanges of moisture and nutrients, energy, and information.

Through these interconnections, the boundary between tree and forest is not solid but porous, such that a tree is no longer understood as an isolated specimen but contextualized within its environment as an inseparable participant in a web of relationships among many other living beings and elements. In much the same way, the personal self can be understood to be inseparable from its context within transpersonal Self.

An implicit indication of this contextual understanding can be seen when Assagioli writes:

> Human beings are not isolated . . . . They may at times feel subjectively isolated, but the extreme existentialistic conception is not true, either psychologically or spiritually . . . . Processes of "psychological osmosis" are going on all the time, both with other human beings and with the general psychic environment.[139]

> Psychosynthesis may also be considered as the individual expression of a wider principle, of a general law of inter-individual and cosmic synthesis. Indeed, the isolated individual does not exist; every person has intimate relationships with other individuals which make them all interdependent. Moreover, each and all are included in and part of the spiritual super-individual Reality.[140]

The above statements indicate a psychological life in which the synthesis of an individual person or personal self, far from being an isolated experience, is understood to be situated within the context of an "inter-individual and cosmic synthesis." While it might sometimes feel as if we are "subjectively isolated", this is "not true, either psychologically or spiritually".

Assagioli goes so far as to state, "The isolated individual does not exist." We can assume by this statement that he is not denying the existence of individuals as somehow unreal or imaginary, but rather, that the *isolated* experience of a personal self does not exist apart from its context in transpersonal Self. This aligns with the earlier statement of the personal self having "no autonomous substantiality" apart from its "source" in transpersonal Self.

The transpersonal Self is therefore not on the same category level as the personal self. It is not just another "self", or separate entity, but rather, the encompassing experiential context within which the personal self exists via a synthesis of relationships across multiple levels to: feelings, thoughts, and sensations; individuals, families, communities, and societies; and places, environments, and ultimately, the whole cosmos.

Just as a tree sapling grows into an ever fuller expression of the forest, so too does the personal self come to "assimilate and implement" an "ever more clear and vivid" expression of transpersonal Self as its "luminous source"—which makes questions about where the personal self ends and transpersonal Self begins, and how to separate the two from each other, somewhat moot.

It is the reason why, in this book, instead of writing "the transpersonal Self", which suggests a singular entity or location, simply "transpersonal Self" is given. In this way, by dropping the definite article (the), a more contextual understanding is better indicated. However, so far, this contextual understanding remains abstract to some degree.

A basis for a more experiential understanding of transpersonal Self will now be discussed in relation to Assagioli's description, in the above statements, of the personal self as the reflection of transpersonal Self. Given that a reflection is a mirror relationship operating in two directions, the practical implications of what we have already discussed about the experience of the personal self will also be applicable to an experiential recognition of transpersonal Self.[141]

Not the Contents

The first reflective similarity between personal self and transpersonal Self is neither being about the "contents of consciousness". If the personal self can be recognized as an awareness of being aware—something that continues regardless of the passing contents of experience—the same is true of transpersonal Self. It is not tied to contents of consciousness, but instead, is present across the full spectrum of human experience.

Whether experiencing a content of transcendent bliss or depressive despair, transpersonal Self will always be reflected in the personal self, in the same way that a puddle in the pavement will equally reflect the brightness of a full moon or the darkness of a new moon.[142]

This is not to suggest that all such experiences are equal. Assagioli writes of the idea of "Self-realization" with respect to an ever deepening experience of transpersonal Self:

> Let us remember . . . that there are not in reality two independent selves. There is one Self—but there are many different and distinct levels of self-realization . . . between the self-identity of the ordinary or normal level of functioning and the full spiritual self-realization there are intermediate stages or levels, ever wider, clearer, fuller.[143]
>
> . . . between the starting point in the lowlands of our ordinary consciousness and the shining peak of self-realization there are intermediate phases, plateaus at various altitudes on which a man may rest or even make his abode, if his lack of strength precludes or his will does not choose a further ascent.[144]

Self-realization is a process of deepening connection to transpersonal Self.[145] It is a journey through successive "intermediate stages or levels" and "plateaus at various altitudes" that will become ever "wider, clearer, fuller."

This provides another link among the seven teaching "experiences", where the intermediate phases or levels of Self-realization can also be recognized as a disidentification process, with Assagioli writing elsewhere that "The intermediate stages imply new identifications."[146] Once again, this is understood to be not just a theory or idea but an experiential process "of natural inner growth, fostered by the manifold experiences of life".

For example, this happens across the life stages when disidentification from being a child results in identification as a teenager, then disidentification from being a teenager results in identification as a young adult, then disidentification from being a young adult results in identification as a middle-aged person. Each successive stage or level of disidentification/identification grants an expanded range of experiential possibilities, as the personal self grows into the fuller potential of transpersonal Self.[147]

However, this process emphasis is not the whole truth. Synthesis is both a process *and* an outcome. And this begs the question: How might understanding this outcome improve an experiential recognition of transpersonal Self? The following statements indicate one way in which Assagioli addresses this question:

> What has to be achieved is to expand the personal consciousness into that of the Self...to unite the lower with the higher Self.[148]
>
> Self-realization . . . means the momentary or more or less temporary identification or blending of the I-consciousness with the spiritual Self, in which . . . there is a forgetfulness of all contents of consciousness . . . there is only the pure intense experience of the Self.[149]
>
> the state of consciousness of the Self-realized individual . . . is a state of consciousness characterized by joy, serenity, inner security, a sense of calm power, clear understanding, and radiant love.[150]
>
> This Self is above, and unaffected by, the flow of the mind-stream or by bodily conditions.[151]

As discussed previously with respect to disidentification and the superconscious, when the outcome of psychosynthesis is emphasized it can become mistaken for a particular content of consciousness.

This can also be seen in the above quoted statements, which suggest that transpersonal Self is a recognizable content—a "pure, intense experience" in contrast with "the ordinary or normal level of functioning" achieved by uniting, blending, and reuniting the "the lower with the higher Self"; whereupon, there is "a forgetfulness of all contents of consciousness".

This is a somewhat ambiguous phrasing, meaning perhaps "not the contents of consciousness" but also suggestive of a non-ordinary or heightened state, as is indicated in the description of "joy, serenity, inner security, a sense of calm power, clear understanding, and radiant love".

And yet, from a principial understanding, this "content" outcome cannot be the case, because claiming an experience of transpersonal Self is a particular state of heightened consciousness indicates a separation not a synthesis.

On a principial basis, transpersonal Self needs to reflect a contextualization of elements coming together in a network of relationships, rather than being separated into discrete contents of experience; therefore, any prioritizing of so-called "higher" over "lower" contents, and a rising above "the flow of the mind-stream" will be in danger of portraying Self-realization as a transcendent decontextualization from mundane reality.

As discussed earlier, in the superconscious section, any such emphasis would be a misunderstanding of Self-realization as a form of "spiritual bypassing", or identification with heightened "contents".[152]

To further discuss this difficulty, and set up a route towards an alternative theoretical understanding, we can return to the point made by Assagioli in the opening of this section: "Language is always inadequate to speak about transpersonal or spiritual experiences."[153]

The difficulty in describing transpersonal Self is due to the limitations of language; in particular, the noun-based structure of modern European languages. While pre-modern languages, spoken by indigenous communities, are verb-based, and therefore, emphasize experiencing the world as an activity or process, modern noun-based languages direct attention towards experiencing a static world of people, places, and things (that is, nouns). This can be seen in Assagioli's use of "the unconscious" as an explanatory metaphor for psychological experience as a subjective interiority or place, filled with "contents", or things (feelings, thoughts, sensations, and so on), and also, sometimes what are called "subpersonalities" (psychological characters or people).

In other words, the experience of the physical world as a place filled with things and persons is transferred metaphorically into how we picture psychological life.

But as discussed earlier, the ubiquitous use of the term "the unconscious" in psychosynthesis theory, and its division into lower, middle, and higher levels, is a radical simplification, an explanatory story, not an actual thing or place that can be experienced. No one has ever measured up the unconscious as a psychological place for a new set of curtains or placed a psychological object under a microscope.

As a psychological place filled with things and people, what the unconscious offers is a set of metaphors to assist in thinking about psychological experiences. This is what Assagioli is offering in writing of the personal self ascending from "the starting point in the lowlands" to finally arrive at "the shining peak of Self-realization". But this should not be taken to assume that there are actually two separate selves, or that Self-realization is literally a journey of ascension.[154]

The metaphor of "the unconscious" immediately confines thinking about transpersonal Self and Self-realization within a container/contents story. Whenever the unconscious is evoked, it presupposes a psychological place or container, whether assumed as a subjective interiority or, more broadly, as a collective unconscious filled with feelings, thoughts, sensations, and image contents.

This obviously has severe limitations with regard to thinking about an experience not recognizable as any particular contents of consciousness. What is therefore needed is an alternative way to theorize about transpersonal Self that goes beyond the noun-based linguistic framing of the unconscious as "container/content".[155]

Let's now examine such an alternative by turning to the second reflective similarity between personal self and transpersonal Self: They are both persons.

Persons in Context

The second reflective similarity is hidden in plain sight. Both the personal self and transpersonal Self are *persons*. If the personal self is an experiencer, a seat of consciousness and will, then in reflective similarity, so too will transpersonal Self be recognizable as a consciousness and will. Transpersonal Self is therefore experienced as a someone, a living subject, a person to whom we can relate.[156]

Assagioli writes:

> In Psychosynthesis, the Self is considered a reality, a living Subject, of which one can have direct and certain awareness.[157]
>
> Accounts of religious experience often speak of a "call" from God, or a "pull" from some Higher Power; this sometimes starts a "dialogue" between the man and this "Higher Source," in which each alternately invokes and evokes the other.[158]
>
> The personal self is generally unaware of the other, even to the point of denying its existence; whereas the other, the true Self, is latent and does not reveal itself directly to our consciousness.[159]

Implicit within Assagioli's presentation is an ongoing relationship between personal self and transpersonal Self.[160] Far from a passive relationship or abstract matter of religious belief, transpersonal Self as a "living subject" is described in the above statements as actively seeking to "start" a communication with the "personal self".[161]

While the personal self is often "generally unaware" of this "pull" from some "Higher Power", it will recognize it in significant moments, when its attention becomes captured by something novel and fresh, beyond habitual expectations, and life seems to offer a "call" to greater awareness and action, such that a "dialogue" ensues in which "each alternately invokes and evokes the other".

With respect to clarifying an experiential recognition, what is perhaps most important in the above statements is that transpersonal Self "does not reveal itself directly" in a singular encounter. To assume any such immediate and direct revelation (perhaps naively pictured as an archetypal, grey-bearded man floating on a cloud) is a misunderstanding. The relationship between personal self and transpersonal Self is not on the same category level as a relationship between Jack and Jill.[162] It is not singular and one to one.

As noted earlier, far from being just another "self", transpersonal Self is better understood as the context of the personal self within an encompassing web of relationships. Each of these relationships can be seen to be acting as "an indirect but true link, a point of connection between the personal man and his higher Self".[163]

In other words, transpersonal Self reveals itself through intermediary relations with, for example:

- other people; that is, partners, family, colleagues, psychotherapists, teachers
- introspection; that is, meditation, memories, dreams, reflection, and study
- sensations; that is, dance, massage, exercise, sex, and so on
- the arts; that is, novels, movies, paintings, music
- the environment; that is, sunsets, billboards, plants, trees, animals

The "call" of transpersonal Self, as a person or living subject, will be experientially recognizable within all the above examples. Many more relational possibilities could be listed, but the principial point to be appreciated is that the experience of personhood is not limited to humans.

As is perhaps most clearly seen in childhood talk with dolls and imaginary friends, human beings have an innate ability to notice and converse with people, places, and things as personified others. And despite adulthood acculturation into a dead world filled with inanimate objects, this childhood personifying ability does not entirely disappear and can be seen to live on in many experiences that we take for granted.

A popular feature of psychosynthesis therapy, to be discussed in some detail in the next chapter, is dialoguing with imagined persons. Assagioli writes of a "principle of personification" whereby "every psychological element . . . tend[s] to personify themselves,"[164] which provides a basis for imagining not just feelings and thoughts but also objects, such as photographs, drawings, sculptures, and teddy bears, as actual persons with whom we enter into dialogue.

This personification continues beyond the consulting room when, for example, a sunset "speaks" to us; a favourite restaurant is considered "a good friend"; when in prayer, or any form of dialogue, such as when writing an e-mail to a friend, the presence of an imagined person is addressed; and when technology breaks down and we say out loud, "You stupid thing!"

In all these ways and more, whenever life seems to be calling us to attention, the experience is mediated via relationships with personified others, whether human or otherwise. And it is by noticing and cultivating these intermediary relationships that the personal self comes into relationship with transpersonal Self.[165] Within this is yet another link between the seven teaching "experiences", to the "ideal model", which is also experienced in a personified form, across a multiplicity of relationships, each providing the realistic possibility of movement towards what we can now recognize as Self-realization.

The transpersonal Self, as the context of the personality, effectively turns inside out common assumptions of a purely inner, or intrapsychic, psychology. As the prefix *trans* suggests—simply meaning "beyond" or "within, through, and across"—transpersonal Self contextualizes psychological life within a network of relationships, both *within* persons and also passing *through, across,* and *beyond* persons. It's a relational perspective that also provides an important principial basis for understanding the process and outcome of psychosynthesis—not as the final attainment of any particular content but rather, as the ongoing development and enhancement of this relational network. It is a journey with no final destination, only successive levels of Self-realization, in the same way that a relationship between Jack and Jill need not be seen to have an endpoint beyond which they have nothing new to learn about each other.[166]

Synthesis

Psychosynthesis theory encompasses two completely different conceptions of "synthesis". It is sometimes applied in one way, then subsequently in quite another; yet, the difference between these two conceptions is seldom acknowledged, such that they are often used interchangeably and conflated as if they were equivalent.[167]

Given that "synthesis" is a guiding principle, the following discussion of the differences between these two conceptions is particularly significant for all aspects of psychosynthesis theory and practice.

As we have also seen with disidentification, the superconscious, and transpersonal Self—each of which also has two understandings—the difference between the two conceptions of "synthesis" come from the type of language employed: one experiential-descriptive and the other abstract-conceptual.

Synthesis of Systems

The experiential-descriptive conception of "synthesis" is the one offered throughout this book, as both the process by which aspects or elements combine into a complex whole and the combination, or whole, created as an outcome of this process.

This conception relates to how psychological life is *experienced* as an ongoing dynamic synthesis of interconnected thoughts, feelings, sensations, perceptions, and actions, which, as the famous saying goes, constitutes "a whole greater than the sum of its parts". In other words, as more elements combine, something qualitatively new is created as a result.

Synthesis is therefore not only a recognition of complexity but also a theory of change—the related premise being that psychosynthesis is an innate tendency of psychological life to move towards ever more satisfying levels of complex organization.

However, the "experience" of synthesis is not just confined to psychological life. Assagioli also conceived of synthesis as a "natural process of growth" evident throughout "all the kingdoms of nature":

> In its most basic sense, psychosynthesis is a name for the conscious attempt to cooperate with the natural process of growth—the tendency in each of us and in our world to harmonize and synthesize various aspects to ever higher levels of organization.[168]

> Synthesis is an organizing and unifying principle which acts in all the kingdoms of nature.[169]

Assagioli's understanding of "synthesis" as "a universal principle"[170] operating on the personal level "in each of us", and also across "all the kingdoms of nature", as briefly mentioned in the Introduction, anticipated the subsequent development of what became "systems theory".

Also known as "complexity theory" or "chaos theory", systems theory is a contemporary scientific understanding of change. It emerged from the modelling of ecological phenomena, such as cloud formations, lightning pathways, and the beatings of the human heart, such that all the way up through the systems of cells, organs, bodies, forests, oceans, and planets circling in the night sky, there can be seen to be a principle of synthesis in operation. This allows the naming of a "synthesis of systems" for this first conception of synthesis.

Synthesis of Opposites

Assagioli was a visionary, a man ahead of his time but also of his time. While psychosynthesis anticipated the subsequent development of systems theory, Assagioli obviously did not have the benefit of these as yet-to-be-invented influences, so he drew upon whatever theoretical influences were available to him on the topic, particularly, the philosophy of dialecticism, which is evident in the following statements:[171]

> . . . psychological life can be regarded as a continual polarization and tension between differing tendencies and functions.[172]
>
> Consideration of the human personality in its totality discloses various fundamental polarities . . . Body–Psyche; Consciousness–the Unconscious ; the lower Unconscious–the Superconscious ; Pathos (Receptivity, Sensitivity, Reactivity)–Ethos (Activity, Dynamism, Will); Eros (Feeling)–Logos (Reason).[173]
>
> . . . an essential attribute . . . is the power to "play with opposites" to regulate the interaction of antipodal forces and functions, thereby establishing a dynamic equilibrium and synthesis.[174]

Dialecticism concerns the forces found in relationships between polar opposites. These are known as "thesis" and "antithesis", which when brought together produce a "synthesis".

With respect to psychological life, this can be seen in Assagioli's understanding of symptoms as "a continual polarization and tension between differing tendencies and functions", such as between body/psyche, conscious/unconscious, receptivity/activity, and feeling/thinking.

An example might be an overly rational person, strongly identified with thinking, who lives in a constant state of tension so as to avoid any awareness or expression of feelings. This tension is addressed by a "synthesis of opposites" to establish "a dynamic equilibrium" that brings together the "thesis" of thinking with the "antithesis" of feeling, thereby removing the tension of polarization.

However, this second conception of synthesis, as a "synthesis of opposites," needs to be recognized as moving away from a principial understanding and practice in two respects: simplification and unification.

Simplification

Pairs of opposites can be helpful coordinates by which to establish a beginning orientation to therapeutic work, framing questions such as: Is this person more comfortable with thinking than with feelings? Do they prefer to give rather than receive? How much of this issue is driven by conscious or unconscious factors?

But beyond this orientational beginning, if we continue to only notice the alternative of one pole or another, the repertoire of experiential life will be considerably reduced. While it is not difficult to point to a difficulty and suggest its opposite pole as a response—feelings requiring thoughts, hungry people needing food, dry soil needing water—this is best appreciated as a simplification.

The tensions between opposites may be one aspect of experience, but there will always be other aspects that do not fit into the polarities of thesis and anti-thesis.[175] Feelings don't just need thoughts; they also need bodies, perceptions, and actions. Hungry people don't just need food; they also need shelter, community, purpose, and meaning. Dry soil doesn't just need water; it also needs air, humus, bacteria, and fungi. There is always a multitude of interacting elements, never just a pair of opposites.

Thesis and anti-thesis are only a beginning description, a rough categorization, not the whole story. In contrast to multiple elements coming together in a "synthesis of systems", the danger in focusing narrowly on just two elements coming together in a "synthesis of opposites" is that it may ignore nuances that don't neatly fit into a polarity framework, with a resulting separation from, rather than a synthesis with, experiential life.

Unification

A "synthesis of opposites" also moves away from a principial understanding with respect to how it conceives the outcome of synthesis.

By now this is perhaps no surprise. The need to avoid, on a principial basis, the outcome of psychosynthesis being mistaken for the achievement of a particular content of consciousness has been discussed already with respect to disidentification, the superconscious, and transpersonal Self.

A similar issue can now also be seen in the following statements from Assagioli indicating the outcome of a "synthesis of opposites":

> Synthesis [is] brought about by a higher element or principle which transforms, sublimates, and reabsorbs the two poles into a higher reality.[176]

> If we examine more closely the specific polarities . . . we can clearly distinguish two main types of solutions. One is realized on the same level; it can be called "the middle way" of compromise, the blending of the two poles. The other solution is achieved at a higher level: it is the fusion of the poles into a higher synthesis . . . . The method of synthesis . . . includes and absorbs the two elements into a higher unity endowed with qualities differing from those of either of them.[177]

> The fundamental duality in the spiritual realm is that existing between the personality and the Transpersonal Self, a polarity which is the cause of many inner conflicts, until harmonious relationships and an increasing blending or unification (spiritual psychosynthesis) are achieved.[178]

The outcome of a "synthesis of opposites" is a unification of the two poles combined.[179] It is a "higher unity", described by Assagioli as "endowed with qualities" different from those elements which it "includes and absorbs". These could be seen to align with a principial understanding, whereby the polarized elements coming together create something greater than the sum of their parts.

But when this synthesis of opposites is understood as a "fusion" that "transforms, sublimates, and reabsorbs the two poles", and the conflict between opposites is seen to be replaced with "harmonious relationships", there is a danger of directing attention towards achieving a particular content outcome.

The outcome described above as a "higher reality" or "higher synthesis" is one in which, for example, an opposition or tension between feeling and thinking becomes somehow fused or blended into a sort of psychological homogenization, as if psychological elements and functions are ingredients in a smoothie.

In other words, there is an attempt to somehow not just rise above the opposition but to transcend feelings and thoughts themselves. To the extent this transcendence results in an experiential movement away from feelings and thoughts, this will obviously be in danger of an outcome separation.

What is therefore needed is an alternative understanding for the outcome of synthesis, one that better allows for the ongoing experience of the polarized elements. The following statements, describing the outcome of a "synthesis of systems" offers some helpful clarification in this respect:

> Psychosynthesis is essentially . . . a bringing together in an organic whole, diverse and sometimes conflicting elements, but in an organic whole in which each element preserves its own individuality and function in operation with all the others, and the faithful human body is the perfect example of bio-synthesis; that is, each cell, each organ, each apparatus concurs to the general health, the vitality of the whole organism, but each completes its own function more or less independently, up to a certain point but in unison; by that I mean organic unity.[180]
>
> The body shows an intelligent cooperation of each element, from the cells to the large functional systems such

> as the circulatory system, the digestive, and so on . . . . Thus, the body is a unified organism, a functional unit of countless diverse parts—a perfect demonstration of unity in diversity. What is the unifying principle that makes this possible? Its real nature escapes us; we can only call it life, but something can be said of its qualities and ways of operating. They have been variously called coordination, interaction, or organic synthesis.[181]

The "bio-synthesis" and "organic synthesis" described above spell out clearly that the outcome of a synthesis of systems does not require the sublimation and transformation of oppositional contents but one "in which each element preserves its own individuality" within "a functional unit of countless diverse parts".

In the same way that a bodily system can achieve "harmony" or "equilibrium" and yet contain tensions—for example, between movement and stillness, eating and fasting, dense bones and soft muscles—so too can psychological life move towards ever more satisfying levels of synthesis, as a *meta-harmony* created by the system as a whole, rather than a *micro-level harmony* between conflicting opposites.

Whether in the systole and diastole of a beating heart, oscillations between receptivity and activity, or periods of feeling and thinking, "what we can only call life" requires polarizations and tensions. Instead of fusing opposites, synthesis can therefore be understood, from a principial basis, as maintaining not only the multiplicity of elements but also the tensions and polarizations within the relationships among those elements—as Assagioli writes, a "unity in diversity", rather than a unification.[182,183]

SYNTHESIS OF TEACHINGS

Assagioli's assertion that the seven psychosynthesis teaching "experiences" are "not isolated" but are seen "to imply others" has now been established by discussing them experientially in synthesis, rather than as theoretical concepts in isolation.

To begin with, we described how the *personal self* is indivisible from the *will*, and vice versa. This led to a description of *disidentification* as an expanded range of consciousness and will becoming available to the *personal self* as it moves towards the potential of its *ideal model*.

This is a change process occasioned by the irruption of *superconscious* experiences from beyond the habitual limitations of the personal self, such that the personal self develops intermediary relationships that act as an indirect but true link to its contextual source within *transpersonal Self*. This results in an expanding *synthesis of systems* across multiple and interconnected levels, within individuals and also between persons and the surrounding society and cosmos.

In this way, a principial perspective on psychosynthesis has been shown to be an *experiential* appreciation of psychological life as ongoing process of *synthesis*. Psychosynthesis teachings therefore are those that help notice, describe, and work with the twin principles of experiential-synthesis, as an expression of "the principles and basic purpose of the entire endeavour".[184]

Whenever Assagioli uses simple everyday descriptive language to communicate this, a firm basis for such a principial understanding has been shown. But this chapter has also discussed where psychosynthesis can be seen to diverge from a principial basis.

The divergence from a principial basis is in large part due to Assagioli continuing with the psychological framework of his time; that is to say, a Freudian psychoanalytical lexicon, rather than inventing a new terminology to describe the subtilties of experiential synthesis.

As we have seen, the metaphors of a psychology of *the unconscious* as a container filled with *contents* offer an abstract-conceptual theoretical terminology. And despite Assagioli's awareness of the distinction between theory and experience, there are significant instances throughout his presentation of these metaphorical ideas; for example, a *centre, higher unconscious*, or *opposites* being conflated with an accurate description of psychological experience.

The result of this is twofold: first, an overly conceptual approach, as a result of mistaking ideas for actual experiences; and second, creating a separation from, rather than a synthesis with, psychological experience.

This chapter has therefore focused upon a description of the experiential complexity of psychosynthesis teachings, so as to distinguish this experience from its theoretical simplifications.

This consideration of teachings is only a beginning, as psychosynthesis is also a practical method of facilitating and enhancing the process and outcome of synthesis in psychological life. The next chapter will further develop the distinctiveness of psychosynthesis by turning the guiding principles of experiential-synthesis back upon its many techniques, methods and exercises.

Chapter 2

Techniques

"Close your eyes, go inside, and find yourself in a meadow."

I closed my eyes. The seminar room grew still as my fellow students focused upon this first experience of the guided imagery technique.

"Allow the meadow to appear . . . . Notice the details . . . the sunlight . . . the breeze."

I tried to focus on my meadow-esque images: a muddy field blurred and morphed into a barren hillside, which then became something like a rainswept football pitch.

"If you have lots of different images, just pick one and focus on it."

Totally, that was my problem. Presumably, we had been invited to visualize a meadow for a reason. But what was so special about a meadow? What did it symbolize? What did it mean? And how would I know if I was picking the right kind of meadow?

"Feel the breeze . . . . Feel the sunlight on your face . . ."

I decided to choose the muddy field version; less a sunlit breeze than a dark sky spitting with rain, but deciding felt like some kind of progress.

"A bus approaches along a road running through the meadow . . ."

I quickly created a narrow road with meandering turns. I could hear a diesel engine approaching around a bend.

"The bus comes to a halt nearby . . ."

Hang on a minute, I thought, *I've not got a bus yet.*

"Two or three of your main subpersonalities get off the bus . . ."

The earlier lesson had introduced "subpersonalities", a psychosynthesis theory about a multiplicity of identities within the personality.

"You observe them . . . noticing their age . . . how they are dressed . . . how they move . . ."

Beside the front wheel of a red double-decker bus stood a small boy in school uniform—shorts, blazer, white shirt, and striped tie. A middle-aged man and woman wandered in the meadow nearby, arguing with each other, but my main attention was held by the schoolboy, leaning up against the bus, kicking the tyre with his heel.

"Decide which subpersonality stands out to you the most, and spend some time with it."

The schoolboy subpersonality glanced over at me and then away again, fingers absentmindedly playing with the strap on his leather satchel. When he wandered down the side of the bus and sat on the running board at the back, it did not feel like I was just making it up anymore.

"Do you feel like speaking with any of the subpersonalities?"

Well, yes, I thought, *that might be a good idea*.

"Consider what you would like to say, and then when you are ready, communicate it to your subpersonality."

I started with a simple *hello*.

The subpersonality just sat there on the back step of the bus, flipping his satchel open and shut, as if he had not even heard me.

I self-consciously repeated *hello*, glad this was all going on in the privacy of my own mind.

"Enter into conversation with the subpersonality. Find out what it needs from you."

Willing the schoolboy to look up and say something, I tried again: *Hello, can you hear me? Hello. Oh, come on . . .*

The schoolboy had nothing to say.

"Okay . . . Take your time . . . Allow the meadow to fade . . . Come back to just being here in the room . . . And when you are ready, open your eyes."

On the wall clock only 15 minutes had passed. My head was buzzing with questions about the technique: Why a meadow? Had I got it right? Why had it felt so forced and made-up? Why had the dialogue failed? And what was the point anyway? What were we trying to achieve? How could I improve? What did I need to learn?

This chapter now set outs to answer these questions by turning the twin principles of experiential-synthesis back upon the techniques of psychosynthesis.

The result will be a broad principial understanding of techniques, not just in set-piece interventions but across everything a psychosynthesis psychotherapist does to creatively adapt the work to the experiential process of synthesis.

Tensions between this creative adaptability and a more formulaic procedural application will be considered across a description of several techniques within the experiential context of psychosynthesis psychotherapy as a creative process.

PROCESSES AND OUTCOMES

Psychosynthesis offers a wealth of therapeutic techniques. Assagioli's first book mentions them in the title, *Psychosynthesis: A Manual of Principles and Techniques*, and goes on to devote two-thirds of its pages to the description of techniques.

The post-Assagioli literature continues this emphasis, offering techniques of meditation and visualization, guided imagery, and ideal models; techniques for the development of imagination, intuition, and the will; and related methods and exercises, such as the "Exercise in Dis-Identification" and the "Exercise in the Blossoming of the Rose".[185]

So popular are some of these techniques that psychosynthesis sometimes becomes identified with them. The near ubiquity of guided imagery and subpersonality work, for instance, has perhaps understandably resulted in psychosynthesis being assumed to be an approach that does guided imagery and subpersonality work, and that applying these so-called "psychosynthesis techniques" is what makes it psychosynthesis therapy.[186]

However, to conflate psychosynthesis with a set of techniques is a misunderstanding. As Assagioli writes:

> Psychosynthesis is not identified with any technique or practice. Despite the fact that in group work use is often

> made of guided imagination and visualization exercises, psychosynthesis can by no means be levelled down to these techniques.[187]

Psychosynthesis psychotherapy can be, and is, practised without recourse to any particular techniques.[188] Indeed, early in my psychotherapy training, I was warned away from applying psychosynthesis techniques.

There was even a number placed upon this technique-free-zone: Six to eight weeks were meant to pass by with a new client before inviting them to explore imagined meadows, make free-drawings or dialogue with "empty chairs". In the meantime, prior to applying such techniques, the opening weeks of therapy were to emphasize getting to know the client and creating a therapeutic relationship, as it was this client-therapist alliance that would form the necessary basis for any future application of techniques.

The implicit message was a cautious one: Techniques can be easily misapplied, and therapy can proceed quite happily without them, and might even benefit from their absence.

Good advice, just not quite the whole story.

The narrow understanding given on my training was of techniques as only a subset of therapeutic interventions, applied to produce a particular and pre-planned outcome; for example: developing a quality or feeling; recognizing a truth or insight; achieving a behaviour or expression.

Due to psychosynthesis techniques often being applied in this way, restricted usage or even avoidance can therefore be understood in regard to the "outcome separation" described in chapter 1. As we saw there, with regard to the "Exercise in Dis-identification", too narrow a focus on the creation of a particular outcome of feeling-thinking-expression (especially if following a formulaic series of pre-planned instructions) may direct attention away from the experiential complexity of the client's process; thereby, creating a separation rather than a synthesis.

But as mentioned, this is only part of the story.

A much fuller story of techniques—that *everything* a therapist does is technique—can be found in the section on "basic comments and general remarks" on the "Techniques of Psychosynthesis" offered in the Introduction to Part Two of Assaglioli's *Psychosynthesis: A Manual of Principles and Techniques.*

In this short and easily overlooked section, only three pages long, Assagioli provides important principles as to how the subsequent 160 pages of techniques are to be understood and applied:

> It is opportune, at the outset, to stress the necessity of relating the different techniques to the overall purpose of psychosynthesis, so that we retain this purpose clearly in mind when we apply the techniques—which are only tools, and as tools can be modified. What is important are the principles and the basic purpose of the entire endeavour . . . all the techniques should be subordinated to this basic goal; they are not a static collection of tools, but can be used and modified at will by therapists and educators, provided we keep in mind the basic purpose of the therapy.[189]

Psychosynthesis techniques will be understood narrowly or broadly depending upon their intended purpose. A basic definition of techniques—from the Greek word *techne*, meaning "an art or craft, a way of making and creating"—is a method or procedure for achieving a particular task or outcome. A similar definition for psychosynthesis techniques given by Assagioli is "a specific psychological procedure used in order to produce a definite effect on some aspect or some function of the psyche".[190]

While a narrow understanding of techniques will focus upon micro-managing a particular content outcome, a broader principial understanding will instead be focused upon facilitating the "overall purpose of psychosynthesis".

But what then is this purpose and how might its principles shape the application of therapeutic technique?

Here is what Assagioli says:

> The basic purpose of psychosynthesis is to release or, let us say, help to release, the energies of the Self. Prior to this the purpose is to help integrate, to synthesize, the individual around the personal self, and then later to effect the synthesis between the personal ego and the Self. [191]

Psychosynthesis techniques applied in service of the "basic purpose of the entire endeavour" will be focused upon effecting "the synthesis" of "the personal self" with "the Self". This is a synthesis that, as discussed in chapter 1, will be an unfolding disidentification process with many intermediate stages or levels and no final destination or content outcome beyond which we can go no farther.

Psychosynthesis techniques in service of this "basic purpose" will therefore be those that provide the necessary therapeutic conditions to facilitate the process of synthesis in whatever direction it so desires, in the same way that a gardener is skilled in providing the conditions for a plant to grow without knowing exactly how many leaves or fruit it will produce.

In this way, the above-described dangers of a narrow outcome focus are avoided by aligning techniques with the broader process of synthesis, as found in the client's moment-to-moment experience.

In this broad process understanding, everything a psychosynthesis psychotherapist does, from the moment a client sits down in the consulting room to the moment they leave at the end of the therapeutic hour, can be considered a "technique", because every question, empathic reflection, and smile, as well as any combination of what are more typically thought of as "psychosynthesis techniques" is offered as a way of making contact with the client's experience and facilitating the underlying process of synthesis.

CREATIVE PROCESS

A broad process understanding of techniques implies a creative application. As quoted above, psychosynthesis techniques are not "a static collection of tools".

In order to "keep in mind the basic purpose of the therapy" any set-piece scripts and step-by-step instructions are only rough guidelines in need of modification by the therapist so as to best support the unpredictable experiential process of synthesis happening in the consulting room between therapist and client.

As Assagioli says:

> In each case, in each existential situation of the patient, I had to use techniques, many existing and others I invented myself or that I combined. It all starts from the living reality, from the immediate situation, so no theory, no preference for one technique or another. In a sense, I say it all depends on who applies it, to whom he applies it, how he applies it, and at what moment which he applies it, so each technique can be helpful or harmful according to these four elements. So that gives a great freedom and pliability, but of course that requires intuition and great practice, but it's easy. I think it's a good policy that it corresponds to an inclusiveness of psychosynthesis.[192]

This statement emphasizes the experiential context of psychosynthesis techniques. What comes first is not the technique but the "living reality" of the "immediate situation". There is "no preference for one technique or another" but rather, an interest and sensitivity to what the "existential situation" requires.

Techniques will therefore be "helpful or harmful" depending on how well they facilitate this experiential context—an experiential context described by Assagioli as encompassing not just the client as an isolated individual but also the therapist and the unfolding "moment" arising within the relationship between therapist and client.

In other words, the client is not an isolated static subject to be manipulated by a decontextualised therapist standing apart from the client's process. Both parties are intimately involved in a dynamic co-creation and therefore any context-independent application, if it neglects this "living reality", will be in danger of imposing upon, rather than aligning with, the process of synthesis.

Assagioli is very clear on this point: "I want to emphasize that every individual is different and no techniques can be applied automatically."[193]

The techniques written in manuals are not intended to be applied automatically in the same way every time, regardless of circumstances. As noted, therapeutic technique is not about following a script, as if we are "painting by numbers". Technical proficiency alone is no guarantee of a client being healed and transformed, just as technical skill in painting is no guarantee of a successful work of art.

While a degree of technical competency is necessary, something else is required, something Assagioli called the "spirit of psychosynthesis".

> One can know all the principal ones [i.e. techniques] and still not have grasped the spirit of psychosynthesis. And vice versa. Real training entails both these factors—intuitive understanding of the spirit of psychosynthesis and a sound technical knowledge.[194]

How this "spirit" is turned into therapeutic practice is not particularly considered in the psychosynthesis literature on techniques. What tends to be emphasized is *what* client issues particular techniques address, and *when* to apply them, but critical discussion of *how* to creatively adapt techniques is somewhat missing.

In particular, this is the case when set-piece techniques are described as a series of steps to be followed, implying an importance of doing the technique "correctly" in the prescribed fashion, thereby obscuring the need for creative adaptation.

This is not the case in the original presentation by Assagioli. It stops short of describing set-piece procedures; instead, it offers principles, rough outlines, and suggestions to be creatively modified by a skilled therapist to the unfolding moment arising between therapist and client, in the same way that a chef with good technique will adapt a recipe to the special dietary requirements of a customer. This means that there is really no such thing as a standardized psychosynthesis technique.

The remainder of this chapter will now focus on an understanding of psychosynthesis psychotherapy as a creative process, and in particular *how* to creatively adapt techniques to the "spirit of psychosynthesis."

This is a somewhat elusive topic, as there is no creativity switch, and trying too hard or coming at it too directly can be more of a hindrance than a help. Nevertheless, there are things we can do.

The first step is to understand the experiential context of creativity, so as to be better able to notice and work with it in clinical practice. To do so we shall be drawing upon a model of the creative process sometimes used by psychosynthesis psychotherapists that outlines an experientially recognizable sequence of five stages: preparation, frustration, incubation, illumination, and elaboration.[195]

The first of these stages, *preparation*, is an effortful thinking-through of available resources within the existing level of knowledge and skills, such as, for example, might happen upon reading about a therapeutic technique in a textbook.

The second stage, *frustration*, arises when an impasse is reached and we do not know how to proceed. At this point we are in danger of giving up. This is what might happen, for example, when the textbook technique produces unexpected results not considered in the written instructions, so that it no longer seems appropriate to proceed as planned, but we don't yet know what else to do. During such moments, it can be helpful to reflect that this is a stage in the creative process, meaning that frustration is to be expected and is not wrong. Indeed, contrary to common-sense assumptions, frustration is a sign that a creative process is underway.

If we can tolerate this frustration stage, we then enter the third stage, *incubation*, which is characterized by the giving up of direct attempts to make something happen and instead, waiting for something to arise. We allow the consequences of the therapeutic technique to unfold and trust a new way forward will eventually emerge.

The fourth stage, *illumination*, is the sudden and effortless arising of a new insight or "aha" moment—a new way forward for the therapeutic technique now being apparent.

In the fifth and final stage, *elaboration*, the insight is shaped into workable form, such as through the choice of words and phrases used to continue delivering the technique.

The advantage of this five-stage model is the way it guides therapeutic attention away from a narrow assumption of "creativity" as a momentary flash of inspiration and towards a broader temporal appreciation. As the following detailed discussion of each stage, and accompanying clinical examples, will now show, a creative adaptation of technique will not just be what happens during a moment of fresh insight but also what leads up to and follows on from it, continuously adjusting to the "immediate situation" and "living reality" of the consulting room, which never stops changing.

The Preparation Stage

The creative process begins with a "preparation stage". While this can include future anticipations or desires, the emphasis is upon describing the current situation. Any rush to outcomes will be in danger of bypassing the important work of clarifying the current issues, questions, and motivations of the client.

The general principal to follow is "from the known to the unknown".[196] While sometimes the preparation stage can spontaneously lead to a creative transformation, the intention is to simply collect information rather than produce anything new.

Only by first establishing what we know about the existing situation will a new way forward duly emerge.

Despite the name, the preparation stage is a continuous aspect of the creative process, as there will always be new information coming into awareness. The opening minutes of any individual session will be a regular "preparation stage", in which the therapist enquires as to how the client has been since the previous session and what they are bringing to the current session. And then, as subsequent experiences emerge during the course of a session, a return to the preparation stage will be what allows them to be acknowledged and described. But most obviously, a "preparation stage" will be evident in the initial assessment and diagnostic period, when the presenting issues and symptoms are first shared by the client.

The preparation stage in these opening sessions maps what Assagioli calls the "preliminary step in psychosynthesis", which he describes as being one of establishing "a thorough knowledge of the conscious and unconscious aspect of one's personality".[197]

While "thorough knowledge" might appear unattainably idealistic, Assagioli later qualifies this by writing, "We do not aim at a thorough, complete, exhaustive exploration of the unconscious."[198] The intention is to address "the immediate situation of the patient" and then allow further assessment "in the course of the preceding treatment . . . as circumstances necessitate, even towards the end of the therapy".[199]

This is another way of saying that the preparation stage never really ends.

Psychosynthesis has many techniques that particularly focus on a "general assessment and exploration of the unconscious".[200] Clients are invited to fill in questionnaires, maintain a reflective journal, record dreams, write autobiographies, make "free drawings", explore guided imagery, and more.

While space does not allow for a full description of all these techniques, what matters is the underlying principles of application. The following description of a guided imagery journey will provide a first example to discuss the creative application and adaptation of psychosynthesis techniques.

"Guided imagery" is a generic term used in psychosynthesis for a range of image-based applications described by Assagioli as "Visualization",[201] "Symbol Utilization",[202] "Imaginative Evocation",[203] and "Initiated Symbol Projection".[204] Each of these techniques offers a slightly different emphasis on image-based work.

We will be approaching these techniques collectively as "guided imagery". This will allow us to focus on the principles they have in common and illustrate the emphasis Assagioli placed on applying techniques flexibly, in "a kind of fluid combination", which, despite appearing to lack order, "is in fact obedient to a higher order of organic development".[205]

A basic principle of guided imagery techniques is that the spontaneously emergent symbolic imagery they reveal is not random but directly reflective of psychological life. As an assessment method, guided imagery therefore allows a means for the "underlying psycho-dynamic organization"[206] of the client to be expressed and described in its perhaps purest formulation:

> To address the unconscious in logical terms is not particularly effective. In order to reach the unconscious . . . we have to speak in its own terms. One should attempt to use the mode in which the unconscious normally operates, which is by way of symbols.[207]

Guided imagery techniques bypass the limitations of conceptual terminology, or "logical terms", thereby meeting the psychological situation of the client directly on "its own terms", by way of symbolic imagery, the benefits of which include, but also go beyond, the initial assessment stage.

> Clinical experience has demonstrated that the source of most psychological maladjustment lies (in "psychological space") on an infantile or primitive, and largely pre-conscious level. On that level thinking appears to take place largely in a "symbolic language" and thus the unresolved conflicts of childhood are best and most easily expressed *and treated* in largely symbolic terms.[208]

Guided imagery techniques are diagnostic and also therapeutic. Working directly with images provides a route into psychological life on what Assagioli calls "the symbolic (non-analytic) level".[209] Once again, the experiential emphasis of psychosynthesis is being made apparent, in the possibility of working directly with the *process* of imaginative experience, treating images as images, without any need to produce a conceptual *outcome* on a theoretical level by turning the images into ideas and interpretations.

The following case study illustrates the guided imagery technique in experiential context.[210] The transcript picks up the work 25 minutes into the second session with a new client. I am the therapist (Th), and Daniel is the client (Cl):

> Th: How about we see what imagery comes up around this issue?
>
> Cl: Sure? But how do you mean "imagery"?
>
> Th: Well, if you were to imagine what we've been talking about as a place . . .

An invitation to "close your eyes" and some kind of relaxation procedure is a common but not always necessary start to the guided imagery technique. Indeed, such a beginning can serve to interrupt the natural flow of the session and produce an unhelpful self-consciousness or performance anxiety for the client. Whereas in the same way we might straightforwardly enquire as to what the client is feeling or thinking, so too we can simply ask what they are imagining, without any need for eyes being closed.

To imagine a scene with the eye of imagination while simultaneously seeing the consulting room is not only perfectly possible, it is also a common occurrence, happening whenever clients explore memories or anticipate future fantasies. The technical name for this is "hypnagogic visions", characterized by a dual consciousness in which the imagined scene overlaps with an awareness of the physical world.[211] The aim of guided imagery is therefore not a complete immersion within an imagined world, but a much more subtle—and realizable—confluence with the physical world.

The only direction given to the client in this example is to picture themselves in an imagined landscape, the principle being that images are places. Whether in a sleeping dream, recollecting a memory, or doing a guided imagery technique, to imagine is to find ourselves within an encompassing story world or environment.

While sometimes a particular opening scene, such as a meadow, is suggested, this is not always necessary or desirable. The principle reason for suggesting an opening scene is to provide "an easy start . . . for the play of their imagination".[212]

However, as the chapter opening showed, even the apparently benign suggestion of a meadow can become an unnecessary distraction, as any such predetermined "content" *outcomes* will always be in danger of steering the client towards what the therapist assumes they should be imagining (a meadow), rather than helping them describe the naturally unfolding imaginative *process* they are already experiencing. Assagioli calls this "autochthonous" imagery, and it is constantly bubbling away at the edges of awareness.[213]

Especially in an assessment period, but also more generally, it is working with this innate autochthonous imagery that most directly embeds the technique within its experiential context. In this way, by allowing the client to spontaneously determine the opening scene, the technique becomes creatively adaptive from the very beginning.[214]

Th: Just take your time, and when you are ready, tell me where you are.

Cl: I'm on a staircase—a stone staircase, rising on and on above me.

Th: A staircase. What kind of stone steps are they?

Cl: Really wide and deep, and old, worn down in the middle; a grey colour.

Th: Uh huh, and what's the quality of the light?

Cl: It's dull. There's an overcast sky, low running clouds. And it's cold.

Th: Cold and overcast. And what can you hear?

Cl: It's really quiet and still on the steps, but there's party noises coming from somewhere nearby.

Th: What kind of party noises?

Cl: Music and chatter and laughter, people having fun. I can see them through a brightly lit window. There's a woman, standing in the shadow of the curtains.

Th: A woman in the shadows.

Cl: Yeah, looking down at me. I'm feeling a bit freaked at being watched.

Th: Freaked?

Cl: Well, unsure; sort of frozen on the spot. Does she want me to be there or not? Does she want me to climb up to the party or not?

Th: So, you're standing on a wide, worn, stone staircase, rising on and on above you. It's cold. The sky is overcast. A woman is looking down at you from a window above, with a party going on in the background. And you are feeling a bit freaked out, not sure whether she wants you to join her or not.

Cl: Yeah, that's right.

Th: What's happening now?

Cl: The woman has stepped out of the shadows, towards the window. She is young, slim, shoulder-length hair. But I can't make out her expression.

Th: Is there anything else you'd like to tell me or do before we move on?

Cl: I'm running up the steps, but they seem endless.

The guided imagery technique requires a fulsome and continuous sensory description of the imagined scene within which the client finds themselves. While the normal world simply exists, whether or not we pay it any attention, an imagined scene needs an attentional effort to maintain the sense of "actually participating in it".[215]

What supports this requirement is an understanding, to be further developed in chapter 4, of imagination as a synthetic experience, one that combines the psychological functions of sensation, feeling, thinking, and intuition.[216] It will be in networking together all these functions that the therapist establishes and stabilizes the required hypnagogic state for the client.

In the above example, as is often the case, due to sight usually being the predominant sense sensation, this networking of psychological functions began with a visual description of the surrounding locale. The "quality of the light" question then bridged into the sensation of touch, with the cold temperature that was felt on the skin as a tactile image. A third sensation was introduced with the description of auditory images or sounds. Olfactory images were neglected but it could have been included by simply asking "What can you smell?"

As Assagioli writes, "combining the evocation of the image with sensations derived from the different senses strengthens the association and the effect."[217]

Once the immediate sensory situation is established, feelings and thoughts often emerge spontaneously, as was the case with Daniel, although if this does not occur the therapist can eventually enquire after them directly.

But notice how the feelings and thoughts described are from within the process of imagining. Any feelings or thoughts from outside the process, which is to say, reflection upon the image "content", such as, for example, "What part of me does the woman represent?", would introduce a theoretical-conceptual approach; therefore, these are best ignored or avoided during the guided imagery session so as not to detract from an experiential emphasis.

A significant difference between Assagioli's guided imagery technique and Carl Jung's somewhat similar "active imagination" is the co-creation between therapist and client.

Jung encouraged his clients "to visualize alone, rather than in the presence of the psychologist" due to a "fear the psychologists presence . . . would reduce the essential spontaneity and value of visualization"; however, Assagioli's experience led him to the opposite conclusion: He felt that a sufficiently skilled therapist could be a supportive rather than distracting presence and assist the client to first develop and then maintain focus upon imagining the scene.[218]

It is this dialogic exchange—closely tracking and shaping the clients *experiencing* of the scene—that allows an ongoing creative adaptation of the technique.

> Th: Okay, take your time, and relax your attention upon the imagery.
>
> Cl: Okay.
>
> Th: And let's have a wonder about the story together?
>
> Cl: How so?
>
> Th: Well, where might you recognize this story in your everyday life? I mean, not literally, but where might you find yourself "as if" standing on a staircase, with this sense of being watched and unsure what to do?

The actual guided imagery journey is not the endpoint of the technique but really only a beginning, and the session continues by exploring connections between the imagined world and the client's everyday life world.

While Daniel will not be expected to find himself walking up an actual stone staircase to meet a mysterious woman at a party it is usually not difficult to find real-life parallels to the nexus of relational patterning shown in the guided imagery.

Assagioli describes how this connection into everyday life is done by analogy:

> . . . it is well to make as clear as possible the relationship between the symbol and the reality which it represents. This relationship is based mainly, if not exclusively, on analogy. Analogy, we might say, is an important psychological link or connection between outer and inner realities . . . a normal and really unavoidable psychological activity.[219]

> The approach of analogy is based on the essential unity of all the aspects of Reality, from the smallest to the largest. Thus, there is a close correspondence between the microcosm and the macrocosm in general.[220]

The spontaneously emergent symbolic imagery revealed by the technique is understood to reflect the "underlying psycho-dynamic organization" of the client and how it connects "between outer and inner realities." In other words, psychological life is not only about "inner" feelings and thoughts but also how those feelings and thoughts shape an experience of the surrounding world and other people.

In this way, the application of analogy as a "psychological link" provides an experiential elaboration of the theoretical understanding of synthesis as a universal principle, evident across multiple scales of attention, within the personality and also relationships to other people, places, and things.

Given that Daniel had presented in therapy seeking help with a depression brought on by losing his job due to a down-turn in the economy, it was perhaps no surprise that his first analogy was to the stone steps of the Bank of England, his previous employer. A related analogy was made between the mysterious woman at the party window and his fiancée, who had left Daniel for another man soon after he lost his job. Both these proximate analogies reflected the symbolic imagery of finding himself on the outside and feeling unclear as to whether he was wanted or not.

There were further analogies, from earlier in Daniel's life, reflecting the running-up-the-steps imagery and him trying hard to get back in as a response to the feeling of being on the outside. These included how he had dealt with the sudden death of a close childhood friend in a car accident by throwing himself into the school football team's training schedule and the time he had dropped out of college, found a job in a bank, and worked hard to gain promotion, eventually climbing all the way to management level.

I also noted a further layer of analogy in Daniel's eagerness to please me. How he always listened carefully, readily answering questions and even asking for "homework" between sessions, all the while having a somewhat quizzical expression, as if waiting to be told his problems were not properly sufficient to continue the therapy. This matched my countertransference (a therapist's response to a client) of feeling unusually strong anxiety during the sessions and having fantasies between sessions that Daniel would not return.

These analogous situations helped formulate my initial assessment of Daniel's current level of identification as the normal mistake of equating selfhood with the "contents of consciousness", as described in chapter 1.

The repeating analogy pattern of being lost on the outside and working hard to try and get back in again suggested identification with manic people-pleasing activity driven by a constant fear of rejection. However, given that the imagery is "directly applicable to therapy without intermediary analysis or interpretation," I did not share the idea of "identification" directly with Daniel.[221]

An "intermediary analysis or interpretation", which is to say a theoretical discussion, may at times be helpful, but it may also be harmful, Assagioli warning of "the temptation of theoretical inquiry and theoretical research—which would be of no benefit to the patient and perhaps harmful, unduly prolonging the treatment or even sidetracking it".[222]

Use of theoretical terminology, such as "identification", would have moved the therapy towards offering explanations and interpretations and away from working directly with the client's experience, thereby creating the danger of "cognitive separation", as presented in the previous chapter.

In order to maintain an experiential emphasis, the case studies in this book avoid the usage of theoretical terminology. While this need not always be the case, application of experiential techniques is most effective if it is conducted using non-specialist everyday descriptive language best suited to meeting the client within the process of synthesis.

It is therefore important for a psychosynthesis therapist to know the difference between theoretical terminology and descriptive speech so that they can consciously decide to apply techniques and avoid sharing conceptual abstractions with the client. This was the case in therapeutic work with Daniel, which proceeded by further description of how the guided imagery *experientially* connected to his everyday life:

> One of the ways in which analogy can systematically be used is in attempting to find new and unusual relationships and to find hypotheses—or ways of looking at things—which one did not have before. It is a method which is full of rich possibilities for creativity . . . . It is linked with that part of the creative process which one might call the "loosening stage", when one allows the unconscious to bring new and creative relationships.[223]

The gathering of analogies is a creative process. In noticing "new and unusual relationships" between the guided imagery symbology and Daniel's life situation, something new was being created, a "way of looking at things which one did not have before". The analogy pattern became a background narrative, or "lens", through which Daniel came to see his whole life more clearly and easily, both past and future, pathology and potential. I understood this to be the beginnings of a "disidentification" process; that is, a growing recognition of his habitual way of being as shaped by past events and limiting "ideal models", something which once learned was now capable of being unlearned.

We will leave a description of Daniel's new possibilities for chapter 4, where we pick up his story next, and for now continue exploring the creative process with other case examples.

The Frustration Stage

Any truly creative process is a voyage into the unknown; therefore, it is always going to entail a necessary measure of unpredictability and surprise, mystery, and strangeness. To set out knowing the destination, and who we will be upon arrival, is merely a projection into the future of an already established position, a repetition, rather than the creation of anything new.

The "frustration stage" begins upon reaching the borderline between the known and the unknown. As mentioned, the dynamic principal of the creative process is one of moving "from the known to the unknown".[224]

During the preparation stage, the effort of gathering known elements is by itself seldom sufficient to create change and transformation, and after a while it seems as if there is a diminishing return for our efforts. The more we push on, the less progress we make.

To the extent we expected otherwise, this leads to feeling frustrated—perhaps in danger of giving up, but frustration about the creative process not working quickly and smoothly need not be a surprise.

It can be helpful to understand the near inevitability of the frustration stage. Creative change is a process, not the flicking of a switch. To expect the momentum of old ways to suddenly stop and a new direction begin, simply because we decided it would be a good idea, is unrealistic. While creative breakthroughs can appear suddenly, assumptions of this always being the case will be in danger of bypassing the frustration stage, which needs to be engaged with, rather than avoided, in order to keep the creative process moving.

Psychosynthesis has many techniques applicable to navigating the frustration stage. Indeed, given that all psychosynthesis techniques can be understood in relation to the disidentification process, during which there is often a struggle to move beyond the familiarity of identification, many are therefore easily related to the frustration stage.

The following case example, with a client called "Rebecca", once again illustrates the creative adaptation of a number of these techniques in combination.

Th: What do you imagine the people in the meeting are thinking about you when you are like this?

Cl: I don't know. I don't think they think very much. *[looks blank and confused]*

Th: How do you mean not "very much"? *[gathering further description]*

Cl: You know, they don't care.

Th: And picking up they don't care leads you into this uncontrollable talking? *[empathic understanding]*

Cl: That's right, I just can't stop talking. It's ridiculous!

Th: And this happened recently in the work meeting, and you are also saying it's happening at other times.

Cl: That's right, it's happening more and more. I get anxious and start blabbing away. People are going to think I'm losing it. I don't know what to do!

The presence of critical judgements from the people in the meeting and the related sense of vulnerability suggested that Rebecca had entered the frustration stage.

In crude terms, whenever change is being taken seriously, as is implicitly happening just by turning up to a therapy session, the frustration stage will become evident in the appearance of critical judgements attempting to shut down the creative process, preventing the client from going beyond the current level of identification. While a direct discussion of this identification on a theoretical level was an option, it would have missed out on the opportunities for working with the process of disidentification experientially.

> Th: These people that don't care about you—in the meeting at work and also at other times—if you were to picture them as just one person, someone to whom you are talking to but they are not really listening, seeming not to care about what you are saying, who would this one person be?
>
> Cl: Well, I don't know.
>
> Th: Just take your time, and see who comes up for this one person [not being surprised by client's uncertainty/keeping the process going by communicating patience and a quiet expectation that an image will come]
>
> Cl: It's my mum.
>
> Th: Your mum?
>
> Cl: Yeah, Mum.
>
> Th: And how is she looking at you? What is her facial expression?
>
> Cl: She's not looking at me but past me, and frowning. Frowning.

While Rebecca had reported feeling judged in the work meeting, there was no actual description of her colleagues being judgemental. Quite possibly they were just bored by the meeting, or maybe even interested in what Rebecca had to say. All we do know for sure is that Rebecca *imagined* that they were critical, and this provided an opening for the technique of personification.[225]

As discussed in chapter 1, Assagioli writes of the experiential basis for this technique, as a "principle of personification" that is "not a theory" but a description of how "every psychological element . . . tend[s] to personify themselves".[226]

By inviting Rebecca to describe the issue as a person, the technique can therefore be seen to align with the natural tendency of psychological life to present itself via personifications. However, the actual language of "personification", or similar theoretical terminology such as "subpersonality" or "part of you", was not introduced.[227] Instead, the technique continued with an experiential emphasis by simply describing the imagined person, not as an abstract idea or concept, but as an in-the-moment encounter within the consulting room.

Th: Given that we are talking about her, and it's therefore sort of as if she is now in the room with us, how about we give her a place and imagine her sitting on this chair *[indicating an empty chair]*

Cl: Er, okay. She's leaning back in the chair, sort of looking down her nose at me.

Th: Looking down her nose at you. *[I'm now looking towards the empty chair, rather than Rebecca, so as to facilitate the personification as a location in the room]*

Cl: Yeah, and sort of tutting, clicking her tongue.

Th: What's she wearing?

Cl: Her housework apron, a pair of jeans, and a cardigan.

Th: And how is it to have her sitting in the room with us?

Cl: Anxious and sort of a resigned feeling, a sense of giving up.

The above section combines the personification and empty chair techniques—not least because they go together very well.

The empty chair provides a placeholder to bring the imagined person more immediately into the client's experience, so that the personification is no longer merely a picture in the mind but a tangible, contextualized presence within the consulting room, all familiar techniques to me as a therapist.

The creative adaptation thus far had not been about the format of the technique itself, having applied it in a similar way many times before, but about subtle modifications to align it with the specific experience of the client. However, as the session proceeded, a new technique emerged, one that just came to me as a good idea, as something I had not done before.

Th: I'm wondering what it would be like to remove the chair from the room? Would you be up for trying that?

Cl: I think so.

Th: Okay. Well, I could move it, or perhaps you would like to do it?

Cl: I'll do it. *[Rebecca gets up and places the chair outside the consulting room, closing the door behind her and sitting back down again in her seat.]*

Th: Okay, notice the empty space now where the chair was before, and when you are ready, let me know how it is to be here now. What difference, if any, does removing the chair make?

Cl: A big difference.

Th: How so?

Cl: Well, it's a relief. I didn't realize before how tense I was feeling, but now my shoulders and stomach are all relaxed. There's a lightness in the room that just wasn't there before.

Th: Anything else going on?

Cl: It's kinda sad, too. An alone feeling. [Her eyes redden, but she does not cry]

Th: I understand. It's a relief, and also there is something sad and lonely about it. And also, I'm noticing how you've really slowed down now, compared to how you were talking earlier. How is it to slow down like this?

Cl: Bit weird.

Th: What kind of weird?

Cl: I don't feel so scared anymore. I'm upset but also a bit angry, not anxious anymore.

The removal of the empty chair was a newly invented technique. In the same way that Assagioli invented his own techniques or adapted existing techniques, so also contemporary psychosynthesis therapists need to do the same. Techniques are not regarded as standardized and complete, to be repeated in the same way each time but as "only tools, and as tools can be modified", so as to apply them to "the overall purpose of psychosynthesis"[228]. An "overall purpose", as discussed earlier, which requires adapting these tools to *a broad and uncertain outcome*.

To the extent that there is a narrowly anticipated or expected outcome, a technique is not creative. For instance, a *narrow outcome* for the removal of the empty chair would have been to facilitate a feeling of relief in Rebecca. As it turned out, this was what happened, but my actual intention was to provide *the process conditions needed for creative change.*

I had the idea of the chair removal being a ritual or psychodrama enactment of a disidentification process. I perceived the critical psychological elements personified in the chair to be keeping Rebecca trapped within the frustration stage, so by creating a physical space or distance from the personification, my hope was to create a parallel psychological space for an expansion of awareness and will; that is, a disidentification process.

The result was uncertain. I had not anticipated what Rebecca would experience as a result of the technique, because disidentification, as discussed in chapter 2, is not about the "contents of consciousness".

In a broad sense the technique did work out as planned. After the removal of the chair, Rebecca went beyond her previously anxious identification to experience a new-found level of confidence, accompanied by an unfamiliar feeling of anger. In other words, she had disidentified. However, this does not mean the technique of removing the empty chair will have the same results with another client.

As Assagioli writes:

> . . . the use of a specific technique or exercise, which may prove useful in one case or in one phase, may be unsuitable or even harmful for other individuals or in different conditions.[229]

The creative adaptation of technique requires an alignment with current psychological "conditions". Happily, the removal of the empty chair aligned well with what turned out to be an emerging assertion in Rebecca. In other words, she was ready to create distance, which is to say "disidentify", from the critical psychological elements personified by the chair. The technique therefore enacted a further facilitation of what was already beginning to happen for her psychologically.

For another person more strongly identified with these critical elements, however, this technique may be less suitable—as would perhaps be evident by their overwhelm and distress on the removal of the empty chair, as opposed to relief and newfound assertion.

To judge whether a client is ready for a particular technique is not straightforward. There is no way to guarantee what will happen ahead of time if we are leaping into the unknown. What is therefore more important than the initial choice of technique is having the necessary creative adaptability to spontaneously follow the process of synthesis wherever it goes.

Incubation Stage

The "incubation stage" is similar but different to the frustration stage. Given that there still remains no new way forward, it is similar, but the significant difference is with respect to how this continuing impasse is dealt with. While the frustration stage may be characterized as trying but failing to control the creative process and pushing on despite diminishing returns, the incubation stage is marked by a recognition of having done all we can do for now, at which point it is time to step back from direct attempts to *make* something happen.

By the time we reach the incubation stage the creative process has a life of its own, and we trust that a new way forward will arise, or at least be more probable, precisely because we have stopped consciously trying to make it happen. This is like a gardener, having prepared the ground and planted seeds, sitting back and waiting for green shoots to emerge.

As Assagioli writes:

> Creativity . . . often requires a period of . . . incubation, during which it is advisable to let the unconscious work without further interference from the conscious will. Paradoxically, paying conscious attention to, or being emotionally preoccupied with, creative processes disturbs them.[230]

In psychosynthesis psychotherapy, the incubation stage can be understood as a continuation of the disidentification process begun in the preceding stages. The frustration stage struggle to remain within the current level of identification has been worked through to allow an acceptance of the need to let go of this old way of being. However, there is still no new identity forthcoming, so the incubation stage is a transitional stage in-between identities:

> . . . this is a period of transition; a passing out of the old condition, without having firmly reached the new, an in-

> termediate stage, in which . . . one is like a caterpillar undergoing the process of transformation into the winged butterfly. The insect must pass through the stage of the chrysalis, a condition of disintegration and helplessness.[231]

The above description of disidentification, quoted already in chapter 1, as analogous to the caterpillar-chrysalis-butterfly cycle, describes well the hiatus of the incubation stage. The previous caterpillar identification having now been fully renounced, the incubation stage finds us within a "chrysalis", in "an intermediate stage", during which we do not yet know what we will become, perhaps having never even looked up at the sky, let alone contemplated the possibility of flight upon colourful wings. All that is still to come.

An important therapeutic consideration during this stage is to allow the necessary time for incubation. This is not always easy or straightforward. Modern life tends to proceed at an incredibly fast pace, often resulting in pressure on therapists and clients to produce reliable results in the shortest possible period, with measurable effects and a cumulative progress in direct proportion to the number of completed sessions.

In this paradigm, any interruption to progress is often deemed to be a "problem", either due to the therapist being "ineffective" or the client being "stuck" and "resistant" to treatment. This can be understood as the result of imagining therapy to be a mechanical process.

Given the ubiquity of machines in modern life it may intuitively make sense to draw upon the mind-as-machine metaphor to speak of "tensions", "pressures," "stresses", and "resistances." These terms can be a helpful terminology for picturing psychological life, but problems arise when they are taken literally, as a whole truth, rather than just a partial comparison—not least because the assumption of mechanical predictability, order, and control will have little place for an incubation stage.

Machines do not pass through a "period of transition" or "intermediate stage". Machines do not grow, develop, or transform themselves into new, improved models. Machines are designed to do a specific task over and over, until they break down and need to be repaired. To imagine therapy as a mechanical process is therefore in danger of assuming that clients are "broken down" and need to return to "productivity" and "effectiveness".

Any therapeutic focus on "repairing" clients will not be a creative process, because the return to a previous state of "working order" is not a journey into the unknown. And any rush towards premature and pre-planned outcomes will bring with it the danger of mishandling the incubation stage by continuing to apply direct efforts, rather than stepping back and giving the creative process the necessary time to do its magic.

Allowing space for an incubation stage requires reimagining periods of apparent non-change. What might appear to be resistance or stuckness need not be a sign of something having gone wrong or indeed, that nothing is happening. Just because we can't see beneath the surface does not mean the "seeds" planted in earlier sessions are not continuing to grow. It takes time for these "seeds" to grow into therapeutic outcomes.

As we have noted, the incubation stage is best imagined via metaphorical comparison to ecological processes—as in the above examples of planting "seeds" and passing through a "chrysalis" hiatus.

The natural world is always passing through cycles of creation and destruction, growth and decay. Both the annual cycle from summer into winter, and the daily rhythms between night and day, feature "a period of transition"—a fallow period of rest—as a necessary precursor to the future growth to come.

Given that human beings are part of nature, not separate from it, it is perhaps not surprising that we turn to these ecological comparisons to help us better understand the creative process. Indeed, "incubation" in itself is an ecological term for the gestation period of eggs.

The incubation stage as a fallow period of waiting does not mean there is nothing to be done. What we are waiting for is a clear *outcome* of direction to arise. In the meantime, a therapist will not just be sitting around "being" with the client in pure silence but rather, continuing to provide the necessary conditions to maintain the creative *process*.

Most obviously, this will involve providing attentive care and empathic understanding towards the client's experience of this somewhat vulnerable in-between time. The above-mentioned ecological metaphors may well be a helpful framework to share with the client, as an antidote to any pressure the client feels to prematurely rush past the incubation stage.

A more structured application of technique can also be introduced during the incubation stage, with two important provisos.

First, the technique will avoid too narrow a focus on creating a particular feeling, insight, or expression—which would force the incubation stage in a predetermined direction—and instead, place emphasis on providing the necessary therapeutic conditions to facilitate the *process* of synthesis in whichever direction it wishes to go.

Second, the choice and timing of any given technique will be seen to arise from the therapist attending to their own creative process, in what we might consider a parallel creative process to that of the client.

Several times during each session, the therapist will return to the preparation stage, gathering their own thoughts, feelings, intuitions, and memories about the work with the client and moving in and out of their own frustration stage in order to disidentify from critical judgements and vulnerable feelings of incompetence and inferiority.

Furthermore, at times during the session, the therapist will enter their own incubation stage, which may be characterized as the faithful expectation that new understanding and ideas about what techniques to follow will emerge in due course, despite not knowing what is happening or what to do about it at this moment.

In this way, the therapist avoids any formulaic repetition of tried-and-tested interventions and remains sensitive to creative adaptations, either within the format of a particular technique or as illustrated above in the empty chair case study, through the invention of entirely new techniques.

This brings us to the fourth stage of the creative process.

Illumination Stage

The opening stages of the creative process precede a breakthrough of sudden insight in the "illumination stage". The effortful preparation, anxious frustration, and patient incubation eventually pay off in a "light bulb" moment.

Out of the blue, all of a sudden, a spark of inspiration arrives—a moment of creative possibility that appears unexpectedly and seemingly without effort, casting the issue or question in a new light and transforming foggy confusion and frustration into clarity and fresh purpose.

Sometimes the illumination stage arrives in bold and obvious fashion, but not always. A welcome appearance of the new is present in a multitude of subtle and even ordinary micro moments within every therapeutic session, just waiting to be noticed at the edges of awareness via seemingly random and fleeting phrases, images, memories, or shifting moods. All of these can be easily overlooked, especially if we are busy searching for a narrow and *predetermined outcome*. The main task of the illumination stage is therefore to be receptive to the subtlety of communications hinting at *unexpected outcomes*.

In psychosynthesis psychotherapy, the illumination stage can be understood in light of several of the teaching "experiences" described in chapter 1. Perhaps most obviously, an illumination is characteristic of an inflow of "superconscious" experience from beyond the habitual limits or identification of the "personal self". The result is a continuation of the process of "disidentification" tracked across the preceding stages and now moving towards its outcome. And whatever form the illumination takes—the variety of which we will soon discuss—the experience is also well characterized by what Assagioli describes as a dialogue between the personal self and "transpersonal Self", which constitutes a "transmission" of "psychological communications" and "enlightening impressions" that are "reaching us all the time":

> The process or mechanism of this transmission is difficult to understand and often its existence is more than many

> people realize or are ready to admit. It apparently involves the whole gestalt of a person's life and the subtle unconscious psychological interplay between the patient and his environment. However, it is not necessary to know the mechanism of transmission—the fact is that sometimes the answer comes seemingly spontaneously through a third person or through a book or other reading matter, or through the development of circumstances themselves. In a certain sense this should not surprise us too much, and it might indicate the fact that enlightening impressions or psychological communications are reaching us all the time, even when not consciously sought. It is we who do not recognize the many and varied "signals." But the fact of formulating a question and being in a state of general expectation helps us to register and recognize what would otherwise remain hidden.[232]

In moments when life seems to be telling you something, the precise "mechanism" by which this happens is not what is most important. How the illumination or answer comes need not be understood on a theoretical level. What Assagioli emphasizes, once again, is the experiential "fact" of these "transmissions", which in perhaps more ways "than many people realize" are to be found in ongoing communications happening via the "interplay between the patient and his environment"—whether in the shape of a "third person", "a book or reading matter", or general "circumstances".

From a transpersonal perspective, psychological life as discussed in chapter 1, is not just "inner" but seen to arise contextually, across a network of relationships, both within persons and also passing through, beyond and between persons, places, and things. It is within these relationships that the subtle signals and hints of the illumination stage will be found.

Psychosynthesis has many techniques applicable to the illumination stage. Of most relevance will be those techniques focused on "spiritual psychosynthesis" and contact with the "superconscious" and "transpersonal Self".

Common to all these techniques is facilitation of the ongoing relationship between the personal self and transpersonal Self. In other words, there is always an "I"-Self relationship. The practical task is therefore not so much to initiate a relationship from scratch but rather, to notice and engage with an already existing exchange of communications.

The following creative adaptation of "The Technique of Dialogue"[233] demonstrates this relational principle within the illumination stage of the creative process.

Assagioli describes the technique of dialogue as a specific application of "the technique of symbol utilization", which was mentioned earlier, in the preparation stage clinical example.[234] A basic first step is to notice the "intermediary" symbol through which "the many and varied 'signals'" from transpersonal Self may be communicating.

As a surrounding contextual network of relationships, transpersonal Self will not be found directly as a discrete entity, but indirectly through these intermediary symbols, which will be recognizable in significant moments, when attention becomes captured by something novel and fresh, beyond the habitual expectations of the personal self.

While there are perhaps an innumerable number of such intermediary symbols, the following list gives an indication of common possibilities to be found in:

- Other people, such as a good conversation or therapy session, and so forth
- The arts, such as novels, movies, paintings
- Sensations and movements, such as dance, massage, exercise, and so forth
- Gaps and discontinuities, such as sudden pauses in speaking, facial expression, gaze

- Introspection, such as meditation, active imagination, reflection and study
- Nature, such as walking in the woods, birdwatching, wild swimming, pets

A case example now introduces the technique of dialogue with my client "Duncan", who had been coming to therapy for long-term depression and suicidal ideation for about five months. The transcript begins with Duncan reporting a significant moment one evening, while out walking his dog.

> Cl: I don't quite know how to describe it.
>
> Th: Where were you when it happened?
>
> Cl: I was out walking the dog and just looked up. Which I never do, but it felt as if something was calling me to look up.
>
> Th: And what did you see?
>
> Cl: Well, it kinda happened all at once. There was this tree, covered in spring blossoms, deep pink ones. And they were sort of framing a full moon. A bright full moon, shining down through this gap in the branches, and it seemed to be—it's stupid really—as if it was looking at me, aware of me.
>
> Th: And what was the moon saying to you?
>
> Cl: I don't know. But it's about what I said, because after a while I turned to the dog and said, "Who wouldn't want to live in a world as beautiful as this?"

A number of elements in the above transcript suggested an opportunity for the technique of dialogue. The report by Duncan of the moon as "calling", "looking", and being "aware" were indicative of ongoing communications.

I therefore assumed the moon to be an intermediary symbol of meaningful significance to Duncan and began the technique of dialogue by inviting a description of what the moon was saying.

But Duncan did not know what it was saying, so at that point, it might have been easy to give up on the technique; however, it is important to be patient. Good things take time.

As Assagioli writes:

> On occasion the answer is immediate and spontaneous; it is received clearly and comes with authority and an absence of all doubt. But this occurs in only the more fortunate cases, for sometimes there appears to be no answer at all. This should not be a reason for discouragement. Sometimes the answer is delayed and comes in an unexpected moment, when the personality is not looking for it and is perhaps occupied with other concerns—a condition that seems to facilitate the reception of the message, because eager expectation and tenseness can constitute an obstacle to receptivity.[235]

While the technique of dialogue is particularly suited to facilitating the illumination stage, as with any given technique, the application will be a creative process, during which all five of the stages will be evident at times.

The above transcript opening shows what could be considered a mini preparation stage, gathering a description of known elements, which then moved into a frustration stage when the dialogue did not proceed in a straightforward way. But recognizing that "This should not be a reason for discouragement" allows a movement into the incubation stage.

Between noticing the moon and talking to his dog, something from beyond the bounds of Duncan's normal identification had entered into awareness. This was the first mention in five months of not only a clear desire from Duncan to continue living but also a reason for doing so, the beauty of the world—both of which suggested an illumination stage communication.

I therefore wanted to continue with the technique of dialogue, as a way to better notice and elaborate upon this illumination. But before doing so, something else needed to happen.

The initial attempt at dialogue had simply been too fast. I had rushed into asking, "What was the moon saying?" without giving sufficient time for Daniel to re-establish himself within the memory. To do so, it is helpful to appreciate how memories are images, an imagining of the past, and therefore, as discussed earlier, with regard to the "guided imagery" technique, it will be important to first establish an experience for the client of finding themselves within this image as an encompassing environment.

Without this experiential context, attempts at dialogue will tend to either result in silence, as occurred in the above case, or with the client unwittingly filling the silence by making up what they think the symbol might say. While such self-invented speech can be an interesting reflective exercise, it will be a dialogue from within the limitations of the current level of identification, rather than a genuine illumination stage communication.

Of course, there is no way to say for sure what is genuine dialogue, but a good indicator will be the accompanying feeling tone. Self-invented speech is characterized by a calm and rational certitude, as opposed to the more edgy, out-of-control spontaneity and surprise of an illumination stage communication.

To better establish the experiential context of the memory, as a precursor for returning to the technique of dialogue, I continued the session with Assagioli's "Live it Again" technique.[236] As the name suggests, this consists in "asking the patient to live again, as realistically as possible, the scene or situation . . . not as an objective event as seen by a spectator but as a participator or living actor".[237]

Assagioli further states that this technique can equally be applied "to future events of which the person may be afraid, the expectation of which evokes anxiety".[238] This means that we have both a "Live it Again" and also a "Live it Already" technique, the rationale being that a present-tense exploration will provide a much stronger experiential emphasis.

In the earlier case examples of guided imagery in the preparation stage and empty-chair work in the frustration stage, a present-tense exploration was assumed, whereas, in the current case example with Duncan, the beginning is taken from a memory, which is initially described in a past-tense perspective; that is, "I was out walking the dog" and "There *was* this tree." If we maintain a past-tense perspective, the result will be a looking back in retrospect, from a once-removed viewpoint, telling the story about what happened.

However, because experiences are a series of "now" moments, this past-tense perspective will act against the application of an experiential technique, in a similar fashion to the separation created by "the observer" position, discussed in chapter 1. To work experientially with memories, or future fantasies, therefore requires switching into a present-tense description so as to create the perspective of "a participator or living actor" from within the situation, living through the various feelings, thoughts, and sensations in real time.

To move from a past memory into the "Live It Again" technique can be approached in two ways. The first is an explicit direction to "step back into the memory" or "imagine it is happening now".

Assagioli offers this opening phrase: "Imagine that you are actually in that situation again—that you are again *living* the experience."[239]

However, such a direct approach can sometimes result in an unhelpful self-consciousness for the client, distracting them from an experiential engagement with performance anxiety concerns as to whether they are accurately reliving the memory or just making it up.

A second approach is much more subtle and indirect, where the therapist initiates speaking *in the present tense*, without any need to mention doing so, in the expectation of the client following suit. In this way, there is no need to interrupt the flow of the session for the client by announcing the beginning of a technique, as can be seen in the following continuation of the case example, where my present tense interventions are highlighted in italics.

Th: I don't think you've ever said that so clearly before. Perhaps tell me a bit more about looking up through the spring blossom at the full moon.

Cl: The moonlight was soft, real gentle. Everything was still and calm. There was just a touch of breeze through the blossoms.

Th: And what *is* the atmosphere or mood *as you look up* at the moon through the blossom?

Cl: Welcoming and easy. Yeah, there was an ease about it.

Th: And the moon *seems* to be aware of you?

Cl: Sort of, yeah.

Th: As if the moon *is* trying to get your attention, even?

Cl: Exactly. It wanted me to stop and look up!

Th: And *as you look up*, what *is* the moon communicating to you? What *is* its message?

Cl: Ha! It's telling me I'm not alone. *[now also in the present tense]*

The technique of dialogue is in combination, or perhaps more precisely an overlapping, with the technique of personification, discussed earlier in the frustration stage clinical example.

As can be seen in the above transcript, Duncan's experience of the moon was decidedly not as an inert chunk of space rock, far less a theoretical concept, but an alive and sentient moon person, not just aware of him but also trying to get his attention. It was a personification that was mirrored by simply referring throughout to "the moon", instead of translating Duncan's experience into theoretical terminology; for example, by speaking of "this moon part of you" or "the moon subpersonality", which would have been to turn the moon person from a living subject into a psychological object and concept.

The basis for this dialogue/personification overlap can be seen in Assagioli drawing upon the work of Martin Buber, whom he saw as calling attention "to a very important deficiency in modern relationships" in the frequent treatment of other persons, not as a "thou" or fellow being, but as an "it" or object.[240]

If we want to develop a relationship with a human, it will be important to treat them with the respect and care due a fellow being, rather than controlling and manipulating them as an object.

Similarly, if we want to form a relationship and communicate with more-than-human imagery, it will also be important to treat them as persons, which is to say autonomous intelligences, with awareness and will, thoughts and feelings, hopes and fears. This is something of a renewal in mature adulthood of that enchanted existence recollected from childhood, when teddy bears, goldfish, and full moons were no different from humans.

The failure of my attempts to dialogue with the schoolboy subpersonality in the opening "meadow" guided-imagery journey at the beginning of this chapter can now be explained as an absence of personification.

Instead of assuming the schoolboy to be a person, the language of "subpersonality" turned him into a psychological object or idea, not a person but an "it", as was more than implied in the teacher's instruction: "Decide which subpersonality stands out to you the most and spend some time with it."

The effect was to remove the meaningfulness of the meeting from its experiential context—that is, with the schoolboy as an autonomous fellow being—and to direct my attention elsewhere, towards what the schoolboy represented: a sub-part of my personal psychology, a symbol of my vulnerability, or an internalization of my actual childhood self. All of which acted against the personification process, suggesting the schoolboy was not properly existing, but simply imaginary or made up, merely a "thing" or "idea".

Unfortunately, this had a silencing effect, the schoolboy understandably not wanting to talk to someone who doubted his reality.

The technique of dialogue can be stopped at any point, but there is always the possibility to continue. Upon receiving the message "I'm not alone", the obvious next step was to facilitate Daniel's return communication to the moon.

Th: How might you like to reply? What might you say to the moon?

Cl: I don't know.

Th: Whatever comes to mind . . .

Cl: I just want to say, "Thank you. Thank you."

Th: And how does the moon respond?

Cl: It's weird. The moon is sort of smiling.

Th: And how is that for you?

Cl: Really moving, surprisingly, moving—like we're friends or something.

The initial invitation to dialogue led to another not-knowing impasse. But again, this was not taken as a setback. A few beats of time and a bit of gentle encouragement led to knowing what to say.

By this stage, we were firmly in a present-tense imagining, partly helped by no longer being a memory. The dialogue continued by inviting a description of how the moon responded to the "thank you", which is effectively a return to the beginning of the dialogue, helping the client to once again notice what is being communicated by the symbol. To which the client can then respond again, and so on, iteratively going back and forth between noticing what is communicated and subsequently responding, until fatigue or distraction suggest an end to the technique.

Elaboration Stage

The "elaboration stage" is about what is done with developments from the illumination stage. Without shaping these developments into workable form and practical expression they will fade away or at best remain unfulfilled fantasies.

The elaboration stage therefore offers recognition to the creative process continuing beyond the merely receptive stage of illumination, and actively bringing to fruition the new insights, visions, and understandings.

A typical example of the close connection between the illumination stage and elaboration stage happened during my assessment of a new client, when a strange and unexpected notion forced its way into my awareness but did not hang around long enough for me to remember what it was. All that remained was an awareness that something important, perhaps an illumination, had come and gone.

I figured it would come back if it was really important and simply continued the assessment, gathering the childhood history, building up a picture of the client's formative years, while simultaneously remaining alert for any unexpected ideas popping back into awareness.

Sure enough, a few minutes later, the idea of "brother" appeared as a recognizable repetition of the earlier fleeting experience; however, this time, it remained long enough for it to develop into an illumination—of my not knowing anything about this client's siblings.

This was surprising, as normally by this stage of the assessment I would have long since asked about siblings as a matter of course, so something strange was going on. The ordinary idea of "brother" was somehow being pushed to the edges of awareness, not wanting to be noticed.

But this absence of information on "brother" was just the illumination stage, so I proceeded to the elaboration stage by simply enquiring, "Did you have any brothers or sisters?" At this, the client shared the history of an incestuous relationship with an older brother, and this relationship subsequently became a significant theme throughout the work.

In psychosynthesis psychotherapy, the elaboration stage can be understood as the fruition of a disidentification process. While the illumination stage eruption of superconscious experiences creates an expanded range of consciousness, this alone is not a full disidentification. To fully disidentify from the previous and limited personal self requires more than just a new level of consciousness or self-awareness.

As discussed in chapter 1, the personal self includes self-awareness and the ability to act upon that self-awareness with the will. The newfound self-awareness of the illumination stage therefore only becomes a full disidentification when it is followed by the elaboration stage, which brings in the will to direct and give expression to developments in the illumination stage.

The technique of ideal models is particularly well suited to the elaboration stage. While Assagioli considered this technique to be indicated "practically for every psychosynthesis and for every patient", he was also clear that it is often best applied "only after or at the final stage of another technique".[241]

Early in the therapeutic process, when a client remains strongly identified, an invitation to visualize an ideal model, as we shall soon discover, would be premature, "a mistake" resulting in "either a repression in the unconscious . . . or the arousing of an active opposition which would forfeit or make difficult the success of the technique".[242]

As with all techniques, timing is important. And the time to apply the ideal models technique is when sufficient disidentification has allowed some movement towards a new way of being, as will be the case after the illumination stage of the creative process.

The ideal models technique rests upon the principial basis established in chapter 1, with the ideal model as a psychosynthesis "experience".

To recap, an "ideal model" can be defined as a personified image or vision of who we wish to become—not as a singular, once-and-for-all, fixed image but as a constantly evolving series of ideal models through which we grow and mature, shaped by the influence of significant role models, such as caregivers, siblings, and teachers, as well as fictional characters from novels and movies.

The purpose of the technique of ideal models is to allow this naturally occurring "experience" to be recognized and consciously reshaped in imagination:

> The purpose is clear: that of utilizing the plastic, creative, dynamic power of images . . . .Here we emphasize the creative aspect of imagination, in the sense that imagination creates mentally and emotionally, and then that which has been imagined and visualized is expressed outwardly through the use of natural means.[243]

The novel possibility realized in the illumination stage can be understood to be an image—a vision or picture of a new way of being or role. Bearing this in mind, the purpose of the ideal models technique is to work with the "plastic, creative, dynamic power" of this image in such a way as to elaborate by "natural means" the initially only "mentally and emotionally" realized image into outward expression in the world.

Put simply, the consulting room becomes a workshop or theatre of the imagination, a context within which the client can reimagine the identities or roles they play and enact new ways of being without the immediacy of everyday life fears and consequences.

Eventually, this consulting room rehearsal will spill over into real-world changes. Assagioli suggested to the client, "Now you see that in imagination you can perform the role. . . now go ahead . . . seek to play it in reality."[244]

But this is not the first step, for the ideal models technique first requires the recognition and freeing of the client from the limitations of the existing ideal model. This is why it rests upon the results of earlier techniques, such as those applied during the assessment stage, when the therapist is working to establish how the current pattern of identification and the connected ideal model shape the client's feeling, thinking, perceptions, and actions in the world.

Several techniques will be applicable to establishing this existing ideal model, as we have seen already in the preparation stage example, which established Daniel's existing ideal model as an identification with a constant anticipation of loss, underlying grief, manic activity, and people-pleasing behaviour and in the frustration stage example, which explored Rebecca's identification and existing ideal model as involving a feeling of powerlessness in a critical world.

To describe the above identifications as "ideal models" might seem strange. Daniel and Rebecca were both struggling with obviously non-ideal ways of being, not living as they would like to. However, the formation of ideal models is not merely a conscious and personal choice. Assagioli writes of the creation of ideal models as an interplay of what "we believe we are" and "what we should like to be" on the one hand, alongside what "others evoke and produce in us" as a result of "what others believe us to be" or "would like us to be" on the other hand.[245]

An ideal model is therefore a complex synthesis of wishes and dreams, expectations and demands, a best-fit version of who we can become, given the mixture of opportunities and restrictions within our current and historical circumstances.

For example, an ideal model will be created when a strict disciplinarian caregiver demands compliant behaviour from a child. Because they are somewhat powerless in their relationship with the caregiver and must maintain the relationship upon which they depend for important needs, the child will learn to align with the caregiver's expectations and become dutiful and compliant. Non-aligned affects, such as assertive exuberance, will become lost to awareness or played out in private fantasies.

This dutiful compliance is an early ideal model, because it allows the child to creatively adapt and better survive psychologically, and also physically, within the conditions in which they find themselves.

Assagioli writes of more positive or "genuine" ideal models as having a "dynamic creative power";[246] that is to say, pointing towards the future and presenting intimations of who we are becoming.

Ideal models will become non-genuine to the extent that this future orientation is absent. When what was once a creative adaptation, a fluid unfolding into the future, becomes congealed and ossified into a rigid structure, perpetuating a fixed way of being, an ideal model turns from facilitating to impeding the process of synthesis, actively foreclosing novel possibilities. This was the case, in varying respects, with Daniel, Rebecca, and Duncan, all of whom were in need of assistance to create new ideal models.

To create a new ideal model is simultaneously an act of destruction. Assagioli writes of this as a "destructive stage of the treatment . . . not directed to influencing the patient *towards* something, but to freeing him from hindrances".[247]

The existing ideal model needs to be destroyed in order to provide space for the creation of a new ideal model. To this end, Assagioli suggests an "aggressive approach", one that consists "of debunking the unworthy model: to show the reality behind the attractive mask".[248] (The word "aggressive" is perhaps unfashionable language, at odds with the relational emphasis of contemporary psychotherapy; a more current phrasing would be "challenge".)

Simply bringing the existing ideal model into awareness is an implicit challenge to the client. The ideal model is described as being a particular and habitual pattern, something created in response to historical conditions, with both advantages and limitations. This moves it away from being "the truth" of who we really are towards something much more provisional, more of a scripted story guiding how we choose to act.

Of course, it won't entirely feel like a choice—at least not to begin with. But over time, when we notice the repeating pattern on ever finer scales of attention, a gap slowly starts to open between choosing to repeat the existing ideal model and trying something else instead, a gap also known as the illumination stage.

At this point, the client and therapist can work together to elaborate the expanded possibilities of a new ideal model:

> Frequently it is a collaboration, in which the therapist tentatively presents the outline of the model and asks if it is acceptable; or he suggests to the patient that he can modify it, and especially that he complete it more "concretely".[249]

By whatever means—a gesture or movement, a feeling or thought, a memory or future imagining—some new possibility, from beyond the bounds of habitual identification, enters into experience and/or expression. All that the therapist needs to do, after noticing this illumination, is to elaborate it into the "outline", or form, of a new ideal model.

Assagioli writes of this with respect to helping the client visualize themselves as "developing an undeveloped psychological function" or focusing upon "a single specified quality or small group of qualities, or abilities".[250] However, to avoid the danger of cognitive separation, these functions and qualities will not be presented in isolation, as a discussion of abstract ideas.

To maintain the experiential emphasis of the technique, the tentative outline of the new ideal model will involve evoking who the client would become were they to embrace the hitherto undeveloped functions and qualities. This involves a personified self-image that contextualizes the function or quality around its related feelings, thoughts, sensations, perceptions, and actions, as shown in the following transcript, continuing the illumination stage example with Duncan:

Th: The moon has become your friend. And you are no longer alone.

Cl: Yeah, something like that.

Th: Sounds like you've stepped into a rather unusual space? What's it like to have a friend, to not be so alone?

Cl: Good.

Th: What kind of good?

Cl: Lighter, as if all this tension has just dropped out of me. I didn't realize I was carrying it around, but I was. And now it's gone . . .

Th: . . . now that it's gone, what's happening?

Cl: Well, maybe I'm not such a bad person after all?

Th: Right. Because you've got a friend now?

Cl: Exactly. I mean, it's not just the moon. There's my dog, my beautiful dog. He was looking up at me in the same way the moon was looking down at me, with a gaze full of love.

Th: You feel loved?

Cl: I didn't want it before, now I'm not so sure. But I'm letting them love me now.

Th: And how is it to let that in?

Cl: Mixed. It's like a relief . . . and also there's something scary about it. I don't quite trust it.

Th: So, this new experience isn't just good; it's also a bit scary. You're feeling loved, less alone, not such a bad person, and lighter, less tensed-up. But you don't quite trust it.

Without any need to reference the technique, or share psychological terminology, the session proceeded by simply inviting Duncan to describe who he was becoming as a result of the illumination. All of this happened rather slowly, as an incremental process, avoiding any rush into an overly perfect and positive ideal model.

Assagioli wrote of a need to align the new ideal model with the "natural development of the given individual" by embracing a "realistic and 'authentic'" model, rather than forcing the process and rushing ahead to create "a neurotic, unreal, 'idealized image'".[251] A "realistic" ideal-models technique is therefore one that allows space for the various doubts, hesitancies, and fears of change:

> If we started with only the positive trend we would not really deal therapeutically with the situation. This explains the chief deficiency in emphasizing only the positive, forgetting and neglecting the negative aspects of human nature. This partially justifies the hostilities in certain circles against the more superficial optimistic advice given for peace of mind and so on . . . . The important point is that we need to deal in imagination with the negative aspects of the individual before we can fully impress the progressive desired good . . . there are certain forces in the individual which run counter to the constructive tendencies, and these resistances need to be dealt with.[252]

My summary of Duncan's new ideal model avoided being superficially optimistic by including both "resistances" and "constructive tendencies". Duncan was feeling loved, not such a bad person anymore, but also a bit scared, with growing self-esteem but not outright, full-blown self-belief. It was a small but significant step away from suicidal ideation towards a tentative belief in the future.

Once a new ideal model becomes sufficiently outlined, the technique continues by translating it into everyday life.

The client is asked or invited to visualize themselves enacting the ideal model, in what Assagioli describes as "a psychodrama-play technique *in imagination*" [original italics].[253]

This act of imagination, in the consulting room, is a necessary precursor to any real-world enactment of the new ideal model. Good ideas and desires to change alone are not sufficient. What is also needed is the ability to imagine those ideas and desires as realistic possibilities in order to bridge from desire into action, illumination into willed elaboration. This is a topic that we will discuss further in chapter 4.

A SYNTHESIS OF TECHNIQUES

By now, it will be apparent that therapeutic "technique" in this book is not meant as a mechanistic or procedural application from a manual. Rooted in the original meaning of the Greek word techne, meaning the craft or skill of making and creating, psychosynthesis techniques are a creative and even artistic endeavour.

While art-based activities, such as writing, drawing, and dramatic performance, may or may not be involved, the primary intention of the technique is not to produce works of art but to facilitate the naturally occurring yet unpredictable experiential process and outcome of synthesis. A technique will therefore be noticeable as a psychosynthesis technique to the degree that it avoids a narrow focus upon preplanned outcomes and instead emphasizes a broad context-dependent and relational-dynamic creative adaptability.

Once again, synthesis and experience have been shown to be the twin principles guiding the psychosynthesis therapist, particularly the creative adaptation or modification of techniques as an experiential-synthesis in at least three respects:

1. The immediate experiential situation unfolding between therapist and client in the consulting room as a synthesis of feelings, thoughts, sensations, perceptions, and actions;
2. Multiple techniques combining to create a bespoke response that best meets the uniqueness of the unfolding experiential process;
3. The synthesis of psychosynthesis teachings informing the therapist's ability to notice and understand this experiential process.

A fourth, and as yet undiscussed, respect in which experiential synthesis shows up will be considered in the next chapter: the synthesis of multiple influences informing the practice of psychosynthesis psychotherapy.

Chapter 3

Influences

Assagioli drew upon a wide variety of influences in the formulation of psychosynthesis, including his own scientific training as a medical doctor, subsequent specialisms in psychiatry and psychoanalysis, and a lifelong interest in religion and philosophy of both the East and West.

Yet, as we shall soon discover, Assagioli's reluctance to discuss these influences has resulted in an ongoing debate as to whether psychosynthesis is a contemporary scientific psychology or a reformulation of historical philosophies and religions.[254]

I remember these debates on the nature of psychosynthesis as being like Zen koans—seemingly impossible to answer directly but somehow serving a purpose, softening me up for an intuitive leap of understanding.

As indeed happened one day, when a teacher said to me: "You just have to work out how *you* want to do psychosynthesis."

I doubt that this was the first time I'd heard this line, as it is something of a psychosynthesis cliché, but for whatever reason—perhaps the gentleness of my teacher's voice or the spring sunshine streaming in through the training room window—something made me sit up and appreciate, as if for the first time, this radical invitation: *Start taking some responsibility. Don't be so passive; you've got something to do here. Everyone does psychosynthesis differently, even you, so go ahead and figure it out.*[255]

No one was going to figure out psychosynthesis for me. It wasn't going to be about blindly following and simply repeating whatever anyone else did, but rather *doing something* with what Assagioli and others had created. It would be in gathering these influences and emulating the creative spirit of Assagioli that the distinctiveness of psychosynthesis would be found—not in general, in the abstract, but in my own lived experience.

When you think about it, any psychosynthesis therapy session will be a synthesis of influences—not only from within psychosynthesis but also from other psychological orientations, as well as further personal influences the therapist brings to the session; and something needs to be done with all this material so as to shape it up into something distinct called "psychosynthesis".

As Assagioli writes:

> While psychosynthesis is offered as a synthesis of various therapies and educational approaches, it is well to keep in mind that it possesses its own original and central essence. This is so as not to present a watered-down and distorted version, or one overcoloured by the concepts and tendencies of the various contemporary schools.[256]

What stops psychosynthesis becoming lost in a multitudinous variety of philosophies and methods is that it has its "own original and central essence". The influences it draws upon are not being shared directly in order to replace psychosynthesis but rather, being applied in such a way as to bring fresh perspectives and possibilities to its teachings and techniques.

And yet, due to the near silence from Assagioli on this matter, exactly what is being done with influences to turn them into psychosynthesis remains largely an implicit modus operandi, or understanding, within the psychosynthesis community.

This chapter therefore sets out to make this an explicit understanding by once again turning the twin principles of experiential-synthesis back upon psychosynthesis itself.

THE DREAM OF A SCIENCE

The initial dream shared by a client can sometimes reveal patterns that resonate across the subsequent months and even years of therapy.

How to work therapeutically with the initial dream story will be discussed further in chapter 4, but for now, the client on the couch is psychosynthesis itself and how it has been dreamed up by Assagioli.

The initial dream of psychosynthesis was for it to be a science. While Assagioli is now somewhat famous for his many decidedly non-scientific influences—matters we shall soon discuss—the considerable influence of his "dream of a science" has largely passed by unnoticed in the literature, allowing it to shape psychosynthesis in ways that are seldom considered.

This is precisely what is happening in a dream state, when the surrounding sights and sounds convince entirely as solid and factual "real" events, and only upon waking do we look back and realize that it was all a dream.

To wake up from the dream of a science requires questioning some basic background assumptions within Assagioli's original presentation of psychosynthesis. This concern may seem somewhat abstract and removed from the nitty gritty of therapeutic healing and transformation and yet, as we have been discussing throughout this book, ideas are not neutral. Implicit assumptions influence not only how we conceive the theory of psychosynthesis but also its experiential possibilities.

In what follows, we shall therefore be looking at a number of statements made by Assagioli and discussing what he did and did not mean by psychosynthesis being a science.

Our first consideration is to frame the discussion within its historical context, and how the dream of a science was a collective dreaming, as Assagioli was just one of many pioneering figures at the beginning of the 20th century who were proposing psychology and psychotherapy as a new scientific discipline.

The opening paragraphs of Assagioli's book *The Act of Will* sets psychosynthesis within this scientific zeitgeist. He describes the fantasy of "a man from a previous civilization", such as "a Plato or Marcus Aurelius", being somehow transported into the present day and how they would, on the one hand, be "dazzled by the material wonders created by advanced technology" but, on the other hand, be surprised and even dismayed by the "very limited" progress made with regard to man's "being", as evident in his relative inability to deal with "emotions, impulses, and desires".[257]

As a corrective to this imbalance, psychosynthesis proposed turning the same scientific methods that had achieved such "advanced technology" towards a study of psychological experiences:

> [Psychosynthesis] is an attitude quite similar, even identical, to that of the natural scientist who objectively, patiently, and persistently observes the natural phenomenon occurring around him . . . If we turn our ability to observe inwards we realize that there is actually an inner world of phenomena.[258]

> May I emphasize the fact that the elements and functions . . . such as aesthetic, ethical, religious experiences, intuition, inspiration states of mystical consciousness, are factual, are real in the pragmatic sense . . . amenable to observation and experiment, through the use of the scientific method.[259]

> It all depends on what you consider science . . . if you take the scientific attitude and method in the way I have put it . . . [psychosynthesis] is proven by its direct experience; it is one of those primary experiences which are the evidences of themselves. Just as colour, a sense of beauty . . . need no explanation. They are primary experiences and therefore have full scientific value, in the broader sense.[260]

The understanding of science adopted by Assagioli "in the broader sense" went beyond scientists' narrow focus on only sensory experiences of the physical world. Instead of studying plants, creatures, and celestial bodies passing across the heavens, psychosynthesis studied the psychological processes of "emotions and feelings", "aesthetic, ethical, religious experiences", and "states of mystical consciousness"—which were seen to be "factual" and "real in the pragmatic sense", and therefore capable of being studied by "the scientific method".

Despite this "inner world of phenomena" not being amenable to simple measurement, the scientific study of the physical world was nevertheless turned inwards, towards a scientific study of subjective psychological experiences, which were deemed to be "evidences of themselves".[261] Here, once more, the experiential emphasis of psychosynthesis shines through.

As a science, psychosynthesis expected the great breakthroughs made by the natural sciences to one day be repeated in psychotherapeutic advances; however, it is important to appreciate Assagioli's understanding of this as being at best a distant horizon for psychosynthesis, taking place sometime in the future.

In other words, his presentation of psychosynthesis was not presented as a settled theoretical position or scientific "truth":

> Let us recognize that we are as yet at the stage of field survey and tentative exploration, of description of results and reports on the use of active methods of verification and development. We are not yet at the stage of "theory building". A great amount of research is required with no "theory building" so that we can remain true to the original scientific purpose and function of psychosynthesis.[262]

> What we hope to see developed over a period of years—and certainly do not claim has yet been achieved—is a science of the Self, of its energies, its manifestations, of how these energies can be released, how they can be contacted, how they can be utilized for constructive and therapeutic work.[263]

The psychosynthesis presented by Assagioli had not yet realized the dream of a science. His psychosynthesis was "as yet at the stage of field survey and tentative exploration". By proposing it as a natural science he was not "theory building"—that is, setting out a firmly established set of psychological laws and principles—but rather, emphasizing the "scientific purpose and function of psychosynthesis" in the application of "active methods" and a further "description of results".

While Assagioli acknowledged the possibility of such a science emerging "over a period of years", it has arguably never existed and given that it has not yet appeared, perhaps never will. But even if one day in the future a "science of the Self" were to be discovered, he writes:

> . . . we must also realize that even if science were able to measure the energies within the constitution of man—which would include emotional, mental, and spiritual energies—this would not make the work of the study of the experience itself less important.[264]

This statement might appear somewhat paradoxical, after all what might be the point of a scientific endeavour if not to establish universal laws and "the truth"? Yet, a true scientific method is only a provisional hypothesis formulation, forever ready to alter its only tentative claims in the face of new evidence, and therefore never arriving at a fixed position or dogmatic reality. Similarly, as we have seen throughout this book, far from settling on "a particular psychological doctrine" or final understanding, psychosynthesis is an open-ended experimentation in "the study" of experience itself.

Hence Assagioli repeatedly warning against mistaking psychosynthesis for any kind of dogma, ideology, or philosophical system, whether religious or scientific:

> Psychosynthesis does not aim nor attempt to give a metaphysical or theological explanation of the great Mystery—it leads to the door, but stops there.[265]

> [Psychosynthesis] does not take any specific position, neither metaphysical nor religious.[266]

> [Psychosynthesis] is based on, and remains adherent to the reality and the situation of each individual. Therefore

> it abstains from formulating theories and creating "systems" or doctrines, even of a scientific kind, or believed to be so.[267]

> In modern life, with the great majority of cases, it is better to stick to the empirical approach of techniques and the actual results of the techniques, eliminating every philosophical or religious question.[268]

Psychosynthesis positively holds back from giving "a metaphysical or theological explanation", "even of a scientific kind" for "the great Mystery"; instead, it offers an approach to "the situation of each individual" and the "actual results of the techniques", which are seen to eliminate "every philosophical or religious question".

In other words, psychosynthesis is not something to *believe in* but something to *do*—a practice that we can engage in on an experiential level, regardless of our background or beliefs.

While the agnosticism of psychosynthesis could be seen to be a belief system in itself, the point being made is not to eradicate or completely avoid holding any beliefs. There are always assumptions, views, theories, and beliefs influencing experience—and psychosynthesis will therefore inevitably draw upon a synthesis of such influences.

However, as has been argued throughout this book, all such influences will only ever be "partial expressions", never complete truths; therefore, while we cannot do without them, it is important to hold them lightly, so as to avoid collapsing the theory/experience gap and mistaking psychosynthesis for a particular belief system rather than a means to engage with the Mystery of experience.[269]

Indeed, another reason for the elusiveness of psychosynthesis is this deliberate embrace of Mystery and a corresponding hesitation to pin things down. It is an openness that, as mentioned in the Introduction, is considered by some to be a weakness. However, it may well be exactly what allows psychosynthesis to help people find themselves within the mystery of life—not as an abstract interpretation but as a direct and meaningful experience; in the same way as viewing a sunset can be a meaningful experience without any need to understand the physics of celestial bodies.

This may not sound dreamy at all, and in fact, psychosynthesis as a natural science appears to be somewhat the opposite—an approach grounded in waking reality. But before discussing the dreamier aspects of psychosynthesis as a science, it will be important to first consider the non-scientific, or esoteric, influences that have also shaped psychosynthesis.

THE WALL OF SILENCE

Assagioli called the presentation of psychosynthesis as a science his "exoteric programme" (*exoteric* meaning "visible" and "shared"). This was the outward-facing programme of lectures and published works he intended for a general audience, but it was not the whole story.

The background to this exoteric scientific presentation drew upon a wealth of non-scientific influences from literary, philosophical, and religious sources.[270] And yet, for reasons to be discussed shortly, these non-scientific influences were only shared with a select inner circle of students and concealed from public view behind what became known as the "wall of silence".[271]

The attempt to maintain this "wall of silence" did not last—perhaps Assagioli referring to these non-scientific influences as "esoteric papers" (in the sense of "invisible" or "secret", implying as it does, something special and beyond the ordinary) was only ever going to attract more attention than it avoided.

With the passage of time, the existence of these esoteric influences inevitably became something of an open secret, and Assagioli eventually acknowledged that the wall of silence "had, and has, many breaches!"[272]

To anyone with more than a passing contemporary interest in psychosynthesis, it will be obvious how many videos, articles, and books are now available offering connections between psychosynthesis theory and various esoteric influences.

For example, the body-feelings-mind structure of the "Exercise in Disidentification" is suggested by Buddhist teachings on the foundations of mindfulness; Assagioli's emphasis on "the Will" is reflected in the Western magical tradition; and the idea of the "I-Self relationship" shows parallels with the mystical traditions of Christianity and Jewish Kabbalah.[273]

The fallen "wall of silence" created a fascinating opportunity to trace the roots of psychosynthesis to Assagioli's original influences. And yet, while this research provides a wealth of interesting material, it also creates something of a problem, given that Assagioli seldom discussed how to apply esoteric influences in respect to psychosynthesis.

Post-Assagioli theorists and psychotherapists have therefore been left with very little guidance as to how to appreciate the place of influences, either within the original presentation by Assagioli or in future developments of psychosynthesis theory and techniques.

The remainder of this chapter will therefore discuss two approaches to bringing down the "wall of silence": First, the "Influences as Origin Story" approach and its limitations, and second, the few statements Assagioli did offer on the subject of influences as the basis for establishing a principial approach to "Influences in Translation".

INFLUENCES AS ORIGIN STORY

The predominant rationale given for the "wall of silence" is the historical context within which Assagioli first presented psychosynthesis.[274]

As discussed earlier, during the early to mid 20th century, Assagioli was one of many figures proposing a new scientific discipline of psychology as a bona fide natural science, similar to that of physics, chemistry, and biology.

Had Assagioli been more forthcoming about his non-scientific esoteric influences at that time, psychosynthesis would have at best been seriously misunderstood, and at worst, been outright rejected from mainstream consideration, thereby holding back its healing and transformative message from the world.

In this light, the "wall of silence" can best be understood as a skilful means by which psychosynthesis was able to gain legitimacy within the prevailing orthodoxy of the scientific world view.

Now that the world (and indeed science itself, as we shall soon discuss) has moved beyond the limitations of a strictly empirical-scientific framework, the "wall of silence" has, according to the above rationale, outserved its original purpose. There is no longer any need to keep secret the esoteric influences that have shaped psychosynthesis—not least because many of these "mystical" and "spiritual" ideas and methods are now aligned with contemporary scientific findings from complexity theory and quantum physics.[275]

With no need to conceal esoteric influences, the "Influences as Origin Story" assumes that there is now an opportunity to discuss and develop a perhaps fuller presentation of psychosynthesis—one that Assagioli would have made, in an alternative history, had he lived in a more sympathetic time.

However, as already noted, while this search behind the "wall of silence" for the "origin story" of psychosynthesis does provide interesting and useful research findings, it is in danger of obscuring the distinctiveness of psychosynthesis in three respects, which we will examine next.

Dynamic Influences

Any conjecture about past influences is always an interpretative leap from the present. The passage of time will bring alterations in culture, language, and ideas that affect how influences from the past are perceived, such that there can never really be a "definitive" understanding, preserved forever like the butterflies of Victorian naturalists in glass display cases.

For example, the original understanding of Buddhist meditation or Christian mysticism will always be a matter of speculation, a viewing of the past filtered through the philosophical and conceptual influences of the present.

Therefore, how Assagioli understood past influences, from his position in the early 20th century, will not only differ from the original understanding of the past but also differ from any contemporary understandings, which are not stationary or fixed, but constantly being reshaped by exposure to new ideas, perspectives, and trends.

So it is then, that any attempt to trace psychosynthesis to its historical influences will, perhaps ironically, also introduce new influences as a result of the contemporary perspectives through which these sources are interpreted.

The conclusion we can draw from this is that there can be no definitive "origin story", because the influences shaping psychosynthesis have always been, and always will be, dynamically shifting and changing. To suggest a "real" or "fuller" psychosynthesis based on a static and ahistorical understanding of past influences, exempt from contingency and set apart from contemporary influences, will be to lose sight of the greater whole created by a synthesis of dynamic influences.

Diverse Influences

Even if it were possible to somehow arrive at a definitive understanding of a particular past influence, any attempt to suggest an authentic "origin story" based upon the salience of a select few past influences will be in danger of losing sight of the greater whole created by the synthesis of diverse influences shaping psychosynthesis.

Any attempt to comprehend the diversity of connections between the original presentation of psychosynthesis and its many influences will never be fully realizable, as to do so would require an impossible 360-degree appreciation of Assagioli's experiential context.

This experiential context includes his classical education, medical training, and significant personal and professional relationships, as well as the many intellectual, social, and technological transformations that occurred between his birth in 1888 and death in 1974.[276] It would also require sifting through not just Assagioli's published works but also his many unpublished notes, letters, and anecdotal material from private conversation, as well as his extensive library.

In addition, any conclusions as to how all these influences might be brought together in synthesis—that is, the relationships among them and how they interact—would once again be an interpretive leap from the present, with no real way of knowing its basis in the original synthesis created by Assagioli.

Philosophical Influences

Approaching psychosynthesis via its "origin story" is also in danger of moving away from, rather than towards, what makes it distinctive, by acting against the stated intentions of Assagioli that it is not a "metaphysical or theological explanation" of "the great Mystery".

Being agnostic towards philosophical and religious beliefs is what allows psychosynthesis to occupy the creative gap between theory and experience—the premise being that psychosynthesis is an experience, rather than any particular system of ideas and concepts. And yet, the many esoteric influences Assagioli drew upon do indeed make propositional claims as to the nature of reality.

With respect to the current discussion, it is therefore important to recognize that the influences shaping psychosynthesis theory and practice are precisely the metaphysical, philosophical, and theological positions that Assagioli is saying psychosynthesis is not.

To name just a few examples: The influence of empirical science is a metaphysics (a branch of philosophy), as we shall soon discuss further; the influence of Hegel's dialectical philosophy, discussed in chapter 1, is obviously a philosophy; while Christianity and Kabbalah are obviously theological influences.

The search for an "origin story" will consequently always need to stop short of suggesting any one or other esoteric influence to be the "fuller" and "authentic" basis for psychosynthesis, as all such equivalences will be in danger of attributing to psychosynthesis the philosophical beliefs of the stated influence, which are primarily abstract ideas about experience.[277]

INFLUENCES IN TRANSLATION

If psychosynthesis cannot be found in any particular set of influences but instead derives from a variety of influences, both historical and contemporary, the question becomes: What did Assagioli do with his influences to turn them into something called "psychosynthesis"?

We will now discuss the process of how influences are applied in psychosynthesis. This will allow the principial understanding that contemporary psychosynthesis therapists need in order to not only appreciate how Assagioli applied influences in the past but also how they can best apply new influences in the present and future.

A suitable place to begin is with the rationale given by Assagioli for adopting the "wall of silence":

> Please pay attention to the distinction between the esoteric papers and the exoteric programme; we have to keep this distinction very clearly and keep the "wall of silence"—as I have said and written in the past—about the presentations. Truth is One, but its presentation is diverse and so has different levels, according to the kind of people to whom we address ourselves. One has to talk to each in their language. We have to be polyglots psychologically and spiritually, learn to be translators; i.e. to translate esoteric teaching in exoteric language.[278]

The need to gain legitimacy as a science, upon which the search for an origin story is based, is not the only reason for the "wall of silence". A second and related reason for adopting the "wall of silence" was a need to translate the esoteric influences into an "exoteric language."

As befits the experiential emphasis of psychosynthesis, this rationale is more methodological than ideological—not so much with regard to an actual silence or complete disavowal of esoteric influences but rather, as a concern over how best to translate the language of philosophy and religion into a form of communication suitable for "the kind of people to whom we address ourselves".

In psychosynthesis psychotherapy, these people are clients—who are generally neither well versed in abstruse philosophical terminology nor turning to therapy expecting to hear a sermon.

In one of Assagioli's chattier communications, "Talks on the Self", a recording of an interview with American students, he again mentions the importance of translation as a means to avoid imposing esoteric language on the client:

> I shall just say something . . . about keeping the clear distinction between psychosynthesis and psychology in general . . . it should always be kept in mind. There are two quite different languages, so we have the privilege of being polyglots, of being able to use both languages. But we should not impose on others a language which they do not know. It is not easy, because the temptation all the time is to slip in some [. . .] matter. I'll tell you by and by how to translate from one language into another . . . we'll make a little dictionary of the different ways of saying the same thing in the two languages. It will be useful.[279]

Assagioli is making a clear distinction between "two different languages" in the above statement: First, the language of psychology, with its specialist terminology, which, alongside philosophy and religion, can be understood as another form of "esoteric" language; and second, the language of the psychosynthesis psychotherapist, who as a "polyglot" is able to use several languages to translate specialist psychological terminology into a form of communication the client understands by finding "different ways of saying the same thing".

The reason for doing the latter is to avoid "the temptation" of slipping into theoretical explanations, rather than addressing the experiential situation of the client, as Assagioli further indicates in the same "Talks on the Self":

> . . . in psychology and philosophy . . . we speak of Will, Love, Mind, thought, etc., but there ain't such a thing. There are only *subjects* who are *willers*, living beings who are lovers. The rest is only pure intellectual abstractions, useful for didactic purposes . . . but there doesn't exist an entity [called] *love*, an entity [called] *will* . . . intelligence is a wonderful thing, but the intellect should not possess us! We should try to be as intelligent as we can (and we can be more intelligent and use our intelligence), but not be possessed by it. And especially realize that any intellectual formulation or theory is merely a description, not a real thing. [It is a question of] semantics, [you see]. The map is not the territory.[280]

Far from being merely a translation from one form of theoretical language into another, the "wall of silence" is a translation process from the "intellectual abstractions" of psychology, philosophy, and religion to a language that best allows a description of the client's lived experience. Theoretical concepts are only a generalized simplification of complex experiences and "not a real thing". They are useful to theorize upon psychosynthesis, but when used therapeutically, without translation into a language the client understands, will be in danger of creating a cognitive separation, merely explaining away presenting issue difficulties within a system called "psychosynthesis".

The concept of "love", for example, will never encapsulate the experience of being loved. It does not tell us about the impact of a gentle smile from a good friend or a glance across a crowded room at a party from an attractive stranger. Even if we refine the concept of love with a sub-concept called "kindness", this will still not be the particular experience but a generalized idea about love.

No number of further sub-concepts—"compassion", "care", "affection", "friendship", "adoration", "intimacy", "desire", "sex"—will adequately capture the experience of love, because love is a living process; not a simple object to be neatly labelled, categorized, and safely tucked away in theoretical boxes. There will therefore always remain a radical gap between a conceptual elaboration of love and a living breathing experience of being loved.

As Assagioli writes:

> All words designating psychological or spiritual conditions or realities are in origin metaphors or symbols . . . Yet symbols have their dangers. In fact, he who takes them literally and does not pass beyond the symbol to reality, but halts before it, does not arrive at the underlying truth.[281]

To "halt before" symbolic theoretical language, and taking it literally, to mistake it for "the underlying truth" alludes to the danger of sharing intellectual abstractions directly with the client. While a therapist might think about and understand a client to be undergoing, for example, a disidentification process, what the client most immediately and directly experiences will be a dynamic amalgam of feelings, thoughts, fantasies, sensations, gestures, and more. To squeeze the multifaceted richness of this experience into a single abstract concept called "disidentification" is therefore a radical simplification, far removed from an up-close description of what the client is experiencing.

While theoretical discussion about disidentification or love or will may have a place at times, if therapy is to heal and transform the client it also needs at some point to "pass beyond the symbol" to the "underlying truth" of experience. To keep thinking about the absence of love in the client's life, and the need for disidentification in order to find this love, may provide lots of interesting interpretations and rational understandings, but without connecting these insights to experiential equivalents the therapy will not provide the necessary conditions for change.

What is needed is a form of communication, a doctrinally neutral therapeutic language, which both avoids imposing a belief system on the client while also embracing an experiential-synthesis. While the nuances of psychological life will never be fully communicable in words, some language styles and ways of speaking will nevertheless be able to close or narrow the theory/experience gap better than others. The simplest route to doing so is achieved by avoiding or at least minimizing theoretical terminology:

> I always insist in psychosynthesis that we shall think experientially, practically, pragmatically. No theory. There is no theory of psychosynthesis! It is a method, an adventure, anything but a theory. Stick to that![282]

> As a general rule it can be said that the patient should only be told that which seems really useful and desirable for the therapeutic purpose; and we should not indulge in the temptation of theoretical inquiry and theoretical research—which would be of no benefit to the patient and perhaps harmful, unduly prolonging the treatment or even sidetracking it. Therefore, the explanations and interpretations which we share with the patient are mainly those necessary for the next technique and stage in the treatment.[283]

By "no theory of psychosynthesis", Assagioli does not literally mean that there is no theory of psychosynthesis (which would obviously be wrong) but rather, that the lexicon of theoretical terminology used to think about psychosynthesis is not necessarily the best language for "the therapeutic purpose" of working with the client's *experience of psychosynthesis*. Theoretical "explanations and interpretations" will be used sparingly, and only in the service of "the next technique and stage in the treatment"; for example, by providing the context for offering an observation, asking a question or beginning a technique.

Apart from these context-building explanations, any purely "theoretical inquiry" is kept to a minimum to maintain an experiential emphasis. Chapter 2 highlighted a number of such techniques, delivered using non-specialist descriptive language, which was chosen to support a specific and vivid evocation of the client's experiential context, thereby avoiding the "perhaps harmful" application of abstract theoretical terminology "which would be of no benefit to the patient".

The foregoing discussion has demonstrated the basis for a general principle of translation, particularly the need to translate "esoteric" into "exoteric" language in therapeutic practice, to the extent of eschewing theoretical terminology altogether. What still remains to be discussed is the translation process needed, prior to therapeutic practice, in order to allow the background influences informing Assagioli, and indeed all post-Assagioli practioners, to be translated into psychosynthesis theory.

THE INFLUENCE/THEORY GAP

Assagioli did not directly discuss his criteria for translating influences into theory. As a result, there are no clear guidelines for maintaining the distinctiveness of psychosynthesis while incorporating new influences into its theory and practice.

Absent of any guidelines in the literature, this book will now propose a recognizable criterion for the translation of any given influence into psychosynthesis theory by reflecting upon the original presentation of psychosynthesis with the twin principles of experiential-synthesis, alongside the introduction of three further sub-principles: holistic, perspectival, and emergent.[284]

As noted earlier, the diverse and dynamic influences shaping psychosynthesis are too numerous to discuss in detail, so we will use the particular influence of natural science (as a continuation of the earlier "dream of a science" discussion) as a case study to demonstrate a principial translation process.

Any influence could have been chosen, but natural science has been considered for two reasons: First, as an exoteric influence (that is, one explicitly embraced by Assagioli) there is no debate as to whether it is indeed an influence; and second, it provides a good example to discuss the importance of maximizing the influence/theory gap.

While the success of a theory lies in how well it aligns with experience, the success of a translation process from influence into theory, on a principial basis, will require maximizing the influence/theory gap.

A translation process is only successful to the extent that it makes a distinction between any abstract-philosophical claims assumed by the influence and the theory into which it is translated. This process therefore allows inspiration from metaphysical, philosophical, and theological sources, without attributing them directly as a basis for psychosynthesis theory and practice—as will become clearer in the following discussion of the holistic, perspectival, and emergent sub-principles.

Holistic

In psychosynthesis everything is connected; there is no separation, only synthesis—the bringing together of all the parts into a greater whole. Therefore, to the extent that psychosynthesis theory draws inspiration from various influences while maintaining the wholeness of this experiential-synthesis, the translation process can be seen to be successful.

A "holistic" understanding and approach is then the first sub-principle criterion for any successful translation process, according to Assagioli:

> In psychosynthesis the emphasis is put on a holistic or integral conception of the treatment, which should always be kept in view and to which every method, exercise, and technique should be subordinated.[285]

> the constant endeavour to keep the entire picture in view, to relate always the part to the whole.[286]

> . . . the harmonization and integration into one functioning whole of all the qualities and functions of the individual must be aimed at and actively fostered.[287]

Psychosynthesis emphasizes "a holistic . . . conception of the treatment", the aim being to gather "all the qualities and functions" into "one functioning whole", an aim that requires always relating "the part to the whole". This was discussed in chapter 1, with regard to the "transpersonal context" of a "synthesis of systems", and in chapter 2, as a context-dependent experiential application of techniques.

But, paradoxically, while the influence of natural science, understood and applied as an experiential method, can be seen to align with this holistic sub-principle, it can also be seen to diverge from it. That's because the particular form of natural science adopted by Assagioli, known as "empiricism", is not only about experience; it is also a metaphysical position:[288]

> One should make everybody understand that psychosynthesis has a positively scientific character, in the empirical and experiential sense.[289]

> My approach . . . is empirical and phenomenological.[290]

> In my opinion, the direct experience of the self . . . is a true, "phenomenological" experience, an inner reality which can be empirically verified and deliberately produced through appropriate techniques.[291]

As a medical doctor, Assagioli would have been familiar with "empiricism", which in the early to mid 20th century was the predominant scientific method. And as is clearly indicated by the close connection being made in the above statements between "empirical and experiential" and "empirical and phenomenological", Assagioli offered empiricism as an experiential method, per the etymological root of "empirical" from the Greek word *empeiria*, which means "experience".

This might seem to align with a principial basis, yet a significant divergence from the holistic sub-principle arises, due to the translation process failing to acknowledge the metaphysical position of empirical science, which posits a fundamental separation between subject and object.

A separation between subject and object, self and world, is what allows the empirical method to isolate or remove the subjective bias of the scientist. In this way, experiments are seen to more accurately observe the natural world, by removing interference from the personal feelings and perceptions of the scientist.

If this appears quite reasonable, it is because the subject-object separation of empiricism has long since become the commonsense world view, a taken-for-granted perspective, in large part born of the success it has had in creating the modern technological world. But any assumption of a separation between self and world is obviously anathema to a "holistic" sub-principle, and the general ethos of psychosynthesis, in which everything is connected, and the part is always related to the whole.

In other words, the scientist, or indeed the psychotherapist, is connected to what they observe, whether it be an experiment on a work bench or a client sitting in a consulting room.

And yet, the influence of this metaphysical separation from empiricism can arguably be seen to have been directly translated into psychosynthesis theory, where the role of the bias-free and objective empirical scientist in the physical world has become internalized as the understanding of a separated "personal self", capable of objectively observing psychological life:

> It means . . . directing the mind's eye, or the observing function, upon the world of psychological facts, of psychological events . . . It could be called the attitude of the observer, the inner observer . . . an attitude quite similar, even identical, to that of the natural scientist who objectively, patiently and persistently observes the natural phenomena occurring around him.[292]

> The changing contents of our consciousness (the sensations, thoughts, feelings, etc.) are one thing, while the "I," the self, the centre of our consciousness is another.[293]

> This Self is above, and unaffected by, the flow of the mind-stream or by bodily conditions; and the personal conscious self should be considered merely as its reflection, its "projection" in the field of the personality.[294]

> The "I" is simple, unchanging, constant.[295]

In the above statements, the "I", or "personal self", as an "inner observer", is assumed to be "an attitude similar, even identical", to the objectivity of the natural scientist.

That which is observed, "the changing contents of our consciousness", is assumed to be "one thing", distinct and separate from this objective "personal self", or "I", which is "another" thing, and seen to be "above, and unaffected" by these changing contents; indeed is itself "unchanging, constant".

In this way, contrary to the holistic sub-principle of always relating the part to the whole, the "personal self" is somehow not contingent upon its experiential context.

Yet even the empirical scientist is only in theory separate from that which is observed. In experience, the empirical scientist will be connected to observations, via feelings, thoughts, and perceptions—all of which inevitably introduce a subjective bias. At best, all that can be attempted is a methodological separation, so as to minimize this subjective influence upon results.

While this methodological separation is possible with respect to physical objects, it is not possible when it comes to psychological experience. The separation between the "personal self" or "I" and the psychological "contents" or "objects" it observes, as we have seen throughout this book, is only a metaphorical separation, not an actual experiential separation.

In other words, it is an imagined separation, a way of thinking about psychological experience as composed of psychological "objects" or "things", in the same way that the world is composed of people, places, and things. This is a radical simplification, not to be confused with the complex reality, where there is no clear line of separation between "contents of consciousness" and an observing "I".

With careful application, a theoretical separation of the "I" from that which it observes and acts upon need not necessarily preclude its usefulness as a psychological theory; however, without a transparent translation process, any usefulness will be offset by unwittingly importing the belief system of the influence.

In this way, psychosynthesis therapists may come to erroneously assume an "inner observer" or "personal self" that stands apart from the wholeness of psychological life and maintains an attitude "identical to that of the natural scientist", as an accurate description of psychological experience.[296, 297]

Perspectival

If the processes and outcomes of experiential-synthesis are a whole created by a network of interconnected parts, each of which is influenced by all the other parts and the system as a whole, then it will not be possible for a neutral or objective observation from any one part or position within the system. Each position of observation will only provide a particular and partial perspective on the whole, never the complete picture or truth.

Alongside the "holistic" sub-principle, a second sub-principle criterion for a successful translation of influences into psychosynthesis theory is therefore the "perspectival" nature of experience.

A perspectival sub-principle can be seen in Assagioli's acknowledgement of the original presentation of psychosynthesis, and all subsequent presentations, as only ever being "partial expressions". No single presentation is definitive, or capable of capturing all that there is to say on psychosynthesis; that is to say, each presentation of psychosynthesis is only one perspective, expressed by a particular person, at a particular time, in a particular place.

The presentation given in this book, for example, offers a self-consciously principial perspective; that is, searching for the whole in the sum of the parts by turning the twin-principles of experiential-synthesis back upon psychosynthesis itself.

And yet, while Assagioli can be seen to embrace a perspectival sub-principle with regard to various psychosynthesis presentations, this is not always the case within the detail of his original presentation.

In particular, this can be seen with regard to the influence of empirical science, and its subject-object separation being directly translated into psychosynthesis theory, with his assumption of being able to observe psychological events from an objectively neutral and bias-free standpoint, with no subjective involvement or perspective:

> One can then—at will, and at any moment— disidentify from any overpowering emotion, annoying thought, inappropriate role, etc., and from the vantage point of the detached observer gain a clearer understanding of the situation, its meaning, its causes, and the most effective way to deal with it.[298]

> In order to dissolve [unconscious complexes] we should use the methods of objectification, of critical analysis, and of discrimination. That is to say, we must employ cold, impersonal observation as if they were mere natural phenomena, occurring outside ourselves. We should create a "psychological distance" between ourselves and them, keeping these images or complexes at arm's length, so to speak, and then quietly consider their origin, their nature, and—their stupidity![299]

While the "observer" might seem an obvious and necessary position to adopt, what matters is *how* we observe. To observe empirically, as a "detached observer" making an "impersonal observation" from a "psychological distance" quite separate from that which is observed, not only diverges from the perspectival sub-principle but also from the understanding of the "personal self" in psychosynthesis theory as a synthesis of awareness and "will".

The synonym of "the observer", as discussed in chapter 1, should therefore not be taken to imply a merely passive and receptive experience. Assagioli writes,

> . . . the self . . . is not only an observer, but also a will-er.[300]

> Observation has to be followed by valuation. Science, particularly psychological science, cannot avoid valuation.[301]

Observation is a combination of two things: the raw experience and how this is actively interpreted or evaluated.

Experiences are not a sort of barcode, to be observed with a scanner, which tells us immediately what it is, as a self-evident or objective fact. They are the result of a *mediatory* process of evaluation; that is to say, an act of will, which shapes this raw data from the world according to the perspective from which it is noticed; for example, raw sensory data of squiggly lines dancing over the rooftops in the middle distance is evaluated as "trees", and perhaps further evaluated as "beautiful trees".

In this way, even scientific statements, especially those of "psychological science", are only ever a working hypothesis, never a complete or objective truth.[302]

The perspectival sub-principle is not a "bug" but an inevitable "feature" of any observation or theoretical position; to be embraced as a basis upon which to enhance experiential-synthesis, rather than eradicated. Only to the extent psychosynthesis theory manages to draw inspiration from various influences while also maintaining this perspectival sub-principle will the translation process be seen to be successful.

Emergent

As we have seen, Assagioli's development of psychosynthesis showed remarkable foresight on his part, as it was not until the second half of the 20th century—first in "systems theory" and then "chaos theory" and "complexity theory"—that a mainstream recognition of synthesis started to appear within the scientific community.

These scientific developments led to a new theory of change called "emergence", which provides a third sub-principle criteria for a successful translation of influences. The basic recognition of "emergence" is that parts coming together in synthesis create spontaneous change through self-organizing processes of adaptation, the outcomes of which are named "emergent".

For example, in weather systems, this occurs when a particular synthesis of shifting climactic conditions—atmospheric pressure, temperature, humidity, and wind—transform a calm and tranquil Atlantic Ocean into a raging storm.

Whether in weather systems, economic systems, social systems, organizational systems, or personal psychological systems, the understanding provided by the sub-principle of "emergence" is that it is not really possible, or perhaps even desirable, to ask which particular part of the system created any given change; for example, whether the storm was created by the drop in temperature or the humidity or wind direction? Instead, emergence is best understood as a product of the participation among all the parts and the system as a whole.

Although this use of emergence was not available to Assagioli as a direct influence, "emergence" as a principial basis for understanding change can nevertheless be seen to be implicit within his presentation of psychosynthesis.

Perhaps the most obvious example of an emergent theory of change in psychosynthesis is the experience and teaching of disidentification.

As presented in chapter 1, the processes and outcomes of "disidentification" follow the delicate self-transformation that results from gathering a synthesis of ever more experiential elements, such that the limitations of "identification" are replaced with what we can now describe as the "emergence" of a new identity.

In this way, simply by introducing previously excluded experiences into awareness, the psychological system as a whole is transformed. But while a difference makes a difference, the advantage of an emergent theory of change is that it does not focus directly upon the causes of change in isolation, such as a new feeling or change in wind direction, but rather, the process of change itself, which will always be seen to be a synthesis of multiple elements.

Given the significance of disidentification throughout psychosynthesis practice, chapter 2 developed this principial understanding with regard to the application of psychosynthesis techniques. These can also easily be seen to align with an emergent theory of change, especially with regard to emphasizing the necessary therapeutic conditions to facilitate the process of synthesis and the emergence of "unexpected outcomes".

The point here is that, while isolated causal inputs, such as ideas or images, may be detectable, the ways in which they impact the system overall are unpredictable.

When techniques were applied as a means to control the production of "expected and pre-determined outcomes", disidentification was shown to diverge from the twin-principles of experiential-synthesis—a divergence that can now be related to the influence of empirical science being directly and unsuccessfully translated into psychosynthesis theory.

The philosophical assumptions of empirical science have so far only been discussed as they relate to bias-free objective observation; when it comes to the current discussion, regarding how change is understood in psychosynthesis theory, what also needs to be addressed is the rationale for why these observations are made; that is, the reason that objective observations are used by empirical science to better predict, and thereby control, the physical world.[303]

The influence of this can easily be seen in psychosynthesis theory:

> We can dominate and control everything from which we disidentify.[304]

> After having discovered all these elements, we have to take possession of them and acquire control over them.[305]

> . . . it is imperative for each man and woman who wants to live consciously to be well aware of those elements or components of their personality—not a dim, passive awareness, but a deliberate assessment, valuation, understanding and control of them.[306]

The translation of empirical science into psychosynthesis theory assumes an "inner observer" capable of not just observing but also controlling psychological experience. In this way, the separation from the whole created between an "inner observer" and observed "contents" is now extended to a separation between controller and controlled.

To attempt any direct control over the outcomes of an emergent process will be in danger of the "control separation" and "outcome separation" described in chapter 1.

And yet, this does not mean simply giving up and going with the flow. A successful translation of the influence of empirical science will be one that takes the inspiration of predictive control without turning it into a philosophical belief.

Such a translation would be aligned to a principial understanding, which can be found by returning to Assagioli's understanding of "control", given in chapter 1, as the ability to guide and regulate experience; that is to say, instead of trying to directly control the outcome of therapy, what therapist and client can more profitably attend to is the guidance and regulation of the therapeutic process itself, thereby facilitating the emergence of unexpected outcomes.

In this way, the emergent sub-principle directs therapeutic attention—not to the predictive control of any particular change from a position of separation outside the system, but rather, the necessary conditions needed to initiate change from within the process of experiential-synthesis itself; that is, by combining ever more experiential elements and allowing the system as a whole to move towards increasingly satisfying yet unpredictable outcomes.[307]

In summary, the translation of empirical science into psychosynthesis requires a "PROCEED WITH CAUTION" warning. If psychosynthesis psychotherapy is primarily an experiential process, not a philosophical position, then it isn't really an empirical scientific method, because while empiricism emphasizes the experiential, it does so within a philosophical framework.

The terminology of "observation" and "control" of an "inner world" introduces a whole set of philosophical assumptions that actively shape not only how psychosynthesis is studied and understood but also how it is experienced. This might not necessarily be a problem, were these assumptions acknowledged and examined within a translation process. However, this is unfortunately not the case within Assagioli's presentation, where the application of empiricism is assumed to eliminate "every philosophical or religious question".[308]

The result of this unexamined application of empiricism is to collapse the influence/theory gap. Instead of using the influence to create a loose hypothesis about the complexity of experiential life, the process is switched around and experiential life is squeezed into the simplifying assumptions of the influence.

In this way, the influence of empiricism becomes a dream story about psychological life. It is so intimately woven into the language and practice of psychosynthesis as to pass unnoticed, thereby unwittingly creating a belief system about an "inner world" filled with "psychological objects" capable of being objectively observed and predictably controlled by an isolated and separate "personal self".

And yet, as we have also seen, an empirical control and objective observation within a decontextualized inner world are not the whole truth of what Assagioli intended. Upon considering his presentation as a whole, subtle qualifications and even opposing perspectives to the philosophical assumptions of empiricism are revealed.

Evidence of empiricism being applied should therefore not be taken to assume a straightforward equivalence with psychosynthesis. The translation of empirical science into psychosynthesis, as with any influence, requires maintaining the gap between its philosophical assumptions and the experiential emphasis of psychosynthesis.

In this way, the application of empiricism can be understood for what it really is: a way to imagine the experience of psychosynthesis "as if" a scientist observing and controlling objects in the physical world. While this imagining is not wrong, and can provide useful insights, maintaining the influence/theory gap allows for the recognition that the comparison is never total. Psychosynthesis is only ever "as if" but never the "same as" empirical science—or indeed any particular influence.

A SYNTHESIS OF INFLUENCES

The debate about whether psychosynthesis is a contemporary scientific psychology or a reformulation of historical philosophies and religions is arguably not one that Assagioli entered into. He did not choose between exoteric and esoteric influences but rather, included both within his formulation of psychosynthesis.[309]

The "wall of silence" is not a complete disavowal of esoteric spiritual, religious, and philosophical influences but rather, a methodological translation of them into the contemporary exoteric language of empirical science. The scientific framing given by Assagioli, far from being untouched by this esoteric background, is therefore the very language with which it was hidden in plain sight, easily recognizable by those wanting to make the connections.

However, making claims about the relative importance of the diverse and dynamic influences shaping psychosynthesis will forever remain a subject of debate. These debates can be creative and informative, but by introducing an impossible simplification—akin to asking whether bread is really made of flour or yeast—can also unwittingly foster more, not less, elusiveness for psychosynthesis. Only by first acknowledging psychosynthesis as a synthesis of influences will its distinctiveness be appreciated.

Psychosynthesis psychotherapists share influences in Assagioli's original presentation, but each therapist will have a more or less different understanding of it, alongside which they will also bring other influences—some coinciding with the influences Assagioli drew upon, some coming from new perspectives, previously unavailable to Assagioli.[310]

However, what stops psychosynthesis becoming lost among this diversity of influences is the extent to which they are not being shared directly, as stand-alone theories and techniques, in order to replace psychosynthesis, but rather, as a way to bring fresh perspectives and possibilities to its expression. In other words, something is being done with these influences that translates them into psychosynthesis.

This chapter has presented a guide for the principial translation of any given influence into the theory and practice of psychosynthesis—a conscious act of translation that allows for the distinctiveness of psychosynthesis to be maintained by neither naively ignoring influences and imagining a "pure" psychosynthesis nor conflating psychosynthesis with any particular influence or set of influences.

In this way, a principial understanding, rooted in the twin principals of experiential-synthesis, and the holistic, perspectival, and emergent sub-principles can be distinguished from the more abstract-conceptual effects of any philosophical, religious, and indeed, scientific influences.

While it will perhaps never be possible, or even desirable, to arrive at a definitive or complete translation of any given influence, such a principial approach will nevertheless be what allows the effectiveness or otherwise of a given influence to at least be evaluated and discussed. This will now be demonstrated in the next and final chapter, which introduces a new partial expression of psychosynthesis as an "act of imagination".

Chapter 4

Imaginings

Training to become a psychotherapist, and in particular a psychosynthesis psychotherapist, was as an attempt to recover my lost imagination. The imaginative richness of my life had been in serious decline for some time.

That innate sense of story-filled possibility and play that I recollected from childhood had long since gone, as had my once taken-for-granted ability to slip into the story world of a good novel or movie. And those precious moments of reverie and wonder, when a cloud formation or sunset captured my whole attention—they too were becoming ever fewer and far between.

Clearly, something had gone wrong. But what? And what to do about it?

It seemed obvious to me that this loss of imaginative life was a decline in my mental health. The depressed, anxious, and alienated person I had become was not the richly imaginative person I remembered; hence, my thinking that training to be a psychotherapist, and becoming a "mental health" practitioner, would be a way to find the practical guidance and advice I needed to turn things around.

Of all the orientations available to me, it was psychosynthesis that caught my attention, due to its clear emphasis upon an image-based approach to therapy. As Assagioli wrote, "The imagination . . . is one of the most important and spontaneously active functions of the human psyche."[311]

But it soon became apparent that training to be a psychosynthesis psychotherapist was not the easy route back to imagination I hoped it would be. The psychosynthesis ideas and techniques regarding imagination were stimulating and practically useful, yet something wasn't quite right.

Despite all the guided imagery journeys, free drawings, and psychodrama enactments, my imaginative life did not immediately recover. Indeed, at times it seemed to slip ever farther away. It was puzzling. Why was a form of psychotherapy that so values imagination not resulting in the restoration of my imaginative life?

This final chapter sets out to answer this question by turning the twin principles of experiential-synthesis back upon psychosynthesis—this time with respect to its understanding and practice of imagination. Once again, a tension will be shown to exist between two contradictory approaches.

We will start with an "inner imagination" approach related to the abstract-conceptual psychosynthesis discussed in chapter 1 and the influence of "inner empiricism" discussed in chapter 3. These will be shown to be what places significant limitations upon psychosynthesis therapists wishing to work with imagination in experiential context.

Despite Assagioli's original presentation emphasizing this "inner imagination", there is nevertheless also the basis for a second more experiential approach of "contextual imaginings". This will be developed in this chapter as the theoretical understanding for a new "image-based" presentation of psychosynthesis.[312]

We will return to the case example of Daniel from chapter 2, then present the clinical application of "contextual imaginings" across a re-imagining of the stages of psychosynthesis in a fourfold sequence of: story identification, story disidentification, story emergence, and living between stories.[313,314,315 316]

The chapter closes with a discussion of the advantages this image-based presentation offers for a psychosynthesis rooted in a comprehensive application of the twin principles of experiential-synthesis.

INNER IMAGINATION

Assagioli clearly recognized the importance of imagination. His teachings and techniques are filled with image-based ideas and methods, some of which were featured in chapter 2.

Nevertheless, despite this emphasis, the original presentation does not directly define imagination. Given Assagioli's avoidance of definitional statements, as discussed in chapter 1, this absence need not be a surprise, and there is no doubt some wisdom in a reticence to explain away the mystery of imagination.

Assagioli's focus is upon establishing the validity of imaginative experience and the important role it has to play in therapeutic practice, but a more explicit theoretical understanding need not necessarily run against this experiential emphasis. Indeed, given ideas and assumptions about imagination can either constrain or enhance the experiential possibilities of imagining, it will be important for an image-based psychosynthesis to establish a satisfactory working understanding of imagination; that is to say, one that best describes imaginative experience.

Within the original presentation of psychosynthesis, the general understanding of imagination is that of an "inner imagination". While not explicitly stated, it can nevertheless be seen in Assagioli's writing.[317] For example, he talks of an "inner dialogue", "inner journey", and "inner program" where possibly we meet a "wise teacher within".[318]

In this view, images are mental pictures—psychological impressions inside the mind—that are separate from the external world of sensory experience. As discussed in chapter 3, this view can be understood with respect to the influence of "inner empiricism" upon Assagioli, whereby the stance taken by empirical scientists towards observing sensory objects in the physical world was internalized by psychotherapists—the contents of psychological life becoming similarly observable within a personal-subjective psychological interiority of "inner" images. However, at best, this inner view is only a partial description of imaginative experience, because images are not just inside.

Imagining connected to a sensory perception of the world is implicit within many psychosynthesis techniques. Whenever an imagined character or situation is granted a presence in the consulting room—for example, perceived in a drawing, sand-tray doll, or "empty chair"—the experience is one of interacting with images situated "out there" in external reality. Indeed, the effectiveness of these techniques positively relies upon participating with the world as an imagined reality.

For example, this can be seen in the case study of Rebecca from chapter 2, where she imagined her mum on the "empty chair"—not as an abstract cypher inside the mind but as a felt presence in the room, affecting her in a similar fashion to a physically present person.[319]

Of course, the "empty chair" is just a chair, a physical constant, but all these therapeutic methods rely upon the imaginative malleability of perception and how, for example, the fixed expression of a teddy bear can appear sad or happy, depending upon how it is imagined.

This activity of images in the world is understood by the inner imagination through the mechanism of psychological projection, which is easily understood by reference to cinematic metaphor.

In the same way that a movie projector produces a sequence of flickering images upon a blank screen, so too is imaginative life seen to project itself outwards from a subjective interiority in the unconscious onto the external world, as can be seen in Assagioli writing of the "outward projection of one's own centre".[320]

The case example with Daniel from chapter 2 (which we will discuss further below) provides a typical example of projection, in how, despite my sincere efforts to convey an empathic understanding and care, Daniel nonetheless came to experience me as a bored, critical, and rejecting therapist.

This gap between my perception of myself and Daniel's perception of me can be understood as him drawing upon a subjective cache of memories stored away in his unconscious to project an image of his critical father from childhood outwards onto the world; that is to say, towards me as the therapist. In short, Daniel did not really perceive *me*; he perceived a projected repetition of his fatherhood relationship from childhood.

In this way, projection provides a helpful way of thinking about the client's presenting issues as an impoverished imagining, based more upon pre-existing notions from the past than fresh possibilities available in the present.

However, as a theoretical basis for an image-based psychosynthesis, this "inner imagination" understanding and related psychology of projection have significant limitations. We will now discuss these across the same four "separations" used in chapter 1 to describe the limitations of the "Exercise in Dis-identification".

Centre Separation

While the "inner imagination" view correctly recognizes the subjective aspect of impoverished imagining and faulty projections as a cause of psychological suffering, it mistakenly assumes that this can be remedied by returning projections to a subjective centre of selfhood, so as to then allow for a purely objective perception, stripped of all imagining.

But as the saying goes, this is to throw the "baby" of imagination out with the "dirty bathwater" of faulty projections.

Imaginative experience obviously includes a subjective aspect, but it does not end there. As we shall soon discover, far from centred within, somehow separated from the external world, imagination is that which actively synthesizes subject and object, self and world.

The "inner imagination" assumption—that projections can be entirely withdrawn from the world in order to arrive at an accurate objective perception—unwittingly directs attention away from the world and towards the contents of a psychological interiority.

This needs to be recognized as an act of separation not synthesis, creating a danger of "centre separation," whereby the simplistic theoretical assumption of a subjective centre of imagining becomes mistaken for the complexity of imagination in experiential context.

Recollect that psychosynthesis understands psychological suffering to be caused by a separation of the part from the whole. Healing and transformation of this suffering are consequently understood to be created by the opposite of this separation; namely a synthesis that combines the parts into a greater whole.

Contrary to this understanding, inner imagination rests upon the fundamental assumption of a separation between person and world; therefore, at best, it is an inadequate basis for healing and at worst, an unhelpful perpetuation of the disconnection that underlies psychological suffering.

Control Separation

Contemporary psychosynthesis psychotherapy positively embraces an empathic and relational stance towards the client's experience. In this way, by simply deepening the client's experience of their feelings, thoughts and sensations, it avoids imposing a controlling agenda upon the client.

But due to inner imagination assumptions, an exception to this approach is often found within psychosynthesis image-based techniques which, far from working to notice, accept, and deepen experience of the client's spontaneously arising imagery, seeks instead to directly change and control what is imagined.

An inner imagination understanding assumes imagining to be an entirely "plastic" power; that is, one with no limits on what can happen in imagination. Techniques based upon this assumption therefore often expect a client to be able to imagine at will whatever scenarios are suggested by the therapist.

For example, during a guided imagery technique, if a client is imagining an anxious, vulnerable character, the therapist might assume that it is the purpose of the technique to directly control this imagery. They might suggest the character take a journey up a mountain path, and upon arriving at the top of the mountain, tell them to imagine a wise being, a bright sun shining down, or some other presumed-to-be transformative symbolic imagery, which will be implied or sometimes explicitly stated, as somehow transforming the anxious character into a confident and assertive one.

In this way, the imagined character is not experienced as a person to relate to but as a psychological object to be controlled and manipulated by the technique into a desired alternative image. This inadvertently creates separation rather than synthesis between the controlled imagery and the client who controls it, a "control separation", due to the assumption of imagination as an entirely subjective reality over which the centre of selfhood has complete control.

Outcome Separation

A third limitation of an inner imagination understanding is the tendency to focus excessively upon the content outcome of *what* is imagined to the neglect of the process of *how* we imagine.

Assuming images to be "inner objects" produces a theory of change, as mentioned earlier, that assumes imagination to be an entirely plastic power, such that the client can simply imagine on demand whatever imagery is suggested by the therapist.

In this way, image work becomes focused upon not only a predetermined outcome but also the particular imagined scenarios and actions by which to get there.

The result will be the forced or made-up feeling of an "outcome separation" due to the emphasis on desired image content either ignoring and/or directing attention away from the process of imagining and those images that are already spontaneously present within the client's experience.

Cognitive Separation

The psychological terminology of an "inner imagination" is just a set of abstract concepts, a way of thinking about imagination. It can be a helpful way of theorizing, but when mistaken for an accurate description of imaginative experience, the result will be "cognitive separation" from that experience.

Imagination is only metaphorically viewed "as if" it is an inner place, filled with image objects or things, capable of control by a centralized observer; however, this metaphorical comparison is not complete.

For example, we might consider how an imagined character in a sleeping dream is experienced by the dreamer as an autonomous "other" in an encompassing imagined reality. It is only on waking from the dream that it is explained from an abstract-conceptual theoretical perspective as an "inner part" or "subpersonality" located within the subjective interiority of "the unconscious".[321]

But when we forget that the theoretical understanding of the inner imagination is just a metaphorical comparison—perhaps through familiarity or the absence of alternative metaphors—and mistake it for an experiential reality, the gap between theory and experience collapses.

In this way images are turned into ideas and imagining into "thinking about" imagining; to the extent that, for example, the edgy presence of an autonomous dream character becomes merely a cypher for a psychological "idea" and its experiential complexity reduced to the theoretical simplicity of an "inner object" or "part", an "archetype" or "subpersonality".

The clinical consequence of this "cognitive separation" moves therapy away from facilitating the transformative meaningfulness of imaginative experience and towards a concern with conceptually figuring out what imagery means, represents, or "stands for". This may lead to lots of interesting interpretations, but without connecting these insights to experiential equivalents, the necessary conditions for change will not be provided.

An inner imagination understanding is at best a partial understanding. The world is not nearly as objective, factual, and devoid of imagining as it suggests. Any exclusively inner understanding is an act of separation not synthesis, and therefore poorly equipped to assist therapists in the application of image-based experiential techniques.

This chapter now continues by developing an alternative theoretical basis that addresses the four separations of "inner imagination"; first, by providing an understanding of imagination as that which brings together self and world, rather than pushes them further apart; second, by providing an understanding more closely aligned with the unpredictable irregularity of dreams than predictive mechanistic control; third, by emphasizing imaginative process, rather than a preoccupation with content outcomes; and fourth, by pointing towards the quality of imaginative experience, rather than thinking about images.

What we will discover is a theory of imagining that not only provides a closer match to imaginative experience but also a fuller expression of the twin principles of experiential-synthesis, a confluence of theory, technique, and principles in the act of imagination.

CONTEXTUAL IMAGININGS AND STORY-WORLDS

To find a more satisfying theoretical basis for an image-based psychosynthesis, one more closely aligned with actual experience, all we need do is what we have done now several times throughout this book; re-examine the metaphorical assumptions of the "inner imagination" understanding and the related psychology of projection.

In particular, we will reappraise the cinematic metaphor of projection and recognize the situation of the viewer, not as somehow inside the projector but as sitting in the cinema theatre, positioned somewhere in between projector and screen.

Contrary to the assumptions of a psychology of projection, the movie experience does not originate in a subjective centre from which it is projected outwards onto the objective world. If it did, there would be no need for scriptwriters, actors, directors, editors, and the whole vast array of artistic contributions that go into a cinematic experience.

To go even farther, there would be no need even for a cinema ticket, seat, projector, and screen. We could just stay at home, close our eyes, and as the director of our "inner" movie, simply conjure it into being as a series of entirely mental pictures.

But of course, this is not the case. While the personal aspect of imaginative projection will result in each viewer having a slightly different experience of a particular movie, this does not mean that the story-world of the movie is an exclusively subjective experience.

Yet neither is the movie an exclusively objective experience. The imaginative experience, while dependent upon the cinema screen, is more than a simple reproduction of physically sensed flickering lights.[322] Imagination goes beyond what is immediately given by the senses.

Paying close attention to the screen will result in it slowly receding into the background of awareness, to the degree that eventually, the viewer will no longer see a flat, static, and inert cinema screen, and awareness of sitting in a cinema watching a screen will be replaced by an awareness of being within an imagined story-world. We become "carried away" and "lost in the movie", wandering around, for example, in a Dickensian London or a sci-fi moon station.

This immersive experience happens to a greater or lesser extent when watching a movie, but what always happens to a complete extent is a continuously immersive imaginative experience of everyday life.

Imaginative experience is best understood as arising between persons and world, neither exclusively subjective nor objective but as a synthesis of both, arising somewhere in between not just viewers and cinema screens but also, for example, in between a reader and the "screen" of a novel's pages, a client and the "screen" of a therapist, or a person on a countryside walk and the "screen" of an autumnal sunset.[323]

This is not to suggest that the everyday experiential world of sense experience is a purely imagined reality. Mountains, rivers, and sky continue to exist without any need for human beings to create them in imagination. Yet the experience of this physical world is never a simple reproduction of what is sensed but rather, what imagination does with sense impressions when they are synthesized with subjective attributes of feelings, beliefs, memories, and so on.

This is why everyone will have a slightly different experience of not just movies but also mountains, rivers, and sky, as there is always a story-world being co-created in the relational entanglement between self and world—an imagined story-world that is neither contained within nor viewed separately as "over there", but is experienced as an encompassing environment within which we find ourselves.

As I wrote in a previous book:

> To walk down any street is an effortless immersion within a fully imagined world. The surrounding image environment appears without any conscious effort to "stand

> back" and "see what is really there". Spindly dark lines in the middle distance, a pale blue expanse overhead, and a nearby translucence are instantaneously narrated into a street story with trees, blue skies, and shop windows.
>
> It does not matter that the trees are seen in profile in the middle distance. We do not perceive two-dimensional trees and say to ourselves in wonder, *How odd!* Imagination goes beyond what is immediately given and presents us with three-dimensional imagined trees. Similarly, it does not matter that the sky is partially obscured by these trees. We do not philosophize as to whether an unseen sky exists or not; imagination fills in this sensory gap, and we imagine a seamless continuation of sky beyond the trees. Nor does it matter that the coffee shop window is dimly lit; we do not leave this darkness as an existential emptiness—imagination pictures an interiority of tables and chairs, staff and customers, music and chatter.
>
> In this way the sights and sounds of the everyday world are stitched together with feeling, thinking, and sensation into an immersive story-world. Despite the concerns of the inner imagination view, we do indeed walk around in a dreamy fashion all the time, as Shakespeare acknowledged when he declared: "We are such stuff as dreams are made on." Everyday reality is an imagined one.[324]

The experiential context of imagination (what we will be calling "contextual imagining") turns the inner-imagination view inside out; such that, far from images being inside, it is we who find ourselves surrounded by images.

Contextual imagining "goes beyond what is immediately given" to produce an "immersive story-world", one that arises in the middle ground that exists between subject and object, with no easily discernible separation between them. In countless large and small ways, these stories are the imaginative patterns within which we live, constantly shaping choices, actions, and relationships.

The contextual imagining of everyday life is always a storyworld. Stories are everywhere, seamlessly woven into the life fabric, passing by unnoticed all the time, not just when we watch movies or read novels but in memories and future plans, as well as practical activities, such as driving across town or cooking a meal.

However, this is not to suggest that all stories are equally valid and that there is nothing to be done. An image-based psychosynthesis understands the client's presenting issue not as a faulty projection but rather, as a limited story about self and world—a story that is ill equipped to contextualize the unscripted symptoms that have now shattered the previously taken-for-granted and habitual imaginative life of the client.

A new story event or character has ushered in an unwelcome dramatic tension into the client's life. It may be, for example, the story of a calm person who is becoming increasingly angry; the story of a trusted life partner who has, out of the blue, filed for divorce; or a serious illness making proximate the previously distant story horizon of mortality and death.

Image-based therapy helps make meaningful sense of these unscripted events and characters by rescripting an expanded story context to place them within. For example, sometimes anger has a place; of course, she was always going to leave me—the evidence was there all along; what matters now is noticing the blossom, living one day at a time.

In this sense, therapy is a time between stories, a slow re-imagining of self and world.

Of course, it is the client's life we are dealing with, and their difficulties cannot be simply wished away as a mere "story", in the sense of something made up or make-believe. But hopefully, it will be clear by now that this conventional view of story is not what is intended.

Before proceeding to the practical application of an image-based psychosynthesis and how to find a new story not by eradicating but rather enhancing imaginative life, it will be important to first clarify the close connection between imagination and story.

THE IMAGINED STORY-WORLD

As seen throughout this book with other terms, a simple definition of "story" is neither straightforward nor sufficient.

What really matters is to indicate the experience, which the following discussion now offers, relating psychosynthesis theory to story in a synthesis of three characteristics: psychological functions, perceptual situation, and dynamic timeline. Together, these characteristics create an imaginative pattern shaping the experience of self and world.[325]

Psychological Functions

The first characteristic of an imagined story-world is as a synthesis of psychological functions.

As might be expected from a psychology based on the principle of "synthesis", psychosynthesis tends to avoid working with the psychological functions in isolation and instead, emphasizes bringing feelings, thoughts, sensations, and intuitions together as different elements of an interconnected whole.

For image-based psychosynthesis, this involves the contextual imagining of a story-world that is experienced not by focusing analytically on any one psychological function in isolation but rather, through a broad, synthesizing attention.

Assagioli writes:

> Imagination is a function which in itself is to some extent synthetic, since imagination can operate at several levels concurrently: those of sensation, feeling, thinking, and intuition.[326]

This statement goes beyond describing imagination as just another psychological function. Assagioli is indicating that imagination, far from operating on its own, is that "which in itself" is constituted from a synthesis of all these other functions.

In this view, feelings, thoughts, sensations, and intuitions are subsidiary psychological functions subsumed within imagination as a synthesizing meta-function operating "at several levels concurrently". This is why Assagioli writes of imagination as "one of the best ways towards a synthesis of the different functions", because imagination is "in itself" a synthesis of these functions.[327]

Put simply, an imagined story-world is not just visual images; it is the experiential context for all the psychological functions. This was demonstrated in the chapter 2 case example with Daniel, where the "guided imagery" technique created an imagined story-world as a synthesis of: visual, auditory, and tactile sensations; feelings; and thoughts.

Perceptual Situation

The second characteristic of an imagined story-world is that it is a "perceptual situation", a place within which we find ourselves.[328]

It is an all-encompassing, three-dimensional environment created by the synthesis of psychological functions. Sensations of sight, hearing, and touch connect us to the colours, sounds, and textures of the story-world; and feelings and thoughts shape our responses to the people, places, and things there.

Whether this perceptual situation is the fictional story-world of a movie or novel, the therapeutic story-world of a "guided imagery" technique, or just the story-world of normal everyday life, this second characteristic indicates that the story-world is always perceived from inside the process of imagining, as an immersion within story as an imagined reality.

Dynamic Timeline

The third characteristic of an imagined story-world indicates how the first two characteristics produce choices and actions that move the story along a "dynamic timeline". A story is not a freeze-frame moment in time but rather, a temporal situation that emerges from a beginning in the past, moves into the present, and continues towards the sense of an ending in the future.

As the process of synthesis itself is also a dynamic movement through time, seeking to emerge into ever more satisfying future possibilities, image-based psychosynthesis therefore recognizes this process of synthesis along the timeline of a story.

While Assagioli did not explicitly theorize about story in this way, the following statements nevertheless show awareness of the need for a synthesis of past, present, and future:

> [Psychosynthesis has an] emphasis on the future, and of its dynamic role in the present.[329]

> There is a basic difference, or rather, contrast between two directions in *time* of the life interest: between the future-oriented, or *forward-verted*, and the past-oriented, or, retro-verted. This opposition between progression and regression is going on all the time in each individual . . .[330]

> In the treatment, three orientations are taken into account: the past, the present, and the future. These are not mutually exclusive, and the goal is to combine them in the right proportions in any case, but the emphasis is on the present; as one author said, "Past, present, and future are merged in the inclusiveness of the moment that IS."[331]

Past, present, and future are "not mutually exclusive", and the aim is "to combine them". Whether the emphasis is on addressing "the future" or "the present", it is important to find the correct "proportions" of combination so that the tension between "future-oriented" and "past-oriented", which is "going on all the time", is synthesized as a constantly unfolding present coming "out of the past", while simultaneously moving "towards the future".

In this way, an imagined story-world is characterized by a consideration of past, present, and future in synthesis along a dynamic timeline.

THE FOUR STAGES OF PSYCHOSYNTHESIS

Before further discussing the advantages offered by an image-based approach for a principial presentation of psychosynthesis, it is important to connect the foregoing theoretical discussion with its clinical application.

Notwithstanding that there are as many possibilities of clinical application as there are clients and therapists, every situation and person requiring a bespoke treatment, in the following discussion we will return to the case example with Daniel to offer a suggested outline for the work.

The intention here is to offer image-based principles and skills as the inspiration for adaptation and combination with other techniques, rather than a set procedure or step-by-step method, which, as noted in chapter 2, would be anathema to the spirit of psychosynthesis.

Stage 1: Story Identification

The opening sessions of any therapeutic process involve gathering an overwhelming quantity of information. Most obviously, there will be the description of the presenting issue or issues—the depression or anxiety, for example, and how, where, and when they manifest; what helps and what makes them worse; whether it is a new or returning experience; and what precipitated the decision to begin therapy.

The answers to these questions will then directly and indirectly convey further contextualizing details of the client's biographical past, current life situation, and hopes and fears of the future.

To the client all these details may appear to be disconnected experiences, just one random thing happening after another, but the therapist will be working to notice the repeating patterns that bring order to the apparent chaos.

Stage 1 of an image-based psychosynthesis involves recognizing this pattern as the client's "story identification". While the original presentation of "identification", described in chapter 1, is characterized as equating selfhood with the "contents of consciousness," in what follows, this understanding of "identification" is re-imagined as living within a restricted and habitual story of self and world.[332]

In the case example with Daniel in chapter 2, I had already introduced the language of "story" as shorthand to suggest the results of the guided-imagery technique at the point when I asked him, "Where might you recognize this story in your everyday life?" And it was only after the subsequent gathering of multiple analogies around this story pattern, such as the repeated description of Daniel's manic people-pleasing activity and constant anticipation of rejection, that I made the following move towards an explicit recognition of the "story identification".

To have done so prior to establishing an experiential basis would have been premature and may have led to an "outcome separation" and related "cognitive separation". However, once I had established a sufficient basis for doing so, directly sharing the "story identification" with Daniel actively served to not just maintain but also deepen the experiential emphasis of the therapy.

Th: We've made quite a few connections to the guided imagery journey now. So let's now consider them together and try to find the underlying story structure they have in common.

Cl: Okay.

Th: I'll go first, then you tell me if you'd add or change anything, and we can find a story that feels right.

Cl: Sure.

Th: I'm hearing a story about a man . . . who has been carrying a heavy burden around for a long time, doing a good job to take the weight of other people . . . but is finding it ever harder to continue and would like to put it down, which makes him worry about what might happen if he does so.

Cl: That's pretty good. You've really stripped it down.

Th: Yes, but is there anything missing?

Cl: The "heavy burden" works, but there's something missing about feeling on the outside, not fitting in.

Th: How about this version: a story about a man feeling on the outside, who has been carrying a heavy burden around for a long time to take the weight of other people, in the hope of being accepted and fitting in, but he's getting tired and wants to put down this burden, and yet, this makes him worry about what might happen.

Cl: I like it.

The above transcript is only a beginning description. As the client reports further experiences in subsequent sessions, an iterative refinement of the "story identification" will be developed. The intention is not to fit into any predetermined story format. What is important is to work flexibly to find the current "best fit" story for the client's experience. Any standardized arrangement is positively avoided by inviting the client to co-create the "story identification". But as the person who knows something about stories, the therapist begins the process, combining the three characteristics of story to create a provisional narrative formulation.

In this example, the *synthesis of psychological functions* is presented not as a list of separate feelings and thoughts but contexualised in an image of Daniel's depression as "carrying a heavy burden"; the *perceptual scenario* not as any one specific setting or list of characters but in a generic narrative relationship to "other people"; and the *dynamic timeline* as an action driven by "the hope of being accepted and fitting in", which is becoming "harder to continue", with future worries "about what might happen".

The rather generic and condensed third-person formulation of a story "about a man" is offered as a way of recognizing a pattern. While a second-person formulation by the therapist is most often employed for an experiential approach and reflects specific details, such as "You are not sure whether she wants you to join her or not," this only provides a close-up point of view from within a particular instance of the "story identification".

However, what is needed to recognize numerous instances of the same story, where the details of place, persons, actions, and responses vary, is a stripping away of all specificity in favour of revealing the underlying narrative structure. What stops this somewhat depersonalized third-person formulation from becoming a separation from experience is that it is intended as an imaginative perspective through which to deepen and clarify experiential life.

We will now discuss this in Stage 2: Story Disidentification.

Stage 2: Story Disidentification

Stage 2 of an image-based psychosynthesis is "story disidentification". While the original presentation of "disidentification", as described in chapter 1, is a cultivation of awareness and will, this is re-imagined in what follows as the cultivation of imaginative life.

The purpose of image-based psychosynthesis, as we have seen, is not to replace story with "reality". The basic assumption is that there is no getting away from stories as imaginative experiences. But not all stories are equally valid. The presenting issue disturbances are due to the limitations of "story identification". What is therefore needed so as to better incorporate the presenting issue difficulties is the cultivation of imaginative capacity needed to re-imagine this "story identification".

Despite writing of the need to regulate and develop imagination, Assagioli does not directly offer principles and methods to do so. What he provides are image-based techniques, such as, for example, the "Technique for the Training and Use of Imagination", the title of which might be taken to suggest a means by which to develop imaginative life.[333]

However, Assagioli's image-based techniques are not a method for developing imagination, per se, but rather, a utilization of images to effect particular therapeutic outcomes. In other words, the emphasis is upon how to use images, while the *process* of how we imagine remains somewhat taken for granted. Nevertheless, an implicit basis for the cultivation of imaginative life as a "story disidentification" can be found within the original presentation of "disidentification" by Assagioli.

Both the original "disidentification" and "story disidentification" methods are concerned with an experiential attention towards "the world of psychological facts of psychological events" as a means of allowing an increasing synthesis of elements into a greater whole.[334]

But, as we saw earlier, a story is composed of three related characteristics, only the first of which, the "psychological functions", might be seen to be included in the original disidentification emphasis on the contents of consciousness as feelings, thoughts, and sensations.

What distinguishes a story disidentification is therefore a directing of attention towards not only the contents of consciousness but also the experiential context created by these contents in the second and third characteristics of story as a "perceptual scenario" unfolding along a "dynamic timeline".

The continuation of the case example with Daniel will now demonstrate the cultivation of imaginative life through a close-up and sustained experiential attention to all three characteristics of story.

Psychological Functions

The following transcript picks up the work with Daniel six months on from the sessions described previously.

Daniel had begun in the normal fashion, with some updates on how he had been since last time we met; in particular, his new job in an accountancy firm, and how he was beginning to regret accepting the initial salary offer. Perhaps he could have gotten more?

But then Daniel suddenly changed topic, speaking with a peculiar hesitancy, such that it wasn't clear at first what he was talking about or why. The below section demonstrates a beginning move towards story disidentification by synthesizing the psychological functions.

Cl: I'm just wondering, you know . . . ? *[voice suddenly quiet and fragile]*

Th: Wondering . . . *[dropping my volume also]*

Cl: I'm still not feeling great.

Th: How are you feeling? *[not sure if "wondering" is just about feeling, but running with it for now]*

Cl: I don't know.

Th: What's it like, not feeling great?

Cl: Confusing.

Th: It's confusing. What you are wondering about is confusing. *[returning to earlier hint at thoughts]*

Cl: Yeah, whether this is working.

Th: Whether this is working... *[a simple reflection to get more information on what "this" means]*

Cl: What's the point of putting all this energy into coming here every week, if it's not working. *[voice even quieter now]*

Th: Ah, okay. You're wondering if the therapy is working.

Cl: I'm just not sure. *[gaze now turned away from me]*

Th: I'm guessing from your tone of voice this probably isn't the easiest topic to bring up. But maybe you were expecting something more definite by now, after all the work you've put in?

The abrupt change in volume and style of speech, more so than the as-yet unclarified topic, suggested the possibility of a naturally occurring disidentification process. Something out of character from beyond the bounds of Daniel's current identification was clearly emerging, and I therefore proceeded to help this process along simply by bringing experiential attention towards a synthesizing of the psychological functions: a feeling of confusion, a thinking about whether the therapy is working, and sensations of speech.

In this way, the client's experience is never approached analytically, by focusing upon any single feeling or belief or bodily sensation, but rather always as a story about self and world created by the synthesis of all these psychological functions, and more.

Perceptual Situation

The "story disidentification" process with Daniel continued by directing attention towards the "perceptual situation" story characteristic; that is to say, how the above-described synthesis of "psychological functions" was actively creating the experiential context of Daniel's relationship to people, places, and things in the surrounding world.

Each of the image-based case examples featured in chapter 2 implicitly worked with this perceptual situation through the "guided imagery", "empty chair", "personification", and "dialogue" techniques, but the people and places imagined were not physically present human persons. Only subsequently were connections made between these consulting room imaginings and the client's everyday life.

However, this case example offers an opportunity to highlight the perceptual situation being directly addressed within the therapeutic relationship as neither a subjective story "in the mind" nor an objective fact but as a contextual imagining arising between Daniel and myself.

> Th: How is it to bring this up, now?
>
> Cl: Not easy, like you say.
>
> Th: Anything in particular "not easy" about it?
>
> Cl: Well, it's not going down well with you.
>
> Th: I see. You reckon I'm disappointed? *[not colluding by confirming his perception, but simply reflecting back so as to gather further description]*

Cl: Yes, of course.

Th: What makes you say that?

Cl: This isn't going anywhere, we've made zero progress, and you are clearly thinking it's just a waste of your time.

Th: How so?

Cl: Ha! It's obvious, right? Here you are, sitting back in your chair, almost half asleep, but always with this slight frown. *[Daniel's voice has regained its usual strength]*

Th: I'm always frowning?

Cl: Sure, yeah. I mean sometimes you laugh, but even then, you're not laughing with me; you're laughing at me.

Th: Okay. Wow, that sounds difficult. It's like I'm bored or something, just thinking this is a waste of time, almost laughable. *[again, not colluding by saying "I am bored" but rather, saying "It's like I'm bored." which allows empathic reflection.]*

Cl: So, what are we going to do about it?

Th: Any suggestions?

Cl: Well, can't we switch it up a gear? I mean, stop holding back on me. Don't pretend; just tell me how it is. I'm up for that. I can do better.

Th: I get it. You're getting worried about the lack of progress and thinking I'm disappointed, and so you are asking if we can turn things up a notch . . . try harder.

How Daniel perceived me is what psychotherapists call "transference", the assumption being that this transference relationship is not random but indicative of the client's wider relational style and history. In terms of the current discussion, the transference is indicative of the story identification, an impoverished re-imagining of the expected, based upon pre-existing notions from the past, rather than any fresh engagement with new experiences in the present.

The expected story identification was first noticeable in the feeling of confusion. In the same way that Daniel had historically felt unsure whether significant others wanted him or not, so too he had come to imagine me as a similarly ambivalent figure.

For this reason, his story had filtered out what was fresh and novel about the therapeutic relationship—which is to say, an encounter with me as someone offering a considerable and sustained level of care and empathy—so as to instead perceive what he expected from me: a repetition of previous unsatisfactory relationships in which fake people will sooner or later let you down.

Initially, this seemed to be a perception of me as a disappointing figure, but it turned out to also be mirrored in Daniel being a disappointment to himself. Daniel's plan to resolve the situation by attempting to regain approval by somehow trying harder and doing "better" completed the repetition of the story identification.

The above transcript shows me working to simply bring attention to the "perceptual situation" characteristic of story. A natural beginning for doing so presented itself when Daniel said, "Well, it's not going down well with you." But if this spontaneous opening had not been forthcoming, the discussion could have been initiated with questions such as, "What do you imagine I might think about that?" or "What is it about me that perhaps brings this up?" Once they have initiated the discussion, a therapist will then continue to be as receptive as possible to the client's perception, simply inviting further description, so as to gather as full a picture as possible. This serves the purpose of deepening the client's experience of the story identification.

The perceptual situation is best approached by neither confirming nor denying its reality. (Recollect that the purpose of story disidentification is not to eliminate imagining from the client's perception of external reality.) While the validity, or otherwise, of the client's perceptions is an important consideration, it will emerge as an *outcome* of first engaging with an experiential process.

It is therefore important that the therapist avoids either confirming or correcting the client's perceptions, as we saw in chapter 2, when my therapeutic use of a variety of image-based techniques in a guided-imagery scene or a personified moon sought not to question the truthfulness or reality of the client's perception but rather, encouraged and enhanced it as an imaginative experience.

However, when the client is describing their experience of the "real world", and especially when this turns towards the transference perception of the therapist, it is all too easy to abandon working with images and imagining and to rush into reality-checking statements, such as "No, I do care" or "No, I'm not bored." But it is only by receiving the transference, and allowing the client to grant sufficient attention to this particular in-session experience of the story identification that a story disidentification process will be provided.

To have either confirmed or corrected the transference would have been to act against Daniel's *imagined reality*. To have confirmed Daniel's transference as an *objective reality* would have been in danger of strengthening story identification. I was therefore careful to acknowledge Daniel's experience by offering simple empathic reflections, such as "You reckon I'm disappointed," rather than confirming it as objectively true, by saying anything declarative such as "You are a disappointment to me."

To have corrected Daniel's transference as merely a *subjective reality* would have been equally problematic, effectively denying rather than bringing further awareness to his experience, thereby undermining the disidentification process.

I therefore did not rush to correct Daniel's transference perception by sharing my growing excitement that this session was actually a significant breakthrough, not a failure at all, given the possibilities offered by the story identification now directly entering the therapeutic relationship, as we shall soon see below.

Dynamic Timeline

A first therapeutic consideration with respect to the "dynamic timeline" characteristic of story is how best to pace the session.

While working to gather the "psychological functions" and "perceptual situation" characteristics, if an overzealous therapist asks multiple questions and offers frequent empathic reflections without leaving spaces between interventions, they will be in danger of not giving the client sufficient time to actually notice and have experiences.

On the other hand, if too much time elapses between therapeutic interventions during the session, the client will be in danger of becoming distracted and drifting away from the experiential context. Therapeutic skill lies in judging the balance between too many and too few interventions.

A second dynamic-timeline consideration will be to avoid a static, or "freeze-frame", experiential attention. Stories are always on the move, whether obviously or imperceptibly, perpetually emerging from the past into the future, but never happening all at once, like a snapshot in a magazine.

For this reason, it will be important to include a description of the underlying motivational decisions, choices, and actions that move the story through time, as shown in the above transcript when I asked: "What makes you say that?" and "Any suggestions?"

A general template for working with dynamic timeline will be a beginning, middle, and end, the current moment always being a "middle" situated between what has gone before, in a past-story "beginning", and the anticipation of future possibilities, in the sense of an ending.

A recognition of story time will be conveyed in the therapist's summaries, which are basically mini-stories, with a beginning, middle, and end, as in my saying above: "You've been getting worried about the lack of progress [beginning] and come to think maybe I'm disappointed in you [middle], and so you are asking if we can turn things up a notch, try harder [anticipated end]."

While these mini-story summaries are *implicit*—that is, not directly named as stories—they can also be worked with explicitly.

The case-example transcript now continues with an explicit application of story by connecting the current session to the earlier work, described above in stage 1 as the "story about a man who . . ."

Cl: But you are disappointed in me, right? I can tell you are.

Th: I get that's what you think.

Cl: But it's not what you are thinking?

Th: What I'm thinking is that how we are getting on in the therapy is probably reflective of other relationships in your life.

Cl: How so?

Th: Remember the "story about a man who . . ." that we came up with a while back?

Cl: Yeah, of course. Oh, my god, yeah, right!

Th: You get it? What's happening right now is another repetition of that story—the story about a man feeling on the outside, carrying a heavy burden to take the weight of other people, in the hope of being accepted and fitting in.

Cl: I'm not fitting in here, with you; that's me thinking this isn't working and you being disappointed in me.

Th: And so, you are wanting to try harder, hoping to become accepted.

Cl: That's crazy.

Th: Why would what happens here be so different to elsewhere?

Cl: Yeah, but isn't that the point of therapy—to change, to learn something new, do life differently?

Th: Sure, and we do that by noticing the story repetition, learning to recognize it as it is happening . . .

Cl: . . . like we are doing right now.

Th: How is it to recognize yourself in the story?

Cl: Weird.

Th: What kind of weird?

Cl: Well, I'm in the story, like you say, but also not anymore. I totally was, a minute ago, but not now, not completely, anyways.

Despite working to maintain an experiential focus upon the "perceptual situation", by neither confirming or correcting its *imagined reality*, sooner or later, it was perhaps inevitable that Daniel, in the transcript opening above, would ask a "reality check" question ("What do you really think and feel about me?")

While answering such questions directly can, with careful handling, be therapeutic, to the extent that the answers do not align with the client's imagined reality they can be a too abrupt challenge to the story identification, and therefore in danger of refuting rather than enhancing experiential attention.

However, a third therapeutic consideration of the "dynamic timeline" story characteristic—working with historical time—allows for a response to the client's "reality check" question, as shown in the above transcript, which maintains the experiential emphasis needed for a disidentification process.

Instead of sharing personal details about my experience of Daniel, I responded to the "reality check" question with my "process" thinking about the session itself ("What I'm thinking is that how we are getting on in the therapy is probably reflective of other relationships in your life.") My intention was to move on from exploring just one instance of the story identification within the transference relationship to multiple instances of the same story as a repeating historical pattern.

Given the subsequent recollected memories will themselves be images, we can maintain an experiential emphasis by simply describing the "psychological functions", "perceptual situation", and "dynamic timeline" characteristics within these earlier stories.

While differing in specific details, these memories will be seen to display the same underlying narrative structure, as explored with Daniel in chapter 2 via the application of analogy as a "psychological link or connection between outer and inner realities".

The paradoxical aim of working with the historical repetition of story identification is to encourage an in-the-moment *recognition of the pattern*. While the initial historical recollections will by definition be in retrospect, continuing to notice the story pattern over a period of time will result in the client becoming ever more sensitized to its repetitions, until eventually they come to notice it as *a lived experience in the moment*. This is what happened in the above transcript, when Daniel said, "Oh, my god, yeah, right!"

The exploration of the transference relationship having provided an in-the-moment and close-up experiential attention to the story identification, it only needed a gentle reminder of the "story about a man who . . ." for Daniel to step into the story as a story in real time; that is to say, the process of imagining became conscious, such that the "perceptual situation" of me in the therapy room was no longer pointing towards an objective reality about a critical therapist but now a much more ambiguous and uncertain imagined reality (*Maybe he's not thinking this is a waste of time?*); simple and sustained experiential attention having cultivated the imaginative capacity needed to disidentify from the limitations of story identification and begin to consider the possibilities of a new story.

Stage 3: Story Emergence

The new story possibilities that spontaneously appear as a result of story disidentification will be noticed and brought into experiential life by way of an uncertain imaginative process.

A conscious predictability and control to the change process may be desirable, but any such attempts by therapeutic techniques to prematurely move into a pre-planned story—perhaps as a healthier, fitter, sober person—will rarely allow for the expected transformation, and will more likely result in an eventual return to the story identification—of junk food and wine on the couch.

Life is an uncertain and open-ended process—something we grow into, like a caterpillar in a chrysalis—and we never quite know what colour or shape our wings will be. But what a therapist can do is learn to notice the story-making process already happening in the client's life as a "story emergence", which requires paying therapeutic attention to those moments of possibility when, as a result of story disidentification, creative gaps begin to appear in the client's habitual story of self and world.

Such emergent possibilities will be evident in any atypical experiences and expressions that do not align with the story identification; for example, an unusual topic, an unfamiliar tone of voice, or an out-of-character strength of feeling. Upon noticing these new story possibilities, the therapist will then work to simply bring them into experiential awareness, as the continuation of the session with Daniel now demonstrates:

Cl: Well, I'm in the story, like you say, but also not anymore. I totally was, a minute ago, but not now; not completely, anyways.

Th: What's different now?

Cl: I'm just not so sure anymore.

Th: About whether the therapy is worth it still?

Cl: No, that was before. Now I'm not sure whether you are disappointed in me.

Th: Right.

Cl: Maybe I'm just imagining your disappointment, because that's what I always do.

Th: So if my disappointment isn't the whole story anymore, what else might be happening?

Cl: You really are going to make me say it?

Th: Not if you don't want to.

Cl: Well, if you are not thinking this is a waste of time,

then maybe I'm not a waste of time, either, you know?

Th: Yes, I understand. And I'm wondering how it is to say that out loud?

Cl: It's like a relief. The tension has just gone. I'm not anxious anymore. I was anxious. I was worried what you were going to say, but not now.

Th: The tension has just gone—as if maybe you've put down your "heavy burden"?

Cl: Ha! Yes. I'm not trying so hard anymore, no.

Th: You don't feel on the outside?

Cl: Not like before, no. There's an acceptance. You seem more supportive now, somehow. Weird.

Th: What's so weird?

Cl: Well before it was like you were definitely bored and grumpy, but now you are not at all.

Th: So, if you are not seeing me as grumpy anymore, and you are no longer feeling like you are a waste of time, what might all this allow to happen next?

Cl: How do you mean?

Th: I mean, right now, you are no longer imagining yourself as a disappointment. You've stepped into a new story where you don't need to try so hard to gain approval. So, I'm just wondering. If this is happening here with us, where else might it be possible, and what might that look like?

The above transcript shows my working with the *imagined reality* created by story disidentification, which required entering into the uncertainty of the new story possibilities and gathering all three story characteristics so as to create the experiential context of the story emergence:

1. In a synthesis of psychological functions, by naming Daniel's emerging thoughts and feelings ("Maybe I'm not a waste of time" and "a relief . . . not anxious anymore");
2. In the emerging "perceptual situation", by describing Daniel's newfound experience of his therapist ("not thinking this is a waste of time" but instead, being "more supportive");
3. By placing these first two characteristics along a dynamic timeline, where the previous future unknown—about what might happen if Daniel put down his "heavy burden" and "not try so hard"—has now been replaced with a present-moment knowing of "not trying so hard anymore." Asking, "What might this allow to happen next?" directed Daniel towards an emerging, as-yet-unrealized future—the "story emergence" being just one more step along the dynamic timeline and therefore, as with all stories, always experienced as a temporal whole, with a past, present, and future.

Stage 4: Living Between Stories

The four stages of an image-based psychosynthesis are best understood as a repeating cycle, in which the client lives through an unfolding sequence of stories, each one offering an expanding range of experiential possibilities. The focus of stage 4 is therefore not upon arriving at the final attainment of a new story but "living between stories".

The emergent possibilities from stage 3, of an alternative to the story identification, are a significant development in need of further elaboration; however, this will be established within the broader context of continuing to cultivate the imaginative capacity the client needs to better participate within not only the current "story emergence" but also all subsequent emerging stories.

The "living between stories" stage is noticeable by an increase in the "story emergence" characteristics first encountered in stage 3, which take the form of atypical feelings, thoughts, perceptions, and actions.

These new story characteristics stand out from, and bring into question, the assumptions of the story identification but are not yet sufficient to create a coherent story pattern strong enough to replace it. This results in a dramatic tension between the continuing dominance of story identification and these seemingly random and disconnected emerging story characteristics.

An image-based psychosynthesis therapist will work to maintain, rather than resolve, the dramatic tension of living between stories. The client is often predisposed to prematurely resolve this dramatic tension by selecting one story over another by either doubling down on the story identification or suppressing it in the hope of achieving a new experience; however, this will miss out on the cultivation of imaginative capacity found within the tension itself, by synthesizing *both* the pre-existing characteristics of "story identification" *and* the new characteristics of "story emergence".

The therapeutic strategy is therefore a "both-and" approach, which allows for a playful acceptance to be conveyed to all story characteristics, with no preference being shown for one story over another.

However seemingly contradictory or incompatible, *both* the pre-existing *and* new story characteristics are brought together in synthesis, as is now demonstrated in a continuation of the case example with Daniel where, two months on from the exchange described in stage 3, he is now discussing a recent meeting with his boss. (Note: Interventions in *italics* show my switching to a present-tense experiential exploration of the memory, as discussed in chapter 2.)

Th: It really does seem a confusing experience. Perhaps tell me a bit more about *sitting in the meeting with your boss.*

Cl: It was just a weekly team meeting around the big table in the conference room. He was sat just next to me, on my right. *[still in past tense]*

Th: And what *is* it like to glance across at your boss?

Cl: It's weird. *[a beginning switch to present tense]*

Th: What kind of weird?

Cl: [Pause] Well . . . the usual sense of disapproval is there . . . in the way he is smirking at me . . . but also . . . something else too . . . because the smirk also suggests he's maybe sort of pleased with me as well . . . as if I'm doing a good job. *[present tense description now established]*

Th: *He seems both pleased with you*, and also not . . .

Cl: That's right . . .

Th: And what is it you *are doing or saying* that he is both pleased with and also not?

Cl: I'm disagreeing with a colleague. She's assuming something about my role which isn't right, and I'm correcting her on it.

Th: And *how are you speaking* to her?

Cl: Confidently, like I'm just totally correct.

Th: So you are speaking confidently, saying what you think. And *what's it like to do that?*

Cl: Again, just weird. I almost said, just wrong! But it's the right thing to do, and it feels good.

Th: As if you are simultaneously both right and wrong at the same time.

Cl: Exactly!

The newfound uncertainty as to whether his boss is approving or disapproving is an imaginative ambiguity, a moment between stories which, by neither confirming nor correcting as true or false, allows the experiential emphasis of psychosynthesis to be maintained, because for Daniel, both past and future possibilities of his boss are simultaneously true within the present *imagined reality.*

In an image-based therapeutic approach, this highlights the importance of always working to include the "dynamic timeline" characteristic of story as a temporal process, unfolding from the past into the present and moving into the future.

While the isolation of any one temporal element is perhaps inevitable at times, when continued over an extended period—whether within a single session or more broadly as a habitual therapeutic style—this will act against imaginative experience in one of three ways:

PRESENT TENSE FOCUS, NEGLECTING PAST AND FUTURE

"Just be here now, in this moment." Any suggestion of a so-called "direct experience" as somehow untouched by the influence of the past or the anticipation of the future will be in danger of creating an eternal "now", disconnected from the consequential sequencing of story.

This does indeed sometimes happen spontaneously; for example, upon waking from an afternoon nap and not knowing what time it is, where we are, and even who we are.

Of course, these gaps in comprehension don't last long, and soon, the present moment will once again become understood in experiential context between past and future events (*I'm here in this strange room, where I've come on holiday, and soon friends will arrive for dinner*).

But to purposefully direct therapeutic attention to these "now" moments is, at best, a misunderstanding of what it means to be in the present and, at worst, an unwitting alienation from imaginative experience. Both memories and future anticipations are contained in the present and therefore to be fully in the moment, we always need to include a synthesis of past, present, and future.

Present and Past Tense Focus, Neglecting the Future

"I can understand how you have come to struggle in this way." Given that, from an image-based perspective, the client has entered therapy precisely because they no longer have a forward-moving story to make sense of events, any undue focus upon only past causes, without the inclusion of a progressive timeline into the future, will be in danger of a static treatment, blocking the process of synthesis.

While an empathic understanding of biographical events will be an important therapeutic ingredient, the client also needs a therapist to help them imagine a new and better future life. Without such a future-oriented perspective, the therapist will fail to notice "story emergence" characteristics and the client will struggle to translate insights about the past into transformative change.

Present and Future Tense Focus, Neglecting the Past

"Your current struggle is going somewhere, a birthing process towards a new way of being." While this statement is not wrong and will be an important aspect of any change process, when offered in isolation from a consideration of the past, the therapy will be in danger of neglecting the formative effects of historical experiences and how they are continuing in the present to hold the client back from future developments.

The symptoms of story identification are not resolved by simply "becoming disidentified", as a static, idealized state of once-and-for-all complete freedom, but in the repeated letting go of the past and stepping into the future possibilities of more expansive identifications, as the process of synthesis continues to move along its dynamic timeline.

In this way, we can recognize Daniel's newfound uncertainty towards his boss as a repetition of the earlier realization at the end of the "story disidentification" stage, when his previous certainty of my being a critical therapist was similarly replaced with an ambiguous imagined reality.

An image-based therapist will therefore be on the lookout for such repetitions, across multiple contexts, of this "living between stories" experience, and once sufficient experiential familiarity has become established to allow the client to begin to notice the connections among these multiple repetitions, the therapist will move on from only working with specific examples to offering a generic story formulation of "living between stories".

Th: So, let's just summarize where we've got to these past few weeks—which is that the story of holding back from upsetting others and worrying about being accepted is continuing, and also there is this growing sense of belonging, of being approved of, and therefore less and less need for you to hold back. How's that?

Cl: Pretty much, that's right, yeah.

Th: Is there anything you would add or change?

Cl: Not so much "hold back"; perhaps "stay quiet" is better.

Th: Okay. You continue to stay quiet . . . and how would you describe what's beginning to happen now?

Cl: Confidence, speaking my mind, just saying what I think, really.

Th: So, you continue to stay quiet, to avoid upsetting others, worrying about being accepted, and also there is this growing sense of belonging and approval, which is allowing you to speak your mind, say what you think—the old story of the outsider and also a new story of acceptance and belonging.

Cl: Yes.

Th: And how is it to be in touch with both these stories at the same time?

Cl: I keep saying it's weird.

Th: You do.

Cl: But in a sort of good way.

Th: Sort of good, so also sort of bad too? *[maintaining the "both/and" tension]*

Cl: Well, the running around scared, worrying about what people think about me, yes that still happens, so that's bad, right. But also, it happens in a different way now. It's not the whole story. It doesn't have the same power over me. I'm worried, but not as worried, you know?

Th: I understand, yes.

Cl: Sometimes, I surprise myself and just come right out and say what I think, without worrying about how it will go down with other people. But then, of course, I do end up worrying.

Th: The worry doesn't stop you, but it sort of kicks in afterwards.

Cl: Yeah, but not like it used to do *[laughs]*

The generic story formulation of "living between stories" is offered so as to further facilitate its recognition as a repeating pattern, such that in-session therapeutic work can then carry over into everyday life, opening up a creative gap between the habitual expectations of "story identification" and the fresh opportunities of "story emergence".

Whether in a disagreement with a work colleague, in the quiet reverie of reading a novel, or choosing what to eat in a restaurant, the imaginative process of meaning-making becomes less repetitive and fixed, and ever more creative and malleable.

Instead of repeatedly falling into the same old routine limitations, the client is ever more able to not just notice but also step into and risk experiencing and expressing the new. And in this way, an ever more satisfying complexity of storied possibilities continues to emerge, allowing the client to better respond to the presenting issue symptoms that brought them into therapy in the first place.

THE ACT OF IMAGINATION

Image-based psychosynthesis presents therapy as a time between stories, such that the previously unscripted events and characters that brought the client into therapy become contextualized within an expanded story about self and world.

But the client on the therapist's couch in this book has not just been an imagined Daniel or Rebecca. The client in this book has also been psychosynthesis itself, and how it has been imagined by Assagioli in a time between stories.

Early in the 20th century, the vision of a psychology based upon an application of synthesis was in many ways a story far ahead of its time. In a world dominated by the controllable mechanistic paradigm of steam engines and telegraph wires, psychosynthesis pointed towards a future recognition, across multiple disciplines, of a networked ecological paradigm in which the actions of any one "part"—whether a butterfly or a viral-video—affect the system as a whole.

But not having the benefit of the many subsequent theoretical developments in this new paradigm, Assagioli made do with those influences available to him. The story of synthesis was therefore presented within an adaptation of the analytical story from Freud—of a psychological life within "the unconscious" and the related influence of an "inner empiricism," as a science of human subjectivity.

However, this book has shown there to be a dramatic tension between the synthetic-experiential and the analytical-empirical stories. The both-and strategy of the book has so far been to describe and maintain the dramatic tension between these two stories. In this way, the argument developed has shown how the principial basis of the synthetic-experiential story is constrained, or even undermined in places, by an uncritical adoption of the analytical-empirical story.

As with any individual client, psychosynthesis is itself passing along a dynamic timeline, one that is unfolding from the past into the present and moving along into the future; therefore, this final chapter seizes the momentum created by earlier chapters to move the discussion on from simply maintaining the dramatic tension between stories.

Significant developments in psychosynthesis theory and practice will never just be an incremental addition to the existing presentations. Any truly creative process depends upon a prior destruction, a clearing-away of the old ways, to make space for the new.

By bringing the analytical-empirical assumptions within psychosynthesis into awareness, they have been revealed as a story identification not a fundamental truism. Recognizing this facilitates the disidentification process needed for the emergence of a new story in the presentation of an image-based psychosynthesis—a presentation that does not perpetuate the limitations of a psychology of "the unconscious" and "inner empiricism".

We will now discuss the advantages of this image-based presentation for a theoretical basis more closely aligned with the twin principles of experiential-synthesis, across four "syntheses" of "contextual imagining".

Contextual Synthesis

Image-based psychosynthesis contextualizes the client's experience within an imagined story world. Whether this is within the eyes-closed imagining of a guided imagery journey, the consulting room imagining of "empty chair" work, the transference relationship, or in the imagining of everyday life, therapeutic work is always understood and approached from the client's perspective within the context of an encompassing story world. Wherever we are, there is always a story.[335]

Any suggestions of avoiding or contraindicating image work, due perhaps to a client having an unstable sense of self or a so-called "over-active" imagination, rests upon the "inner imagination" assumption of imagining being a discrete psychological function that can be ignored in favour of an exclusively cognitive, emotional, or body-based approach.[336]

But for an image-based psychosynthesis resting upon a "contextual imagining" understanding, the choice is not between *whether* to work with images or not, but only a matter of *how* best to do so.

As we saw in the case example with Daniel, the holistic principial basis for any image-based approach will be one of gathering the story characteristics of the client's narrative across multiple contexts in search of the underlying pattern of "story identification". At the appropriate moment, once sufficient experiential evidence has been established to recognize this story, we can then offer it to the client in a generic formulation as a story "about a man [or woman] who . . .". This story template provides the imaginative perspective needed to work through the subsequent stages of psychosynthesis.

It is important to note that, although it aligns with the original presentation of psychosynthesis on a principial basis, the contextual-synthesis of an image-based approach presents a significant theoretical divergence. In the original presentation, an important hypothesis is the idea of the "personal self" as a "centre of consciousness and will", with the related therapeutic aim of building "a new personality—coherent, organized, and unified" around this "unifying centre".[337]

Perhaps due to its ubiquity, this idea is often mistaken for an accurate description of the experience of psychosynthesis; however, it is best understood as a working hypothesis, just one way of theorizing about psychosynthesis, an abstract conceptualization rather than "the truth".

In the same way that the human body is no longer understood as having a centre of control in the brain but rather, a distributed system of regulation spread across a synthesis of cells and organs that together create a complex whole, so it is that psychosynthesis also need not be restricted to being understood as revolving around a "centre".

As post-Assagioli psychosynthesis theorist Molly Young Brown writes:

> A subsystem may specialize to perform needed functions of coordination, but we would hardly say the nervous system is the "boss" of our body. It simply carries messages around about what is happening elsewhere and what responses are required. In psychosynthesis, we might see the self and the will as the "boss" of the system, but I believe this is a distortion arising from our cultural bias towards hierarchy. The self is the system and the system is the self; it is not some distinct part of us that rules the rest.[338]

Psychosynthesis becomes decentred when understood as a contextual synthesis. The notion in the above statement of "the self is the system, and the system is the self" offers another layer of reflection to the recognition from chapter 1 of the "personal self" and "transpersonal Self" as "not really two selves, two independent and separate entities".[339] This recognition directs attention towards an understanding of "transpersonal Self" as the encompassing experiential context within which the "personal self" exists.

In other words, "transpersonal Self", far from being a discrete entity, or centre, is seen to be a decentralized network of intermediary relationships—with people, places, and things and feelings, thoughts, and memories—and it is by noticing and strengthening these relationships that we cultivate the "personal self".

Building upon the understanding, again from chapter 1, of this "personal self" and "transpersonal Self" being a reflection of each other, we can now go one step farther and recognize that in the same way that "transpersonal Self" is not a discrete entity, or centre, "some distinct part of us that rules the rest", so too can the "personal self" be understood in a decentralized fashion to be distributed across the whole system of relationships.

The presentation in this chapter, of the imagined story-world as the experiential context within which the client exists, can therefore now be seen to reflect this decentralized understanding of "personal self". This is why an image-based psychosynthesis does not search for a source of imagining centred within the client, nor projected outwards onto the world from such a centre, but rather, as a decentralized experience arising in between self and world.

In the same way that the relationship between "personal self" and "transpersonal Self" was described in chapter 1 as experienced via a network of intermediary relationships, so too chapter 4 has described the act of imagination.

Whether it be the story-world of a movie created in the relationship between viewer and screen or the story-world of psychological life created in the relationship between persons and the "screen" of other people, places, and things, there is always an imagined reality. Indeed, we can say that a relationship, far from being a simple and static "thing" or "object" with a centre, is an imagined reality constituted by a contextual web of dynamic processes.

The advantage of an imagined story-world as a decentralized experience is therefore an antidote to the "inner imagination" limitation of "centre separation".

Instead of further isolating the client, by unwittingly encouraging an identification with a centre of control in a decontextualized "inner world", an image-based psychosynthesis provides a theoretical and methodological basis aligned to the twin principles of experiential-synthesis and the act of imagination, which moves the client towards wholeness, bringing self and world together, not farther apart.[340]

Participatory Synthesis

Image-based psychosynthesis participates with images as persons. This may strike some as a somewhat strange and even dangerous notion, more suggestive of a regressive return to childhood naivety than a healing of psychological suffering in adulthood, but once again, the ground from which we build is experience.

Putting aside the assumptions of an "inner imagination" understanding, and considered clearly, imaginative experience can easily be recognized as one of relating and participating with images as persons.

How we imagine the therapist in the transference relationship, and indeed any other human being, is most obviously a participation with an imagined person. Other obvious examples are those imagined persons found in the characters of movies, plays, novels, paintings, and sleeping dreams, and of course, the everyday experience of writing a letter, email, or text may also be viewed as participating with the imagined person we are addressing in the writing process. We also communicate with imagined persons during any form of prayer or self-talk.

But the experience of imagined persons is not limited to humans. When a bright full moon "speaks" to us, a favourite city park or country walk is considered "a faithful companion", or we entreat a broken-down car, saying "Oh, come on. Give me a break!", we are relating to the surrounding physical environment of the everyday story-world as if it were populated with imagined persons.

The principial basis for this participation with image-persons was established earlier in the book. Chapters 1 and 2 quoted Assagioli describing a "principle of personification" in how "every psychological element . . . tend[s] to personify themselves".[341]

In this understanding, psychological life is not experienced as discrete feelings and thoughts but rather, as the personified images that contextualize these feelings and thoughts in imagination, as was shown in the chapter 2 case example questions, such as, "How about we see what imagery comes up around this issue?" and "These people that don't care about you . . . if you were to picture them as just one person . . . who would this one person be?"

However, what really matters is not so much the discovery of personified images but how they are related to and the aims of this relationship. Here, the aims of an image-based psychosynthesis align with the original presentation of psychosynthesis by developing a relationship between the "personal self" and "transpersonal Self", both of which are *persons*.

The experience of "transpersonal Self", as discussed in chapter 1, is not a direct and one-to-one encounter but rather, via a network of intermediate relationships that act as "an indirect but true link, a point of connection between the personal man and his higher Self".[342]

The important principial point made in chapter 1 is that these "intermediate relationships" are not limited to only human persons but also to be found in personified encounters with movies and novels, sunsets and billboards, trees and technologies. In other words, the principle of personification by which "the call of Self" is experienced is the same as that established above for an image-based psychosynthesis.

The advantage of emphasizing a participatory-synthesis is that it avoids the "control separation" limitation of "inner imagination". To assume images are merely "inner objects", part of a subjective reality entirely controllable by a centre of selfhood, will tend towards a relationship of domination and manipulation that will, at best, only serve to obscure and distort the connection to "transpersonal Self".

Only by participating with images, not as an "it" or object to be controlled but as a "thou" of fellow being to be valued and respected, as someone from whom we might have something important to learn, will it be possible to establish and strengthen the "intermediate relationships" between the "personal self" and "transpersonal Self".[343] These constitute a personhood of images that, as we have seen, is not a forced make-believe but simply an accurate reflection of imaginative experience.

Emergent Synthesis

Image-based psychosynthesis emphasizes an emergent-synthesis approach to change. The client's presenting issue is understood as the eruption of unscripted story characters and events (also known as "superconscious" experiences). These require a re-imagining of the client's story-world—a re-imagining that will follow the unpredictable process of synthesis, allowing it to emerge along its dynamic timeline, rather than attempting to establish a pre-determined story outcome.

The process of "emergence", as introduced in chapter 3, is one of parts coming together in synthesis to create spontaneous change through a self-organizing process of adaptation, the outcome of which is called "emergent".

This book has therefore presented image-based techniques and principles that direct therapeutic attention towards facilitating emergence, simply by attending directly to the process of synthesis itself.

Whether creating a guided imagery story-world, dialoguing with an imagined character on an "empty chair", or engaging with transference projections, an image-based therapist engaged in networking synthesized experiential elements will constantly be on the alert for atypical expressions.

These atypical expressions may take the form of out-of-character feelings or thoughts or a sudden pause or unusual facial expression and indicate the stage of "story emergence", or "the call of Self", as discussed in chapter 1. Bringing these atypical expressions farther into awareness and synthesizing them will allow for the imaginative shaping of a new story-world, or "ideal model".

Assagioli writes, "When will and imagination come into conflict imagination wins."[344] Simply put, no matter how strongly change is willed, if this change can't be imagined it's not going to happen. To just have a desire to change, however strong, is not enough. Without the ability to imagine a future event or way of being as a realistic opportunity, it will be all too easy to avoid the uncertainty of the new and return to the familiar and habitual.

In this way, hopes and dreams remain unrealized fantasies about what could have been; whereas if the uncertainty of the new can be tolerated, in the dramatic tension between stories, then these possibilities will carry over into expression as an act of imagination—an imaginative transformation understood to be created, not by any single part or centre of control but rather, by the process of synthesis and the emergent self-organizing behaviour of the system as a whole.

Emphasizing such an emergent-synthesis will therefore avoid the "inner imagination" limitation of "outcome separation".

Experiential Synthesis

Image-based psychosynthesis primarily emphasizes the experience of images, the premise being that imaginative experience is in itself healing and transformative.

For example, we might recognize this when we consider the image of a beautiful sunset, and how by simply gazing into the sunset and watching as it gently disappears over the horizon, all manner of transformations might arise in us: cathartic grief and letting go; a new perspective on an old problem; or wonder and awe and a sense of connection to a greater whole beyond individual existence.

But whatever the sunset's effects, they will arise spontaneously, as a total experience, without needing us to figure them out. Indeed, grasping after the sunset, wanting to know "what it means", would probably get in the way of the experience.

To recreate the transformative effects of not just sunsets but any aesthetic or artistic experience, the techniques and therapeutic principles conveyed throughout this book have endeavoured to showcase an approach that emphasizes working with images as imaginative experiences, rather than turning images into theoretical ideas.

It is the difference between, for example, spending time contemplating an actual painting in an art gallery and reading about it in a textbook. While the textbook gives a quick hit of understanding, with information about the painter's subject, style, and influences, this is really only "thinking about" the painting, a set of ideas about it as an object or thing, not the imaginative experience created by entering into the mood and atmosphere of the actual painting as a story-world.

In this way, an image-based psychosynthesis is perhaps best understood as an art-form rather than a science, given that the primary intention is to facilitate a meaningfulness of imaginative experience, rather than any attempts to analyze, interpret, or explain what imagery means.

The main strategy for this image-based experiential focus has been to eschew theoretical terminology.

While a therapist might understand a client to be in the midst of a "disidentification" process from a "subpersonality" and trying out a new "ideal model", to share this terminology directly with a client will be a movement away from the primacy of imaginative experience. The theories and ideas about the imagery will mean that it is no longer really a meaningful experience in and of itself but rather, a symbol for a secondary meaning to be found elsewhere.

Of course, such theoretical discussions have a place, particularly as a way to gain perspective from overwhelming experience, but this will need to be understood by the therapist as only a partial and temporary aspect of the therapy, an orientation for the subsequent experiential engagement needed to facilitate the process of psychosynthesis.

Instead of theoretical terminology, an image-based approach favours a richly descriptive everyday language capable of synthesizing together the various contextual layers needed to notice, validate, and enhance the client's experience of an imagined story-world.

A therapist will therefore work to synthesize the three characteristics of story by bringing descriptive attention to the client's sensations, thoughts, and feelings and the perceptual situation they find themselves in while also passing along a dynamic timeline, emerging from the past into the present and moving along into the future.

As described in chapter 2, such image-based work was understood by Assagioli as not only a direct diagnostic insight into the "underlying psycho-dynamic organization" of the client but also a therapeutic means by which to bypass the abstractions of theoretical terminology, meeting the psychological situation of the client directly on "its own terms".[345] In this way, emphasizing an experiential-synthesis will avoid the "inner imagination" limitations of a "cognitive separation".

A SYNTHESIS OF STORIES

Stories are commonly understood as fiction, a fantasy tale conjured up by novels and movies, something to kill time in airports and entertainment at the end of the workday, something that, if it has an existence, is a subjective one, an inner realm quite separate from practical matters and "real life".

According to this view, sensible adults are guided by reason and facts rather than stories. Yet this view is itself a story.

The history of ideas is littered with once simple truths we now call "stories" or "myths". Creationism, flat-earth-ism, and geocentric theory (the sun orbits the earth) were the science of their day, latterday assumptions about the nature of reality.[346]

With the benefit of evolution, geology, and modern astronomy, it is perhaps easy to dismiss these previous world-views as fictions and to believe we moderns are guided not by stories but "by the science". However, breakthroughs in quantum physics and complexity theory have shown the common-sense reality of everyday life, with its strict empirical division between subject and object, to be what it really is: just another story.

At the experimental edge of science, the world is a much more joined-up and mysterious place than allowed for by this empirical story, and no doubt by the time common-sense understanding catches up with this quantum story, if it ever does, science will have moved on again and be telling an ever weirder new story.

In the broad understanding set out here, stories are not the opposite of the real; instead, they are what allow us to decide what is real.[347] Stories are the imaginative patterns within which we live. In countless large and small ways, the narratives of story guide everyday choices. Whether voting in an election, arguing with a partner, or playing a game of hide-and-seek, the information focused upon (and neglected) and how this is shaped into understanding and behaviour is determined by the parameters of story.

Human beings are storytellers. We live and communicate through stories all the time, which is what makes them so important.

A healthy psychological life depends upon a synthesis of stories. Telling stories and listening to stories are what connect us to the fabric of life; whereas, to not be able to share our story or listen to other people's stories is a restricted existence, isolated from the fuller potential of who we are and vital connections to other people and the surrounding world, akin to a pot-bound geranium drying out on a windowsill in the hot summer sun.

Set apart from the medium of stories, there is neither the vision nor the means for creative growth, healing, and transformation.

An image-based psychosynthesis is therefore most simply understood as storytelling. At the beginning, it will be the telling of ill-fitting stories that poorly equip us to understand and navigate the difficulties of our presenting issue. And it will be in the very sharing of these limited stories, by simply participating within the medium of storytelling itself, that imaginative capacity begins to grow—an imaginative capacity that slowly allows the current life situation to be seen for the provisional and contingent story it really is, rather than the truth and certainty it was previously assumed to be. This creates a new-found imaginative malleability of perception that opens up a creative gap for the emergence of a much more satisfying and meaning-filled life of storied possibility and play.

Epilogue

What Does Psychosynthesis Do?

When readers come to the end of a book, it is easy to imagine that the author set out from the very beginning with a clear plan of everything to be written and how to write it down.

But of course, the process is not like that.

In reality—as is also the case with practising psychotherapy—the writing of a book proceeds in uncertain fits and starts, across a series of unexpected and vague intuitions, only growing with clarity and coherence slowly, almost imperceptibly, in the course of thousands of word choices, into the creation of something new, which had no previous existence.

There comes a point when the writing down of this process needs to end—but this is not quite that point, and there is still time for a few closing reflections.

It seems appropriate at the end of the book to return to the opening description in the Prologue of an eclectic multiplicity of "partial expressions" making the distinctiveness of psychosynthesis difficult to appreciate, an elusiveness that begged the question: What is psychosynthesis?

It may have seemed like a reasonable enough question, even a necessary one, but it was only answerable in one of two ways, neither of which offered a satisfactory description of psychosynthesis.

An easy first answer was to claim a particular set of teachings, techniques, and influences is what constitutes the true, and perhaps even original, authentic psychosynthesis. In this view, there is no elusiveness, only dogmatic certainty.

But there were two serious problems with this answer. First, it immediately comes into conflict with other psychosynthesis therapists, each of whom will have a different flavour of understanding and style of practice. Second, and perhaps more importantly, this answer requires ignoring the positively non-dogmatic emphasis of Assagioli's presentation:

> There is no orthodoxy in Psychosynthesis and no one, beginning with myself, should claim to be its real or true representative, its head or leader. Each of its exponents tries to express and apply it as well as he or she is able to, and all who read or listen to the message, or receive the benefit of the methods of Psychosynthesis, can decide how successful any exponent has been or will be in expressing its "spirits".[348]

A more nuanced second answer understood that psychosynthesis was not to be confused with the forms of any one of its various presentations. In this view, echoing the "Exercise in Dis-Identification" affirmations, we might say that psychosynthesis has teachings, techniques, and influences, but it is not those teachings, techniques, and influences.

Once again, this was not an entirely satisfactory answer, because it only emphasized what psychosynthesis is not, rather than what it is.

In principle, this answer allowed the possibility of two different presentations—for example, the original Assagioli version and the adaption of it by Firman and Gila—to both equally be psychosynthesis, but it did not tell us what makes them so.[349]

Assagioli's claim of psychosynthesis being an innate and natural *experience* is what allowed a common ground to be established between presentations. Despite conceptual differences, what connects various theoretical formulations is that they are only different ways to notice and think about the same underlying experience of psychosynthesis. And what connects all of the various techniques is that they are different ways to co-operate therapeutically with this same experience.

According to this understanding, "experience" was established as the first principle of psychosynthesis.

But what kind of experience?

A related second principle of "synthesis" was then described, so as to indicate the particular experience of psychosynthesis: as the process of gathering multiple elements into an ever greater whole.

Upon establishing this principial basis, the book then proceeded to offer its main contribution to the development of psychosynthesis theory and practice. By turning the twin principles of experiential-synthesis back upon psychosynthesis itself, and in particular the original Assagioli presentation, it was shown that far from being a coherent and unified system, there is a tension within it between two contradictory approaches or stories.

While Assagioli does in places show some awareness of the tensions between these two approaches, mostly they remain unacknowledged. However, the two approaches were nevertheless shown to be noticeable by the type of language employed in each case, which is why a concern with language has been such a significant theme throughout this book—words not just being a matter of speech but also that which shapes understanding and experience.

The first of the two approaches, a synthetic-experiential story, is noticeable by its usage of non-jargonistic everyday descriptive language.

In this approach, psychosynthesis is understood and practised as a dynamic process of participation within the flux and flow of experiential life, never settling upon any fixed point of understanding or practice, always moving, passing through successive identifications, in an unending sequence with no final destination or outcome.

As Assagioli writes:

> Psychosynthesis is an open system; there is no end to it, but only temporary halting places . . . It is therefore unrealistic to speak in terms of "having understood or not having understood". Understanding being ever partial, belief in having understood all indicates lack of understanding. It is a question of a gradual process.[350]

It is an approach that eschews static dogmas and definitions and understands that reality is ultimately ungraspable, something permanently mobile and mysterious, a constant state of becoming.

The description of this first approach, as an experiential-synthesis, subtly moved the book away from the question of "What is psychosynthesis?" to asking "What does psychosynthesis do?"

Despite not being directly asked, this can be seen to be the main question addressed by the book. This is the case not least because the underlying experience of synthesis held in common by psychosynthesis psychotherapists (to the extent that what they are practising is psychosynthesis) will be recognizable—not on the level of theory and technique but rather, in what a therapist does with the various ideas and methods to notice and participate in the synthesizing of experiential elements into an ever increasing whole.

What really matters is not the actual presentation, per se, but how it is expressed and actively put into practice within an experiential context. This means that psychosynthesis is best understood as an action verb, meaning that it is something we do—in the same way that we run, jump, eat, and sleep so also do we "psychosynthesis".

The second of the two approaches, an analytical-empirical story, is notable for its use of abstract-conceptual language. Psychosynthesis is presented not only through the use of everyday descriptive language but also through a more abstract, theoretical terminology, based in large part upon a psychology of "the unconscious".

To speak of the unconscious as a psychological interiority, or *place*, filled with psychological objects, or *things*, and sometimes occupied by psychological *persons*, or "subpersonalities", is to picture psychosynthesis as a collection of common nouns; that is, places, persons, and things.

But "the unconscious" is not a literal psychological interiority, or place; the "personal self" or a "subpersonality", for example, are not actual inner persons, and neither is a feeling or thought an actual inner object, thing or "content" of consciousness. Use of these "inner" nouns is merely a theoretical construction, an explanatory story, or "working hypothesis", and therefore a radical simplification, not to be mistaken for the actual experiential complexity.

However, when mistaken for "the truth", this abstract-conceptual terminology easily becomes a belief system, which is not only anathema to the non-dogmatic emphasis of psychosynthesis but also one of the main reasons for its apparent elusiveness. It leads to the impossibility of psychosynthesis being approached as a graspable and discrete noun, some form of psychological "content" or "thing" or "person", when really it is an experiential process, an activity, a verb:

> There are only *subjects* who are *willers*, living beings who are lovers. The rest is only pure intellectual abstractions, useful for didactic purposes . . . but there doesn't exist an entity *love*, an entity *will* . . . intelligence is a wonderful thing, but the intellect should not possess us! We should try to be as intelligent as we can (and we can be more intelligent and use our intelligence) but not be possessed by it. And especially realize that any intellectual formulation or theory is merely a description, not a real thing. [It is a question of] semantics, [you see]. The map is not the territory.[351]

> As for language, the reader will find the word "will" used as a noun throughout. This has been done for the purpose of simplifying the text. However, it should be noted at the outset that no "metaphysical" claim is being made either for or against the proposition that the "will" exists. My approach, dealing as it does with "willers" and "willed acts," is empirical and phenomenological.[352]

The abstract-conceptual language of psychology has been shown to be an "esoteric", or specialist, terminology in danger of turning psychosynthesis into a theoretical explanation rather than an experiential process and practice. The principial approach to psychosynthesis presented in this book has therefore emphasized the need to translate theoretical terminology into a language best suited to meet the client's experience.

But while the theory being used by the therapist to think about the therapeutic process is not shared directly with the client, it will nevertheless indirectly influence what experiences are noticed and validated, how they are engaged with, and to what ends.

Not all theories are created equally. Some will more satisfactorily facilitate the experiential process of psychosynthesis better than others. The better presentations will be those that reduce the theory/experience gap by more closely aligning conceptual understanding with the actual experience.[353]

To this end, this book has therefore proposed an image-based approach to theory and practice, so as to release psychosynthesis from the limitations of a psychology of "the unconscious" and the related influence of "inner empiricism".

While an effort has been made to evidence the discussion directly from statements made by Assagioli, this has been a selective process, which will have inevitably emphasized and elaborated certain points while quietly ignoring others.

For example, no attention has been given to the ubiquitous "oval diagram" or "egg diagram". However, it has been ignored, partly due to its overuse, so as to show it is not axiomatic, and also because of Assagioli's own critique:

> [the egg diagram] is, of course, a crude and elementary picture that can give only a structural, static, almost "anatomical" representation of our inner constitution, while it leaves out its dynamic aspect, which is the most important and essential one.[354]

But whatever particular theories and techniques have been included or omitted, the criteria for selection has been to choose statements that support the argument for a principial basis to psychosynthesis.

As Assagioli writes, what we call psychosynthesis, "should not be looked upon as a particular psychological doctrine, nor as a single technical procedure",[355] but rather, "What is important are the principles and the basic purpose of the entire endeavour."[356]

The whole point of a principial approach, as will be apparent by now, is that there is no such thing as a definitive understanding. Psychosynthesis is a living process, an experiential activity, not a static "thing" capable of being definitively pinned down in words.

But this does not mean that we stop trying to improve upon the understanding we do have. How we think about psychosynthesis is not just a theoretical but also a practical matter.

The conceptual elaboration in this book has sought to clarify ideas that limit the experiential context of psychosynthesis and to offer alternatives that set it free; however, it is by no means intended as any kind of final word on the matter.

In the same way that this work has built upon many previous contributions, my hope is that it will sufficiently convey the "spirit" of psychosynthesis to capture the inspiration of readers, some of whom will perhaps take it as a basis for future works. It is therefore intended as another step on an ever unfolding journey.

It is not the truth. It is not the end.

Notes

PROLOGUE

1. "There is no orthodoxy in Psychosynthesis and no one, beginning with myself, should claim to be its real or true representative, its head or leader. Each of its exponents tries to express and apply it as well as he or she is able to, and all who read or listen to the message, or receive the benefit of the methods of Psychosynthesis, can decide how successful any exponent has been or will be in expressing its 'spirits'." (Assagioli, "Relationships Between the Various Foundations, Institutions, and Centers" / "Letter of Freedom").

2. "I consider [psychosynthesis] as a child—or at the most as an adolescent—with many aspects still incomplete: yet with a great and promising potential for growth. I make a cordial appeal to all therapists, psychologists, and educators to actively engage in the needed work of research, experimentation and application. Let us feel and obey the urge aroused by the great need of healing the serious ills which at present are affecting humanity: let us realize the contribution we can make to the creation of a new civilization characterized by an harmonious integration and cooperation, pervaded by the spirit of synthesis." (Assagioli, *Psychosynthesis: A Manual of Principles and Techniques*,9.)

3. While the following was written in 1983, it arguably maintains its relevance today: "Psychosynthesis . . . is in the early adolescent stage of development. The coming of age, the maturing [will require a questioning] of the established ideas and models and to see the need for serious research and debate. I think many of the existing psychosynthesis models have been taken too literally and are I believe often used somewhat naively today. I think we need at this time to be more rigorous in our thinking about psychosynthesis theories and models and particularly in how we use them." (Evans, *Mirages of the Mind: Yearbook Vol. III*, 7.)

4. Psychosynthesis therapists "now operate in a very different world than the one in which [Assagioli] developed his theories . . .". (Millichamp, *Transpersonal Dynamics: The Relational Field, Depth Work and the Unconscious*,19.)

5. Assagioli, "Training: A Statement by Roberto Assagioli", point 11.

6. Assagioli, *Psychosynthesis: A Manual of Principles and Techniques*, 30.

INTRODUCTION: WHAT IS PSYCHOSYNTHESIS?

7. Assagioli, quoted in Guggisberg Nocelli, *Know, Love, Transform Yourself: Theory, Techniques and New Developments in Psychosynthesis, Vol.1*, 117.

8. "Maps are not the territory. We all know that, yet we often forget it. Maps are merely representations drawn from individual experience, measurements, observations, and estimations. Yet we know that maps give us ideas about what to look for, landmarks to notice and gauge our progress by, and a way of planning with some degree of accuracy." (Young Brown, *Unfolding Self: The Practice of Psychosynthesis*, 99.)

9. Diana Whitmore, private e-mail correspondence with author, 15 November 2021.

10. Assagioli, *Psychosynthesis: A Manual of Principles and Techniques*, 65.

11. Assagioli, *"Talks on the Self"*.

12. Assagioli, *Psychosynthesis: A Manual of Principles and Techniques*, 11.

13. Guggisberg Nocelli, *The Way of Psychosynthesis*, 147–148.

14. Assagioli, *Psychosynthesis: A Manual of Principles and Techniques*, 280.

15. "It is useful to remember that the word theory is derived from the ancient Greek *theorein*, which means "to see". A theory, then, is a "way of seeing" a topic, and different people will have different theories, depending on how they experience reality. Some theories will be more general, some more specific. All theories are biased and limited in some way. Therefore, the work of developing theory is to find a way of seeing that seems to fit the phenomena under observation and at the same time can gain enough consensus among fellow "seers" to be generally accepted. All theories are at best approximations and therefore never true in an absolute sense. They can, however, help us to see what is "there" to the best of our knowledge at the time. As we "see" more clearly over time, we can modify our theories or we can reject them as they cease to be useful. At any point in time, certain theories will inform the "seeing" of the majority while other theories will have a more marginal existence, either because they are becoming obsolete or because they have not yet been recognized as holding a way of seeing that reveals reality. Examining a theory, then, involves studying how people see certain phenomena and assessing how useful this way of seeing is in its capacity to illuminate and explain the aspect of reality under scrutiny." (Yeomans, *Readings in Psychosynthesis: Theory, Process & Practice, Volume 2*, 251.)

16. www.collinsdictionary.com.

17. "Interview on Psychosynthesis with Roberto Assagioli", accessed April 8, 2023, https://www.youtube.com/watch?v=e9rVWAxE2hQ

18. Vargiu, *Synthesis 3/4, The Realization of the Self*, 144.

19. Assagioli, "Relationships Between the Various Foundations, Institutions, and Centers" / "Letter of Freedom".

20. Assagioli, *Psychosynthesis: A Manual of Principles and Techniques*, 30–31.

21. "This inclusive understanding is not eclectic; it is synthetic—psychosynthesis holds all approaches and methods within a coherent view of the person and the person's unfoldment. However, unless this overarching synthetic viewpoint is made clear, individual concepts and techniques become the focus and the broader perspective is lost." (Firman and Gila, "Assagioli's Seven Core Concepts for Psychosynthesis Training", 1.)

22. Assagioli, "The Golden Mean of Roberto Assagioli", interview by Sam Keen in *Psychology Today*.

23. Assagioli, "Training: a statement by Roberto Assagioli", point 8.

24. "It is one of the beauties of psychosynthesis that it is not a closed system with rigid, crystallized methods. It provides an open structure that can integrate effective methods from other disciplines and leaves room for the creativity of the practitioner." (Martha Crampton, quoted in Young Brown, *Unfolding Self: The Practice of Psychosynthesis*, 73.)

25. Assagioli, "Training: A Statement by Roberto Assagioli", point 3.

26. "A tradition that just transmits the teachings of the founder is already dead." (Pierro Ferruci, Foreword to Guggisberg Nocelli, *Know, Love, Transform Yourself: Theory: Techniques and New Developments in Psychosynthesis, Vol.1*, 23.)

CHAPTER 1: TEACHINGS

The Core Concepts

27. Assagioli, "Training: A Statement by Roberto Assagioli".

28. Firman and Gila, "Assagioli's Seven Core Concepts for Psychosynthesis Training".

29. Sørensen, *The Soul of Psychosynthesis: The Seven Core Concepts.*

30. Firman and Gila, "Assagioli's Seven Core Concepts for Psychosynthesis Training", 1–2.

31. "These are the seven 'facts' and fundamental features of Psychosynthesis that must be part of Psychosynthesis training and its education syllabus. These core concepts are what we can call 'the soul of Psychosynthesis'." (Sørensen, *The Soul of Psychosynthesis: The Seven Core Concepts*, 19.)

32. "While [Assagioli] is not saying that psychosynthesis training should be limited to these seven core concepts, he is saying unequivocally that without these concepts one does not have psychosynthesis training." (Firman and Gila, "Assagioli's Seven Core Concepts for Psychosynthesis Training", 2.)

33. Assagioli, "Training: A Statement by Roberto Assagioli", point 2.

Concepts and Experiences

34. To be fair, this issue is not completely overlooked within the core-concepts framework. "Psychosynthesis is about 'mapping' the 'terrain' of human experience, and all our elaboration of the models of psychosynthesis have been inspired by the need to have these models more accurately represent lived human experience." (Firman and Gila, "Assagioli's Seven Core Concepts for Psychosynthesis Training", 4).

35. Quotation marks will henceforth distinguish between generic experiences and the seven teaching "experiences".

36. Assagioli, "Training: A Statement by Roberto Assagioli", Point 2.

37. Assagioli, "Training: A Statement by Roberto Assagioli", Point 3.

38. "Significant attention has been paid to Assagioli's 'Training' document, a late writing he did that elaborated what he considered to be the seven core 'experiences' of psychosynthesis. In the wonderfully integrated way that psychosynthesis exists as a whole which is greater than the sum of its parts, it would be hard to pull any one of the experiences apart from the others. They are of a piece." (Guggisberg Nocelli, *Know, Love, Transform Yourself: Theory, Techniques, and New Developments in Psychosynthesis, Vol. 1*, 572.)

Teachings in Context

39. Assagioli, "Relationships Between the Various Foundations, Institutions, and Centers" / "Letter of Freedom".

40. Assagioli, *The Act of Will*, 7.

41. "Interview on Psychosynthesis with Roberto Assagioli", accessed April 8, 2023, https://www.youtube.com/watch?v=e9rVWAxE2hQ

42. Assagioli, "The Balancing and Synthesis of Opposites."

The personal self

43. Assagioli, *Psychosynthesis: A Manual of Principles and Techniques*, 5.

44. Assagioli, *Psychosynthesis: A Manual of Principles and Techniques*, 18.

45. Assagioli, *Psychosynthesis: A Manual of Principles and Techniques*, 116.

46. Also sometimes called "self-consciousness", which is not meant in the colloquial sense of shyness or embarrassment, but as a consciousness of being conscious.

47. Assagioli, *Psychosynthesis: A Manual of Principles and Techniques*, 18.

48. Assagioli, *The Act of Will*, 101.

The will: strong, skilful, good

49. "The will as an anxiety-ridden sense of duty, as condemnation, as repression of a part of ourselves, as a refusal of what we are, is always a kind of will that is a detriment to something and thus represses. Instead, the will that originates from the center of our being does nothing at the expense of something else; does not impose but coordinates, does not push, does not force, does not condemn or repress, but simply directs." (Piero Ferrucci, quoted in Guggisberg Nocelli, *The Way of Psychosynthesis*, 264.)

50. Assagioli, interview with Stuart Miller, quoted by Guggisberg Nocelli, *The Way of Psychosynthesis*, 264–265.

51. Assagioli, *The Act of Will*, 10.

52. Assagioli, *The Act of Will*, 35.

53. Assagioli, *The Act of Will*, 47.

54. Assagioli, *Psychosynthesis: A Manual of Principles and Techniques*, 30–31.

55. Assagioli, *The Act of Will*, 86.

Disidentification

56. Assagioli, *Psychosynthesis: A Manual of Principles and Techniques*, 116–125; Assagioli, *The Act of Will*, 213–217.

57. Assagioli, *The Act of Will*, 211.

58. Assagioli, *Psychosynthesis: A Manual of Principles and Techniques*, 112.

59. "While disidentificaton can be associated with experiences of freedom, peace, and serenity . . . it may just as easily involve turmoil, inner conflict, and anxiety . . . a crisis of transformation . . . not a calm quiet, centred experience . . . Disidentification simply moves us towards a deeper experience of our existence, and this may or may not be serene or even pleasant." (Firman and Gila, *Psychosynthesis: A Psychology of the Spirit*, 99.)

60. Assagioli, *Psychosynthesis: A Manual of Principles and Techniques*, 50.

61. Assagioli, *Psychosynthesis: A Manual of Principles and Techniques*, 22; Assagioli, *The Act of Will*, 211.

62. Assagioli, *Psychosynthesis: A Manual of Principles and Techniques*, 114–116.

63. Assagioli, *Psychosynthesis: A Manual of Principles and Techniques*, 116.

64. "In therapy the technique of self-identification should be used as early as possible, because its use by the patient facilitates and fosters the use of all the other techniques of psychosynthesis." (Assagioli, *Psychosynthesis: A Manual of Principles and Techniques*, 119.)

65. There are slight variances between the two versions of the "Exercise" given by Assagioli: one in *Psychosynthesis: A Manual of Principles and Techniques*, 116–119; and another in *The Act of Will*, 214–217.

66. Assagioli, *The Act of Will*, 214.

67. Assagioli, *Psychosynthesis: A Manual of Principles and Techniques*, 118–119.

68. Assagioli, *Psychosynthesis: A Manual of Principles and Techniques*, 129.

69. Assagioli, *Psychosynthesis: A Manual of Principles and Techniques*, 114–116.

70. "Although Assagioli insists on the importance of disidentification, one might not often realize that it is not just a technique but a long and complex process that requires great commitment and some degree of mental health in the absence of which this practice can even become iatrogenic and be used as a means of division and isolation." (Guggisberg Nocelli, *The Way of Psychosynthesis*, 239.)

71. Assagioli, *The Act of Will*, 216.

72. An example of disidentification as an idealized state of complete freedom and choice: "This empathic experience with your friend allows an experience of *disidentification*. That is, you are not stuck in, *identified* with, any particular pattern of feeling, thought, and behaviour but can shift and move

among all of them. You are clearly distinct-but- not-separate from the various contents of your inner world; that is, *disidentified* from them all." (Firman and Gila, "Assagioli's Seven Core Concepts for Psychosynthesis Training", 5.)

73. An example of disidentification as an idealized state of complete freedom and choice: "Disidentifying means, above all, creating a psychic space where all the elements of our personality (all of our sensations, desires, emotions, thoughts, and various subpersonalities) can be known, welcomed, and integrated. When we disidentify, we adopt the attitude of the observer, and can become the directors of our lives, emancipating ourselves from addictive and automatic behaviours." (Guggisberg Nocelli, *Know, Love, Transform Yourself: Theory, Techniques, and New Developments in Psychosynthesis, Vol. 1*, 100.)

74. Assagioli, *Psychosynthesis: A Manual of Principles and Techniques*, 117.

75. Assagioli, *Psychosynthesis: A Manual of Principles and Techniques*, 122.

76. Assagioli, *The Act of Will*, 220.

77. Another example of "control separation" language from Assagioli: "In the fields of drives, emotions, and feelings, the balancing of opposite qualities requires the intervention of a higher regulating principle of a mental or transpersonal nature. The first task is to prevent the drives and the emotions from overwhelming and submerging the reason and the will. The best way to achieve this is to learn how to disidentify oneself from them at will, in order to be free at any time to maintain the 'I', the centre of consciousness, on a higher level above them, in order to be able to observe and evaluate them, and to wisely regulate them as needed . . . A clear understanding of this process of synthesis enables one to achieve it more easily and rapidly. The essential requirement, as previously mentioned, is to avoid identifying oneself with either of the two opposite poles, and to control, transmute, and direct their energies from a higher centre of awareness and power." (Assagioli, "The Balancing and Synthesis of Opposites".)

78. The following statement from Assagioli on "control" as a desired outcome is of interest at this point due to the language of "psychological distance" , which can be seen to imply a "separation", in the acknowledgement of the danger of such a distancing perspective creating a "suppression or repression" and a critical perspective paralyzing and killing our "emotions and feelings", which is clearly not Assagioli's intention: "In order to dissolve [unconscious complexes] we should use the methods of objectification, of critical analysis, and of discrimination. That is to say, we must employ cold, impersonal observation as if they were mere natural phenomena, occurring outside ourselves. We should

create a "psychological distance" between ourselves and them, keeping these images or complexes at arm's length, so to speak, and then quietly consider their origin, their nature and— their stupidity! This does not mean the suppression or repression of the energies inherent in those manifestations but their control and redirection into constructive channels." (Assagioli, *Psychosynthesis: A Manual of Principles and Techniques*, 23.)

79. Assagioli, *The Act of Will*, 22.

80. Assagioli, *The Act of Will*, 10

81. Assagioli, *The Act of Will*, 211.

82. Assagioli, *Psychosynthesis: A Manual of Principles and Techniques*, 119.

83. Assagioli, *Psychosynthesis: A Manual of Principles and Techniques*, 114.

84. Assagioli, *Psychosynthesis: A Manual of Principles and Techniques*, 117.

85. "*The self can also be defined as the only part of us which remains forever the same*. It is this sameness which, once found and fully experienced, acts as an ever-present pivot point for the rest of the personality, an inner stronghold to which we can always refer in order to regain a sense of poise and self-consistency. Then we can see that the self remains the same in ecstasy and despair, in peace and turmoil, in pain and pleasure, in victory and defeat." (Piero Ferrucci, *What We May Be*, 61.) [original italics]

86. Assagioli, *The Act of Will*, 212.

87. Assagioli, *Psychosynthesis: A Manual of Principles and Techniques*, 18.

88. The following from Firman & Gila is a welcome attempt to reframe an objectification of psychological experience: "The reader will note too that we have here followed our usual convention of not using definite articles or possessive pronouns with the psychosynthesis terms, 'I', 'will', or 'Self'. We believe that the use of such articles and pronouns in phrases such as, 'my' 'I,' 'the will', or 'the Self' tends to suggest an object of awareness, rather than the pure subjectivity these terms are meant to convey. We have found that attention to these seeming minor details has been useful in representing—always imperfectly—the illusive and ineffable mysteries of 'I', 'will', and 'Self'." (Firman and Gila, "Assagioli's Seven Core Concepts for Psychosynthesis Training", 4.)

89. Assagioli, *The Act of Will*, 215.

90. "When we are "off-centre", when we forget ourselves, we live on the margins of our being, and we fall prey to many ghosts. Then, destructive impulses, emotions difficult to deal with, anguishing thoughts and fantasies, and images of us that make us suffer take possession of our self that, identifying

with them, becomes those impulses, those emotions, those thoughts or fantasies. Instead, Piero Ferrucci explains that the "centre" "is that part in us that is always healthy, corresponds to our true identity, and always remains true to itself. (. . . In the Centre, we are masters of ourselves, we feel at home rather than slaves exiled in a far-off land; we are alert instead of falling prey to anguishing dreams; we are ourselves, we are not something or someone else. The Centre is our 'I'. Finding your own deep centre, your true 'I' gives a strong sense of mastery." (Guggisberg Nocelli, *The Way of Psychosynthesis*, 248.)

91. "If during these times [of disidentification] we attempt to maintain a centred, choosing, self-actualizing persona, we are in effect dissociating from the depths of our own humanness." (Firman and Gila, "Assagioli's Seven Core Concepts for Psychosynthesis Training", 15.)

92. "If we confuse disidentification with any particular type of experience, there is a danger that we will begin to confuse 'I' with particular types of experience: "When I disidentify, I feel ________, therefore, 'my true I' is _________." The problem here is that 'I' is becoming objectified. 'I' is here understood not as who we are, but as a psychological place, an attainment, a certain type of experience. In other words, 'I' is misunderstood as a potential mode of consciousness rather than as the *one who experiences* all modes of consciousness." (Firman and Gila, "Assagioli's Seven Core Concepts for Psychosynthesis Training", 8.)

93. Assagioli, *Psychosynthesis: A Manual of Principles and Techniques*, 116.

94. ". . . [the Exercise in Dis-Identification technique] may not be indicated, or should be used with care, in the case of patients who are ever too prone to self-observation and self-analysis, with patients who are or become too much interested in the observation of their inner world—which may prove more pleasing and less strenuous than active participation in the outer life." (Assagioli, *Psychosynthesis: A Manual of Principles and Techniques*, 122.)

95. "The effect of this shift is that the experiential authenticity of the actual introspective experience—the simple observation of inner events—is quietly transferred to the more abstract philosophical belief." (Firman, *"I" and Self: Re-visioning Psychosynthesis*, 22.)

96. "Disidentification must not of course be confused with any sort of mental analysis of the inner world. Such an inner stance is not a disidentification at all, but quite the opposite—it is an identification with the process of mental analysis. Although such a mental identification is often referred to as 'objectivity' it is clearly biased towards the thinking function, and operationally cuts off 'I' from immediate experience of other dimensions of the psyche-soma, such

as sensations, feelings, images, or intuition . . . Here I experience that I am mental analysis. This identification then conditions my total awareness as if analysis were the 'lens' through which I experience everything. (And too, I would here relate not only to the inner world via analysis, but to the outer world of relationships and events as well)." (Firman, *"I" and Self: Re-visioning Psychosynthesis*, 46-47.)

97. "If this discrimination between the authentic self and super-egoic subpersonality is not fully understood and experienced, disidentification risks being used as a means to distance oneself from unacceptable or overly painful psychic contents. It becomes a system to protect oneself from the intense emotional reactions caused by such content. This way of practising disidentification, far from facilitating a process of integration and self-transformation, merely pushes the intolerable parts of oneself toward the lower unconscious, thereby increasing the internal division." (Guggisberg Nocelli, *The Way of Psychosynthesis*, 239.)

The ideal model

98. Assagioli, *Psychosynthesis: A Manual of Principles and Techniques*, 166.

99. Assagioli, *Psychosynthesis: A Manual of Principles and Techniques*, 168.

100. Assagioli, *Psychosynthesis: A Manual of Principles and Techniques*, 25.

101. Assagioli, *Psychosynthesis: A Manual of Principles and Techniques*, 26.

102. Assagioli, *Psychosynthesis: A Manual of Principles and Techniques*, 27.

The superconscious

103. Assagioli, *Psychosynthesis: A Manual of Principles and Techniques*, 194.

104. Assagioli, *Psychosynthesis: A Manual of Principles and Techniques*, 6.

105. "Early psychoanalytic theory was fraught with 19th-century positivism and a reductionism vis-à-vis spiritual experience." (Firman, *"I" and Self: Re-visioning Psychosynthesis*, 31.)

106. Assagioli, *Psychosynthesis: A Manual of Principles and Techniques*, 198.

107. The post-Assagioli psychosynthesis theory of "bifocal vision", conceived by Steve Krull in 1970s San Francisco, encompasses a simultaneous understanding of psychological symptoms as being shaped by past personal-biographical

events and also as having a future potential or purpose which is seeking to emerge through the symptom. (Thom Yeomans, private e-mail correspondence with author, 30 September 2024.)

108. Assagioli, *Psychosynthesis: A Manual of Principles and Techniques*, 193.

109. Assagioli, *Psychosynthesis: A Manual of Principles and Techniques*, 198.

110. Assagioli, *Psychosynthesis: A Manual of Principles and Techniques*, 43.

111. Assagioli, *Transpersonal Development*, 28.

112. Assagioli, *Psychosynthesis: A Manual of Principles and Techniques*, 39.

113. Assagioli, *Transpersonal Development*, 27.

114. Assagioli, *Psychosynthesis: A Manual of Principles and Techniques*, 43.

115. Assagioli, *Psychosynthesis: A Manual of Principles and Techniques*, 112.

116. "In psychosynthesis we maintain *that nothing has to be condemned, or destroyed, or eliminated.* As I said before, 'we can benefit from and utilize every function and element of our psyche, provided we understand its nature and purpose, and place in it its right relation with the greater whole.'" (Assagioli, "The Superconscious and the Self".)

117. Assagioli, "The Superconscious and the Self."

118. Assagioli, *Psychosynthesis: A Manual of Principles and Techniques*, 38.

119. Assagioli, *Psychosynthesis: A Manual of Principles and Techniques*, 17–18.

120. Assagioli, *Psychosynthesis: A Manual of Principles and Techniques*, 198.

121. Assagioli, *Psychosynthesis: A Manual of Principles and Techniques*, 38.

122. Assagioli, *Psychosynthesis: A Manual of Principles and Techniques*, 198.

123. Assagioli, *Psychosynthesis: A Manual of Principles and Techniques*, 17, 197–198.

124. Assagioli, Psychosynthesis: *A Manual of Principles and Techniques*, 198.

125."To be spiritual does not mean only to be able to transcend the little self in a 'vertical' direction . . . It includes also a 'horizontal' attitude; that is, communion of thought and love and harmonious collaboration with all fellow-creatures. This expansion is achieved through "concentric circles," which gradually include ever larger groups, from the family to humanity as a whole." (Assagioli, "Psychosynthesis in Education".)

126. "Assagioli still implies a progression away from the lower unconscious and towards the higher unconscious. One seemingly moves from the assessment, through personal psychosynthesis, and finally to spiritual or transpersonal psychosynthesis. This tends to suggest the Gnostic progression up the 'ladder of enlightenment' or 'scale of being'. There is little sense here that lower unconscious dynamics are an integral, pervasive, and ongoing aspect of all human growth, no matter how spiritual one's life becomes." (Firman, *"I" and Self: Re-visioning Psychosynthesis*, 31.)

127. Firman and Gila write of this as a "transpersonal identification": "Such an identification can be developed after powerful peak experiences, immersion in religious and spiritual study, and/or in becoming adepts at practices such as prayer and meditation." (Firman and Gila, *Psychosynthesis: A Psychology of the Spirit*, 100.)

128. "What distinguishes psychosynthesis from many other attempts at psychological understanding is the position that we take as to the existence of a spiritual Self and of a superconscious." (Assagioli, *Psychosynthesis: A Manual of Principles and Techniques*, 193.)

129. Assagioli, *Psychosynthesis: A manual of principles and techniques*, 197–198.

THE TRANSPERSONAL SELF

130. Assagioli, *Psychosynthesis: A Manual of Principles and Techniques*, 19.

131. Assagioli, "The Golden Mean of Roberto Assagioli." Interview by Sam Keen in *Psychology Today*.

132. Assagioli, "Training: A statement by Roberto Assagioli", point 2.

133. Assagioli, *Psychosynthesis: A Manual of Principles and Techniques*, 37.

134. Assagioli, *Psychosynthesis: A Manual of Principles and Techniques*, 20.

135. Self is "the context of the personality". (Hardy, *A Psychology with a Soul*, 30.)

136. "I propose that the 'Self' described in psychosynthesis is closely akin to the 'Ecological Self' described by deep ecologist Arne Naess and others—a sense of self encompassing all of nature, all of life, and acting from this very inclusive perspective. Sadly, many psychosynthesis practitioners confine Self to the 'higher realms'. They tend to go 'up' for guidance and inspiration, and avoid touching—both literally and figuratively—the soil beneath their feet. Assagioli himself called Self 'the Higher Self' and most of his students carried on this tra-

dition, at least until recently. John Firman and Ann Gila (1997) have described vividly how this perspective can create a split within an individual between the 'good' self on high, and the 'bad' self below. It also reinforces the unfortunate tendency in our culture to divide Spirit from Nature, mind from body, heaven from earth." (Young Brown, "Ecopsychosynthesis: Meeting the Crisis of Our Times".)

137. "The successful outcome of psychosynthesis counselling may be described as an expanded sense of identity, in which the Self . . . is viewed as the context of life experience. This expanded sense of identity often awakens a motivation which includes self-enhancement but one which interfaces with the larger whole. What is good for the individual is good for the larger whole and ego boundaries enlarge towards more social and global wellbeing. Increased tolerance for paradox and ambiguity is exhibited, and inner and outer experience becomes more harmonious and confluent." (Whitmore, *Psychosynthesis Counselling in Action*, 157–158.)

138. "[The Self] can be seen as being . . . the context of the personality." (Shorrock, *The Transpersonal in Psychology, Psychotherapy, and Counselling*, 160.)

139. Assagioli, *Psychosynthesis: A Manual of Principles and Techniques*, 19.

140. Assagioli, *Psychosynthesis: A Manual of Principles and Techniques*, 30–31.

141. "Assagioli was quite clear that he considered 'I' to be a 'projection' or 'reflection' of Self. This concept gives us a way to approach Self via the method of analogy, a method used by Assagioli himself . . . That is, if 'I' is an image of Self, we can use the experiential understanding gained from studying 'I' to speculate about the nature of Self." (Firman and Gila, "Assagioli's Seven Core Concepts for Psychosynthesis Training", 29.)

142. "Self can therefore be thought of as ever-present and actively loving, whether one is experiencing a traumatic memory from the lower unconscious, a peak experience in the higher unconscious, working with middle unconscious patterns, engaging existential issues of mortality and meaning, or expressing oneself in the world. As the direct and immediate source of 'I' Self is always present as a source of dialogue, support, and guidance, no matter what our experience, no matter what our stage of development, no matter what our life situation." (Firman and Gila, "Assagioli's Seven Core Concepts for Psychosynthesis Training", 29.)

143. Assagioli, *Psychosynthesis: A manual of principles and techniques*, 113.

144. Assagioli, *Psychosynthesis: A manual of principles and techniques*, 24.

145. Assagioli distinguishes "Self-realization" from a similar notion of "self-actualization" given by Abraham Maslow. The distinction is most easily understood as one in which "Self-realization" incorporates but goes beyond the experience of "self-actualization". Self-realization includes the awakening of personal potential that is "self-actualization" in parallel to and as a means to "the experience and awareness of the synthesizing spiritual Centre"; in other words, an experience of "transpersonal Self", which as the context within which the "personal self" exists provides a language for experiences of connection to a wider sense of meaning and purpose beyond the personal-individual level. (Assagioli, *Psychosynthesis: A Manual of Principles and Techniques*, 37.)

146. Assagioli, *Psychosynthesis: A Manual of Principles and Techniques*, 24.

147. "The phenomenon of identification accompanies the entire course of all human existence. In fact, any growth path can be considered as an evolution departing from a series of partial identifications to identities with increasingly complex and inclusive elements . . .The process of identification only becomes pathological if it becomes arrested at a particular stage, impeding advancement towards successive disidentification and, consequently, the entire process of development which is constantly followed by the individual." (Guggisberg Nocelli, *The Way of Psychosynthesis*, 233.)

148. Assagioli, *Psychosynthesis: A Manual of Principles and Techniques*, 24.

149. Assagioli, *Psychosynthesis: A Manual of Principles and Techniques*, 202.

150. Assagioli, *Psychosynthesis: A Manual of Principles and Techniques*, 53.

151. Assagioli, *Psychosynthesis: A Manual of Principles and Techniques*, 19.

152. "It should also be pointed out that the reaching up into the realm of the superconscious and its exploration, while approaching the consciousness of the Self, may sometimes even constitute an obstacle to full Self-realization, to the reaching of the summit where the personal-I awareness blends into awareness of the spiritual Self. One can become so fascinated by the wonders of the superconscious realm, so absorbed in it, so identified with some of its special aspects or manifestations as to lose or paralyze the urge to reach the summit of Self-realization." (Assagioli, *Psychosynthesis: A Manual of Principles and Techniques*, 38.)

153. Assagioli, "The Golden Mean of Roberto Assagioli". Interview by Sam Keen in *Psychology Today*.

154. "It is not difficult to point out *theoretically* how to reach this aim [of Self-realization]" (Assagioli, *Psychosynthesis: A Manual of Principles and Techniques*, 24.) [original italics]

155. John Firman offers the notion of "transcendence-immanence" to convey an understanding of "transpersonal Self", which is not about any particular "contents": "Self, like 'I', is not to be associated with any particular state of consciousness at all. Self is transcendent of any state of consciousness, and therefore can be immanent in any and all states—Self can experience bliss or agony, unity or disintegration . . . In fact, my experience of isolation and pain may not mean I have distanced from Self at all, but quite the contrary, that I am joining Self in a radical openness to the depths of human suffering." (Firman, *"I" and Self: Re-visioning Psychosynthesis*, 82–83.)

156. The transpersonal Self is considered to be the person's "spiritual Self who already knows his problems, his crisis, his perplexity". (Assagioli, *Psychosynthesis: A Manual of Principles and Techniques,* 204.)

157. Assagioli, "Jung and Psychosynthesis". (Quote translated from Italian in Guggisberg Nocelli, *The Way of Psychosynthesis*, 261.)

158. Assagioli, *The Act of Will*, 114.

159. Assagioli, *Psychosynthesis: A Manual of Principles and Techniques,* 20.

160. Assagioli's implied relationship between "personal self" and "transpersonal Self" is later made explicit by Firman and Gila, who coined the phrase "I-Self relationship". (Firman and Gila, *Psychosynthesis: A Psychology of the Spirit,* 38-42.

161. "Transpersonal Self" provides "the source of personal being but [also] a directionality for individual unfoldment and meaningful engagement with the world", (Firman and Gila, *The Primal Wound,* 43); Self is not passive but "capable of a profound and meaningful empathic relationship with an individual's everyday experience of life". (Whitmore, *Psychosynthesis Counselling in Action*, 18.)

162. "It is worth raising the question of whether the Self is individual at all, but rather is the point at which the personality makes contact with the creative process of life itself." (Millichamp, *Transpersonal Dynamics*, 18.)

163. Assagioli, *Psychosynthesis: A Manual of Principles and Techniques*, 25.

164. Assagioli, "Talks on the Self".

165. Firman and Gila (*The Primal Wound,* 44) write of the Self as being constantly in relationship with the "I", and that this I-Self relationship is itself "dis-

tinct from any specific relationship in life, yet it is embedded in these relationships at the same time".

166. "It should be pointed out that, for humanist psychologists, self-realization is an ideal goal that is expressed as a process and as a tendency rather than as a truly achievable stage. Maslow, aware of the fundamental difficulty associated with this concept, does very much to redefine the term by clarifying that self-realization is not a definitive or final situation, or a distant goal, but rather a dynamic, active process that lasts all through a person's existence." (Guggisberg Nocelli, *The Way of Psychosynthesis*, 101.)

Synthesis

167. The following quotations illustrate the two conceptions of synthesis being implied as more or less similar classes of the same synthesis:

- "Synthesis is, in fact, an organic process. We cannot force it or make it happen, but what we can do is co-operate with and facilitate the process as it organically unfolds. One way of achieving a move towards actualizing this potential that we all have is to work at balancing and synthesizing the opposites that exist within us." (Parfitt, *The Elements of Psychosynthesis*, loc1529, Kindle Edition.)
- "Regarding the principle of the synthesis of opposites, I'm treating it separately since it is a more general type of synthesis compared to the others." (Guggisberg Nocelli, *The Way of Psychosynthesis*, 286.)

168. Vargiu, *Synthesis 3/4, The Realization of the Self*, 144.

169. Assagioli, quoted in Sørensen, *The Soul of Psychosynthesis*, 170.

170. Assagioli, quoted in Guggisberg Nocelli, *The Way of Psychosynthesis*, 281.

171. "The argument of the synthesis of opposites means reinforcing the intuition that, from Heraclitus to Plato to Hegel, through Nicola Cusano and Giordano Bruno, has been transmitted to us by Western philosophy." (Guggisberg Nocelli, The Way of Psychosynthesis, 285–286.)

172. Assagioli, "The Balancing and Synthesis of Opposites."

173. Assagioli, "The Balancing and Synthesis of Opposites."

174. Assagioli, *The Act of Will*, 103–104.

175. "Such relationships are not confined to the tension between the classic polarities of thesis and antithesis, although such polarities may be one mani-

festation of phenomena. These relationships may be between a number of psychological elements that derive from quite different levels of ontological experience." (Peter Hubbard, "Shaping a Psychospiritual Participatory Paradigm" in Simpson and Evans, *Essays on the Theory and Practice of a Psychospiritual Psychology: Volume 1*, 55–64.)

176. Assagioli, "The Balancing and Synthesis of Opposites".

177. Assagioli, "The Balancing and Synthesis of Opposites".

178. Assagioli, "The Balancing and Synthesis of Opposites".

179. "But as we move toward the Self, unity replaces multiplicity. The psychological life becomes harmonized as the diversity of its parts fuses into a synthesis" (Pierro Ferrucci, *What We May Be*, 134); ". . . as we examine the two poles of a dichotomy ever more carefully, we come to see that the contrast between them lessens...till they converge and fuse into a synthesis" (Pierro Ferrucci, What We May Be, 205); and "the synthesis of opposites, and the creative moment is characterized by the encounter of two forces, which combine at a higher level. Thus, the process of growth and evolution of our personality depends for its dynamics on the tension of multiple polarities, for which it is necessary to find ever more differentiated levels of synthesis". (Guggisberg Nocelli, *The Way of Psychosynthesis,* 287.)

180. "Interview on Psychosynthesis with Roberto Assagioli", accessed April 8, 2023, https://www.youtube.com/watch?v=e9rVWAxE2hQ

181. Assagioli, *The Act of Will*, 32.

182. ". . . the aliveness and unity of such expression flows not from an undifferentiated fusion of these perspectives into a larger whole, but from a sense of self able to engage the full diversified range of this multiplicity . . . The principle of personality integration is here not so much that of unity as of relationship". (Firman and Gila, *The Primal Wound*, 8.5)

183. "This growing de-emphasis on harmony, integration, and union is quite like the change in the United States from the notion of the country as a 'melting pot' of diverse ethnic groups, to concepts of diversity and multiculturalism in which ethnic and cultural identity is respected and preserved. Here the norm becomes acceptance of differences and tolerance of the tension and conflict that may be caused by these differences. But is not the synthesis of parts into larger and larger wholes a fundamental meaning of the very word 'psychosynthesis'? It depends on what is meant by 'synthesis' and 'larger whole.'" (Firman and Gila, "Assagioli's Seven Core Concepts for Psychosynthesis Training", 21.)

Synthesis of Teachings

184. Assagioli, *Psychosynthesis: A Manual of Principles and Techniques*, 65.

CHAPTER 2: TECHNIQUES

Processes and Outcomes

185. While Assagioli makes a distinction among techniques, exercises, and methods, this chapter discusses them collectively, as does Assagioli in his writing of exercises and methods as subsets of techniques; exercises being "the combination or association of various techniques in order to produce a general effect"; and methods being "a combination of techniques and exercises used in a specific succession or alternation . . . in order to achieve the therapeutic or educational aim considered necessary or valuable". (Assagioli, *Psychosynthesis: A Manual of Principles and Techniques*, 66.)

186. "Because we're human and fallible, we do tend to identify psychosynthesis tangibly, with guided imagery and subpersonality work, or something like that. And to the extent we do that, we do in fact create this little, finite piece, which is useful, but is only useful for some people in some situations. People sometimes say to me, 'Psychosynthesis is only useful for some people.' Yes, as it is commonly practised, that's true. But I think psychosynthesis is more than that. I think it is, in the first place, a comprehensive psychology which acknowledges that people are at different places in their development, and have different needs, and that you don't apply the same technique to everybody." (Molly Young Brown, quoted in Schuller, *Psychosynthesis in North America: The Story of the Movement, the People, and the Issues*.)

187. Assagioli, "Training: A Statement by Roberto Assagioli", point 5.

188. ". . . keep in mind that psychosynthesis therapy denotes an overall orientation to the therapeutic process and is not a particular technique or methodology. It is rather a context within which any and all appropriate methods may be employed, depending on the training of the therapist. Foreground here is not technique, but the unique person of the client". (Firman and Gila, *The Primal Wound*, 209.)

189. Assagioli, Psychosynthesis: *A Manual of Principles and Techniques*, 65.

190. Assagioli, Psychosynthesis: *A Manual of Principles and Techniques*, 66.

191. Assagioli, Psychosynthesis: *A Manual of Principles and Techniques*, 65.

CREATIVE PROCESS

192. "Interview on Psychosynthesis with Roberto Assagioli", accessed April 8, 2023, https://www.youtube.com/watch?v=e9rVWAxE2hQ

193. Assagioli, "The Golden Mean of Roberto Assagioli". Interview by Sam Keen in *Psychology Today*.

194. Assagioli, "Training: A Statement by Roberto Assagioli", point 6.

195. While Assagioli ("Creative Expression in Education: Its Purpose, Process, Techniques, and Results") wrote of a creative process model, across the three stages of conception, gestation, and birth, the five-stage model described here was first developed by psychosynthesis theorist James Vargiu (*Synthesis ¾: The Realization of the Self*) building upon earlier work by the social psychologist Graham Wallas, who, in 1926, presented a four-stage creative process: preparation, incubation, illumination, and verification. (Wallas, *The Art of Thought.*)

THE PREPARATION STAGE

196. Assagioli, *Psychosynthesis: A Manual of Principles and Techniques*, 68.

197. Assagioli, *Psychosynthesis: A Manual of Principles and Techniques*, 68.

198. Assagioli, *Psychosynthesis: A Manual of Principles and Techniques*, 100.

199. Assagioli, *Psychosynthesis: A Manual of Principles and Techniques*, 100.

200. Assagioli, *Psychosynthesis: A Manual of Principles and Techniques*, 68.

201. Assagioli, *Psychosynthesis: A Manual of Principles and Techniques*, 145.

202. Assagioli, *Psychosynthesis: A Manual of Principles and Techniques*, 177.

203. Assagioli, *Psychosynthesis: A Manual of Principles and Techniques*, 225.

204. Assagioli, *Psychosynthesis: A Manual of Principles and Techniques*, 287.

205. Assagioli, *Psychosynthesis: A Manual of Principles and Techniques*, 176.

206. Assagioli, *Psychosynthesis: A Manual of Principles and Techniques*, 291.

207. Assagioli, *Psychosynthesis: A Manual of Principles and Techniques*, 180.

208. Assagioli, *Psychosynthesis: A Manual of Principles and Techniques*, 292

209. Assagioli, *Psychosynthesis: A manual of principles and Techniques*, 292.

210. All client examples are anonymized composites of work with multiple clients.

211. Assagioli, *Psychosynthesis: A manual of principles and techniques*, 293.

212. Assagioli, *Psychosynthesis: A manual of principles and techniques*, 294.

213. Assagioli, *Psychosynthesis: A manual of principles and techniques*, 293.

214. To allow the imagery which already exists in psychological life to come into awareness is what Diana Whitmore calls "evocative imagery" (Whitmore, *Psychosynthesis Counselling in Action*, 54).

215. Assagioli, *Psychosynthesis: A manual of principles and techniques*, 226.

216. Assagioli, *Psychosynthesis: A manual of principles and techniques*, 143.

217. Assagioli, *Psychosynthesis: A manual of principles and techniques*, 158.

218. Assagioli, *Psychosynthesis: A manual of principles and techniques*, 289-290.

219. Assagioli, *Psychosynthesis: A manual of principles and techniques*, 178.

220. Assagioli, *The Act of Will*, 124-125.

221. Assagioli, *Psychosynthesis: A manual of principles and techniques*, 302.

222. Assagioli, *Psychosynthesis: A manual of principles and techniques*, 94.

223. Assagioli, *Psychosynthesis: A manual of principles and techniques*, 178-179.

THE FRUSTRATION STAGE

224. Assagioli, *Psychosynthesis: A Manual of Principles and Techniques*, 68.

225. While based upon the "principles of personification" the "technique of personification" is not an original Assagioli technique but invented by myself, although something similar is discussed in the literature as a "method of personification" in Guggisberg Nocelli, *Know, Love, Transform Yourself: Theory, Techniques, and New Developments in Psychosynthesis, Vol 1*, 642.

226. Assagioli, "Talks on the Self".

227. Imagined persons—whether encountered in a consulting room, dream, or memory—are clearly an aspect of psychological life. However, the way in which these experiences are variously understood needs to be recognized as a theoretical explanation. We can see this, for example, when we consider how it is only upon waking from a dream that the experience of imagined dream people becomes theorized as "subpersonalities", "personifications", psychodynamic "inner-objects", or internalizations of personal-biographical figures, and

so on. And that's just the modern psychological explanations, none of which would be the go-to understanding of, for example, an aboriginal Australian, who might understand a dream person as an ancestor or a spirit guide. But whatever theoretical perspective is taken it needs to be recognized as just one way of understanding the actual experience, rather than being conflated with it, whereupon it becomes a belief system; that is, we literally believe the imagined person is a "part", a subpersonality, a spirit guide, or whatever. While there is a time and a place for such theorizing about imagined persons, this is best done separately from experiential techniques, in which the focus needs to be upon the actual encounter and relationship to the person as a person, not an idea or concept.

228. Assagioli, *Psychosynthesis: A Manual of Principles and Techniques*, 65-66.

229. Assagioli, *Psychosynthesis: A Manual of Principles and Techniques,* 66.

The Incubation Stage

230. Assagioli, *The Act of Will,* 59.

231. Assagioli, *Psychosynthesis: A Manual of principles and techniques*, 50.

The Illumination Stage

232. Assagioli, *Psychosynthesis: A Manual of Principles and Techniques,* 204–205.

233. Assagioli, *Psychosynthesis: A Manual of Principles and Techniques*, 204.

234. Assagioli, *Psychosynthesis: A Manual of Principles and Techniques,* 177.

235. Assagioli, *Psychosynthesis: A Manual of Principles and Techniques*, 204.

236. Assagioli, *Psychosynthesis: A Manual of Principles and Techniques,* 101.

237. Assagioli, *Psychosynthesis: A Manual of Principles and Techniques,* 101-102.

238. Assagioli, *Psychosynthesis: A Manual of Principles and Techniques*, 102.

239. Assagioli, *Psychosynthesis: A Manual of Principles and Techniques,* 102.

240. Assagioli, *Psychosynthesis: A Manual of Principles and Techniques*, 205.

The Elaboration Stage

241. Assagioli, *Psychosynthesis: A Manual of Principles and Techniques*, 173–174.

242. Assagioli, *Psychosynthesis: A Manual of Principles and Techniques*, 174.

243. Assagioli, *Psychosynthesis: A Manual of Principles and Techniques*, 166.

244. Assagioli, *Psychosynthesis: A Manual of Principles and Techniques*, 172.

245. Assagioli, *Psychosynthesis: A Manual of Principles and Techniques*, 167.

246. Assagioli, *Psychosynthesis: A Manual of Principles and Techniques*, 26.

247. Assagioli, *Psychosynthesis: A Manual of Principles and Techniques*, 170.

248. Assagioli, *Psychosynthesis: A Manual of Principles and Techniques*, 169.

249. Assagioli, *Psychosynthesis: A Manual of Principles and Techniques*, 171.

250. Assagioli, *Psychosynthesis: A Manual of Principles and Techniques*, 170.

251. Assagioli, *Psychosynthesis: A Manual of Principles and Techniques*, 26.

252. Assagioli, *Psychosynthesis: A Manual of Principles and Techniques*, 175.

253. Assagioli, *Psychosynthesis: A Manual of principles and Techniques*, 171.

CHAPTER 3: INFLUENCES

254. An example of psychosynthesis presentation that emphasizes its particular philosophical/religious/metaphysical influences is given by Kenneth Sørensen, who writes, "Reading Assagioli's books and articles, it becomes clear that his work is steeped in metaphysical considerations. He opens the door wide to ideas of Cosmic Synthesis, Emanation, Involution and Evolution, Atman, Brahman, Universal Self, etc. Assagioli's approach to spirituality is clearly theistic. God, Brahman, the Universal Self, is a reality for him . . . I believe the best description of Assagioli's metaphysics is Evolutionary Pantheism." (Sorensen, *The Soul of Psychosynthesis*, 8–9.)

255. "There is no orthodoxy in psychosynthesis and no one, beginning with myself, should be considered as its exclusive representative or leader. Each of its exponents tries to express and apply it as well as he or she is able to, and all who read or listen to the message, or receive the benefit of the use of the methods of psychosynthesis can decide how successful any exponent has been or will be in expressing its 'spirit'." (Assagioli, "Relationships Between the Various Foundations, Institutions, and Centers" / "Letter of Freedom".)

256. Assagioli, "Training: A Statement by Roberto Assagioli", point 2.

The Dream of a Science

257. Assagioli, *The Act of Will*, 3–4.

258. Assagioli, *Psychosynthesis: A Manual of Principles and Techniques*, 114.

259. Assagioli, *Psychosynthesis: A Manual of Principles and Techniques*, 6.

260. Assagioli, "Talks on the Self".

261. "Science and the scientific method have been seen in this period in the West as the way to truly objective knowledge. The science that is the basis of modern Western culture is inductive—in other words, it is based on observation and experimentation and . . . from observations . . . generalizations and laws are created . . . This assumption has been carried over from the natural sciences to the social sciences, into the study of the individual in psychology." (Hardy, *A Psychology with a Soul*, 97.)

262. Assagioli, *Psychosynthesis: A Manual of Principles and Techniques*, 197.

263. Assagioli, *Psychosynthesis: A Manual of Principles and Techniques*, 194.

264. Assagioli, *Psychosynthesis: A Manual of Principles and Techniques*, 194.

265. Assagioli, *Psychosynthesis: A Manual of Principles and Techniques*, 6–7.

266. Assagioli, "Bio-Psychosynthesis".

267. Assagioli, personal correspondence quoted in Ferruci, "On the Threshold of Mystery".

268. Assagioli, *Psychosynthesis: A Manual of Principles and Techniques*, 206.

269. "I am not arguing against belief systems. We need them to give us structure and meaning in our lives. I'm drawing attention to what happens when we totally identify with them, leaving no room for doubt . . . An aspect of belief systems is that they usually allow one experience and forbid another, so any new information or possibilities is not allowed to emerge . . ." (Fee, "*Through, With, and In.*")

The Wall of Silence

270. "Assagioli was influenced by many spiritual and philosophical traditions and people, such as the Russian esotericist P.D. Ouspensky; the Sufi mystic Inayat Khan Rehmat Kahn Pathan; Carl Jung; Martin Buber, who developed the I-Thou relationship theory; the founder of Logotherapy Viktor Frankl; and Alice Bailey, with whom he was a close friend." (Millichamp, *Transpersonal Dynamics*, 14.)

271. Hackwood, "Beyond the Wall of Silence."

272. Assagioli, personal correspondence quoted in Ferruci, "On the Threshold of Mystery".

273. See Hardy, *A Psychology with a Soul.*

INFLUENCES AS ORIGIN STORY

274. See Hardy, *A Psychology with a Soul.*

275. Some suggested reading on the application of contemporary scientific paradigms within psychotherapy: Frater, *Waking Dreams*; Marks-Tarlow, *Psyche's Veil*; Hill and Dahlitz, *The Practitioner's Guide to the Science of Psychotherapy*; Mindell, *The Quantum Mind and Healing*; and Totton, *Wild Therapy*.

276. Assagioli spends the opening pages of *Psychosynthesis: A Manual of Principles and Techniques* acknowledging his debt to the "vast amount of studies and research" available to him at the time of writing, accrued "in the course of the last seventy years", listing the influential persons from medicine, psychology, and culture who have contributed to the formulation of psychosynthesis. (Assagioli, *Psychosynthesis: A Manual of Principles and Techniques*, 11–16.)

277. "Thinking of psychosynthesis as a version of esotericism for the masses not only gives a false idea of psychosynthesis. It also diminishes Assagioli's originality .... In psychosynthesis you can find echoes of many different traditions and systems .... All these influences inspired him to create an original synthesis. He worked at it from 1909 (or even before) to the time of his death in August 1974. That's more than 65 years. Why on earth would Assagioli take the trouble to create psychosynthesis; i.e. construct a school of psychology with its own themes and guidelines, enter the tricky arena of contemporary psychology and pedagogy, communing with some of the greatest minds in twentieth century psychology and psychiatry, in this way participating to not one, but two revolutions in psychology's short history (psychoanalysis and humanistic-transpersonal psychology), get busy with starting centres and activities and publications throughout the world—if it turned out to be nothing more than a watered down brand of esotericism? ... Psychosynthesis is indeed inspired by spiritual traditions down the ages. But if we conceive it as deriving its raison d'être from another source, a source to which only some people and not all have access, we entirely deprive it of its inherent power." (Ferruci, "On the Threshold of Mystery".)

Influences in Translation

278. Assagioli, quoted in Hackwood, "Beyond the Wall of Silence".

279. Assagioli, "Talks on the Self".

280. Assagioli, "Talks on the Self".

281. Assagioli, "Symbols of Transpersonal Experiences".

282. Assagioli, "Talks on the Self".

283. Assagioli, *Psychosynthesis: A Manual of Principles and Techniques,* 94.

The Influence/Theory Gap

284. The choice of these three sub-principles of holistic, perspectival, and emergent is influenced by the characteristics granted to any "system" by "systems theory", which, as discussed in chapter 1 in the "Synthesis of Systems" section, is a contemporary scientific understanding, anticipated by Assagioli's work. For a useful introduction from a psychosynthesis perspective, see Horowitz, *The Dance of We*.

285. Assagioli, *Psychosynthesis: A Manual of Principles and Techniques*, 66.

286. Assagioli, *Psychosynthesis: A Manual of Principles and Techniques*, 67.

287. Assagioli, *Psychosynthesis: A Manual of Principles and Techniques,* 7.

288. "If spirituality was essentially a subjective experience, and if the only valid knowledge was the empirical one, then the epistemic legitimacy of transpersonal studies had to be defended in terms of a 'science of human experience', an 'inner empiricism' . . . a 'subjective epistemology', a 'science of consciousness' or, more recently, a 'science of spiritual experience'." (Ferrer, *Revisioning Transpersonal Theory*, 20.)

289. Assagioli, personal correspondence quoted in Ferruci, "On the Threshold of Mystery".

290. Assagioli, *The Act of Will*, vi.

291. Assagioli, *Psychosynthesis: A Manual of Principles and Techniques*, 5.

292. Assagioli, *Psychosynthesis: A Manual of Principles and Techniques*, 114.

293. Assagioli, *Psychosynthesis: A Manual of Principles and Techniques*, 18.

294. Assagioli, *Psychosynthesis: A Manual of Principles and Techniques*, 19.

295. Assagioli, *Psychosynthesis: A Manual of Principles and Techniques*, 117.

296. "The 'soul' or 'self' here thus becomes a pure spiritual essence, an invisible homunculus living somewhere within the psyche-soma. We shall see that this . . . is an ideological belief held by Assagioli, and that this belief is not proven by phenomenological observation as he claims." (Firman, *"I" and Self: Re-visioning Psychosynthesis*,12.)

297. "The effect of this shift is that the experiential authenticity of the actual introspective experience—the simple observation of inner events—is quietly transferred to the more abstract philosophical belief." (Firman, *"I" and Self: Re-visioning Psychosynthesis*, 22.)

298. Assagioli, *The Act of Will*, 216.

299. Assagioli, *Psychosynthesis: A Manual of Principles and Techniques*, 23.

300. Assagioli, *The Act of Will*, 101.

301. Assagioli, *The Act of Will*, 60.

302. "Yet scientific psychology, while claiming to eliminate evaluations, has frequently (and indeed almost inevitably) formulated evaluations without being aware of it. As Maslow has said, 'Science is based on human values and is itself a value system.'" (Assagioli, *The Act of Will*, 98.)

303. See Hardy (*A Psychology with a Soul*) writing of science as "the search for certainty and control" (169) . . . and science as "based on a premise of growth and of control—the more we can find out, the more power and control we have over the nature of things"(97).

304. Assagioli, *Psychosynthesis: A Manual of Principles and Techniques*, 22; Assagioli, *The Act of Will*, 211.

305. Assagioli, *Psychosynthesis: A Manual of Principles and Techniques*, 22.

306. Assagioli, *Psychosynthesis: A Manual of Principles and Techniques*, 68.

307. "It is important to emphasize that, for many scholars, the new vision of the universe designed by quantum physics is perfectly matched with the theories developed over time by great mystics and esotericists. Quantum mechanics, in fact, reveals the essential interconnection of the universe and makes us realize that we cannot break the world into elementary units having independent existences." (Guggisberg Nocelli, *The Way of Psychosynthesis*, 136–137.)

308. Assagioli, *Psychosynthesis: A Manual of Principles and Techniques*, 206.

Synthesis of Influences

309. "Inherent in the development of [Assagioli's] ideas are both a scientific and a mystical approach, though he tended to play down the more mystical aspects of his work, intent on gaining scientific validity for his theories." (Millichamp, *Transpersonal Dynamics*,13).

310. "This inclusive understanding is not eclectic; it is synthetic—psychosynthesis holds all approaches and methods within a coherent view of the person and the person's unfoldment. However, unless this overarching synthetic viewpoint is made clear, individual concepts and techniques become the focus and the broader perspective is lost." (Firman and Gila, "Assagioli's Seven Core Concepts for Psychosynthesis Training", 1).

CHAPTER 4: IMAGININGS

311. Assagioli, *Psychosynthesis: A Manual of Principles and Techniques*, 144.

312. This new "image-based" presentation draws upon influences from beyond psychosynthesis; however, in order to provide a principial rationale for it being a *psychosynthesis* presentation, rather than suggesting equivalence to these background influences, this chapter will continue to focus upon statements by Assagioli, and for those who are interested, the *non-psychosynthesis* influences will be listed here in the Notes section.

313. Assagioli's original version of the four stages is as follows: 1. Thorough knowledge of one's personality; 2. Control of its various elements; 3. Realization of one's true Self: The discovery or creation of a unifying centre; and 4. Psychosynthesis: the formation or reconstruction of the personality around the new center (Assagioli, *Psychosynthesis: A Manual of Principles and Techniques*, 21).

314. These stages have also been adapted by Firman and Gila in "Assagioli's Seven Core Concepts for Psychosynthesis Training", 17–20.

315. Therapeutic change is more akin to the irregularity of dreams than the mechanistic predictability of a stage-by-stage linear progression. The four stages are therefore best considered as rough guide to help notice and work with the unpredictable richness of imaginative process in therapeutic practice. The qualification by Assagioli of his original formulation therefore remains an important proviso: "It should be made clear that all the various stages . . . are closely interrelated and need not be followed in a strict succession of distinct periods or phases." (Assagioli, *Psychosynthesis: A Manual of Principles and Techniques*, 29.)

316. "It is important to keep in mind that although the linear progression of the stages does make logical sense, these stages may not in fact be experienced in this sequence; they are not a ladder to climb but integral aspects of a single process. Further, it seems that one never outgrows these stages; any stage can be present at any moment no matter how long one has trod the way of Self-realization." (Firman and Gila, "Assagioli's Seven Core Concepts for Psychosynthesis Training", 17–18.)

Inner Imagination

317. An "inner imagination" usage can clearly be seen in the following comparison between psychosynthesis and the psychology of Carl Jung. While Jung conceived of imagination broadly, as synonymous with all psychological life (see note 335 below), and therefore found within all aspects or functions, such as feeling and thinking, and also perception of the sensory world, Assagioli instead offers a much narrower understanding, as a distinct psychological function, which is strictly related to "inner" imagining, and therefore not related to "the function of sensation" and "impacts coming from the external world". He writes: "An important difference from psychosynthesis exists in connection with the psychological functions. Psychosynthesis maintains that Jung's four fundamental functions do not provide for a complete description of the psychological life; but that there are other functions as fundamental, which merit inclusion as well. The first is the *imagination*. Jung's lack of recognition of the imaginative function appears strange in view of his attributing such great importance to images and symbols. The explanation lies in his belief that imaginative activity can evidence itself in all the four other functions. But he asserts this without demonstrating it or dealing with it. It seems impossible to admit that fantasy or imagination can be manifested in the function of sensation, which is a perception, by means of the senses, of the so-called external reality; that is, of impacts coming from the external world. On the other hand, other psychologists correctly give the imagination a fundamental place in psychological life." (Assagioli, "Jung and Psychosynthesis".)

318. Assagioli, *Psychosynthesis: A Manual of Principles and Techniques*, 26, 204, 205, 206.

319. Assagioli, *Psychosynthesis: A Manual of Principles and Techniques*, 226.

320. Assagioli, *Psychosynthesis: A Manual of Principles and Techniques*, 25.

321. See note 227 on "imagined persons".

Contextual Imaginings and Story-Worlds

322. As Jungian therapist Mary Watkins writes, imagination "does not simply represent the given . . . but creates or brings something new into being". (Watkins, *Invisible Guests*, 68).

323. Several influences come together in establishing this understanding of "contextual imagining". The following selection of quotes and references provides an indicative sample:

- "Imagination bridges the gap between matter and mind." (Cheetham, *Imaginal Love*, 95.)
- "It is essential to understand the mediating role of imagination . . . we are not contrasting an 'inner' realm of fantasy with an 'outer' world of reality." (Levine, *Poiesis*, 33.)
- "Imagination can be said to be the 'bridge' between self and world; but we are always 'on' this bridge." (Levine, *Poiesis*, 41.)
- "Since we can know only fantasy images directly and immediately, and from these images create our worlds and call them realities, we live in a world that is neither 'inner' nor 'outer.'" (Hillman, *Re-Visioning Psychology*, 23.)

324. Frater, *Waking Dreams*, 52–53.

The Imagined Story-World

325. Several influences have informed this list of story characteristics, including:

- Narrative sociologist Arthur W. Frank writes, "My working understanding—not a definition—of narrative is simply this: one thing happens in consequence of another." (Frank, *Letting Stories Breathe*, 41).
- Social scientist Margaret Somers writes of four story "features": "(1) relationality of parts; (2) causal emplotment; (3) selective appropriation; and (4) temporality, sequence, and place. Above all, narratives are constellations of relationships (connected parts) embedded in time and space, constituted by what I call causal emplotment." (Somers, "Narrativity, Narrative Identity, and Social Action: Rethinking the English Working-Class Formation", 601.)
- Zack Stein and Marc Gafni (writing together under the pseudonym

"David J. Temple") write of five story elements: a thread of action, an implicit set of desired outcomes, a sense of reality and importance, a degree of freedom and evolution, and the resolution or climax of a crisis. (Temple, *First Principles and First Values*, 10.)

326. Assagioli, *Psychosynthesis: A Manual of Principles and Techniques*, 143.

327. Assagioli, *Psychosynthesis: A Manual of Principles and Techniques*, 144.

328. "An image is a place, an environment in which we find ourselves." (Bosnak, *Embodiment*, 9).

329. Assagioli, *Psychosynthesis: A Manual of Principles and Techniques*, 4.

330. Assagioli, *The Act of Will*, 258.

331. Assagioli, "Psychosynthesis: Its Essential Components."

The Four Stages of Psychosynthesis

332. Identification is similarly described by post-Assagioli psychosynthesist Molly Young Brown as a state in which we become "victims of a single world view and self image". (Young Brown, *Unfolding Self*, 40.)

333. Assagioli, *Psychosynthesis: A Manual of Principles and Techniques*, 143.

334. Assagioli, *Psychosynthesis: A Manual of Principles and Techniques*, 114.

The Act of Imagination

335. This understanding implies a close connection between imagination and psychological life, in general, which has in part been influenced by psychologist Carl Jung and post-Jungian writers, as can be seen in the following quotations:

- Carl Jung wrote that "Every psychic process is an image and imagining" (CW 11, para 889), or more emphatically and simply, "Psyche is image" (CW 13, para 75).
- James Hillman wrote that "The primary activity of the psyche is imagining . . . we humans are primarily acts of imagination, images . . . what we are really, and the reality we live in, is our psychic reality, which is nothing but the poetic imagination going on day and night; we are such stuff as dreams are made of." (Hillman, *We've Had a Hundred Years of Psychotherapy and the World's Getting Worse*, 62.)

- Robert Romanyshyn wrote: "Between subject and object a story appears, which is expressed in a way of seeing and of speaking about the world. The story which appears is the appearance of psychological life." (Romanyshyn, *Psychological Life*, 16.)
- Donald Kalsched wrote: "By the reality of the psyche, I mean an intermediate realm of experience which serves as a ligament connecting the inner self and the outer world by means of symbolic processes which communicate a sense of 'meaning.'" (Kalsched, *The Inner World of Trauma*, 6–7.)

336. See, for example, Diana Whitmore in *Psychosynthesis Counselling in Action*: "Perhaps more than any other technique, mental imagery has strong contraindication . . . With clients who may be psychotic or borderline it should never be used. With those lacking any solid sense of identity it must be used with caution . . . For this type of client there is already an excessive amount of free-floating images, and imagery work would only add to the chaos." (Whitmore, *Psychosynthesis Counselling in Action*, 56.)

337. Assagioli, *Psychosynthesis: A Manual of Principles and Techniques*, 26.

338. Molly Young Brown writes of the similarities between psychosynthesis and systems theory: "In one of the classes I took in systems thinking, a student spoke of the need for a systems-based psychology. I believe we have one in psychosynthesis, a psychology firmly based in an understanding of our essential relatedness . . . although they may be articulated in different languages, the same principles inform psychosynthesis and General Systems Theory." (Young Brown, ("Psychosynthesis: A Systems Psychology?".)

339. Assagioli, *Psychosynthesis: A Manual of Principles and Techniques*, 20.

340. Psychosynthesis psychotherapist Massimo Roselli, wrote of what he called "psychoenergetics" in which "the object of study is no longer the individual separated from their relational context but, according to an ecological and interdependent perspective of life, the individual as being in a relationship, not only with their own self and with others in the family group, but with society and all humanity, as well as with all the energies of the planet and of the cosmos". (Guggisberg Nocelli, *The Way of Psychosynthesis*, 136.)

341. Assagioli, "Talks on the Self".

342. Assagioli, *Psychosynthesis: A Manual of Principles and Techniques*, 25.

343. As discussed in chapter 2, with respect to the inspiration Assagioli derived from Martin Buber.

344. Assagioli, *Psychosynthesis: A Manual of Principles and Techniques*, 144.

345. Assagioli, *Psychosynthesis: A Manual of Principles and Techniques*, 180.

A SYNTHESIS OF STORIES

346. As psychotherapist James Hillman writes, "The myths we believe and are in the middle of, we call them 'fact', 'reality', 'science.'" [no source available]

347. As philosopher Mary Midgley puts it: "Myths are not lies. Nor are they detached stories. They are imaginative patterns, networks of powerful symbols that suggest particular ways of interpreting the world. They shape its meaning." (Midgley, *The Myths We Live By*, 1.)

EPILOGUE

348. Assagioli, "Relationships Between the Various Foundations, Institutions, and Centers" / "Letter of Freedom"

349. Firman & Gila. See, for example: Psychosynthesis: *A Psychology of the Spirit* (2002) and *The Primal Wound* (1997).

350. Assagioli, "Training: A Statement by Roberto Assagioli", points 8 and 3.

351. Assagioli, "Talks on the Self".

352. Assagioli, *The Act of Will*, vi.

353. "Scientific descriptions, explanations, and laws cannot claim any 'objectivity' in the ordinary sense; they are nothing but schemes and concepts of our mind, the value of which consists in being good 'working hypotheses', comfortable 'shortcuts', possibilities of 'economy of thought', useful artifices to be able to clarify the differences between phenomena. Psychologists are therefore deluded into believing that they are either 'explaining' or even describing subconscious phenomena in a more exact and objective way . . . Instead, the question must be raised: which group of concepts best responds to the purposes mentioned." (Assagioli, "The Subconscious")

354. Assagioli, *Psychosynthesis: A Manual of Principles and Techniques*, 16.

355. Assagioli, *Psychosynthesis: A Manual of Principles and Techniques*, 30.

356. Assagioli, *Psychosynthesis: A Manual of Principles and Techniques*, 65.

Bibliography

Note: Assagioli articles marked * can be accessed at
https://kennethsorensen.dk/en/
(with thanks to Kenneth Sørensen).

Assagioli, Roberto. "The Subconscious", from The Assagioli Archives Florence, 1911.*

Assagioli, Roberto. "Creative Expression in Education: Its Purpose, Process, Techniques, and Results." Psychosynthesis Research Foundation, 1963.*

Assagioli, Roberto. *Psychosynthesis: A Manual of Principles and Techniques*. Psychosynthesis Research Foundation, 1965, 1995 edition.

Assagioli, Roberto. "Bio-Psychosynthesis", Doc.#23617, Assagioli Archives Florence, 1966.*

Assagioli, Roberto. "Relationships Between the Various Foundations, Institutions, and Centers" (also known as "Letter of Freedom"), originally sent, in 1967, to the presidents, members of the boards of directors, and other officials of the foundations, institutes, and centres of psychosynthesis. First published in *Psychosynthesis Digest* Vol. I, No. 1, 1981, reprinted in Psychosynthesis International Directory, 1988.*

Assagioli, Roberto. "Jung and Psychosynthesis." Psychosynthesis Research Foundation. Issue No.19, 1967b. *

Assagioli, Roberto. "Symbols of Transpersonal Experiences." Psychosynthesis Research Foundation, Reprint No. 11, 1969. *

Assagioli, Roberto. "The Balancing and Synthesis of Opposites." Psychosynthesis Research Foundation, Issue No. 29, 1972a.*

Assagioli, Roberto. "Psychosynthesis: Its Essential Components." Assagioli Archives Doc. #24288, 1972b.*

Assagioli, Roberto. *The Act of Will: A Guide to Self-actualization and Self-realization.* Turnstone Press, 1974a, 2002 edition.

Assagioli, Roberto. "Training: A statement by Roberto Assagioli." Instituto di Psicosintesi, 1974b.*

Assagioli, Roberto. "The Golden Mean of Roberto Assagioli." Interview by Sam Keen, *Psychology Today*, 1974c.

Assagioli, Roberto. *Transpersonal Development: The Dimension Beyond Psychosynthesis*, Inner Way Productions, 2007.

Assagioli, Roberto. "Talks on the Self." Handout from The Psychosynthesis and Education Trust, London, undated 1.*

Assagioli, Roberto. "The Superconscious and the Self." Handout from The Psychosynthesis and Education Trust, London. Written by Jim Vargiu, based on interview with Assagioli, undated 2.*

Assagioli, Roberto. "Psychosynthesis in Education." Psychosynthesis Research Foundation, Reprint No.2. Undated 3.*

Bosnak, Robert. *Embodiment: Creative Imagination in Medicine, Art and Travel.* Routledge, 2007.

Cheetham, Tom. *Imaginal Love: The Meanings of Imagination in Henry Corbin and James Hillman*. Spring Publications, 2020.

Evans, Roger. *Mirages of the Mind: Yearbook Vol. III*, Institute of Psychosynthesis, 1983.

Fee, Angie. *"Through, With, and In."* Psychosynthesis Trust, 2022, accessed 18 January 2023
https://psychosynthesistrust.org.uk/through-with-and-in/k/en/

Ferrer, Jorge N. *Revisioning Transpersonal Theory: A Participatory Vision of Human Spirituality*. State University of New York Press, 2001.

Ferrucci, Piero. *What We May Be: Techniques for Psychological and Spiritual Growth Through Psychosynthesis*. Tarcher/Putnam, 1982.

Ferrucci, Piero. "On the Threshold of Mystery." Psychosynthesis Trust, 2018, accessed 2 November 2022
https://psychosynthesistrust.org.uk/on-the-threshold-of-mystery/

Firman, John. *"I" and Self: Re-visioning Psychosynthesis. Psychosynthesis Palo Alto*, 1991.

Firman, John, and Ann Gila. *The Primal Wound: A Transpersonal View of Trauma, Addiction, and Growth*. State University of New York Press, 1997.

Firman, John, and Ann Gila. *Psychosynthesis: A Psychology of the Spirit*. State University of New York Press, 2002.

Firman, John and Ann Gila. "Assagioli's Seven Core Concepts for Psychosynthesis Training." Psychosynthesis Palo Alto, 2007
https://www.synthesiscenter.org/PDF/Seven%20Concepts.pdf

Frank, Arthur W. *Letting Stories Breathe: A Socio-Narratology*. The University of Chicago Press, 2010.

Frater, Allan, *Waking Dreams: Imagination in Psychotherapy and Everyday Life*. Transpersonal Press, 2021.

Guggisberg Nocelli, Petra. *The Way of Psychosynthesis: A Complete Guide to Origins, Concepts, and the Fundamental Experiences, with a Biography of Roberto Assagioli.* Synthesis Insights, Kindle edition, 2019.

Guggisberg Nocelli, Petra. *Know, Love, Transform Yourself: Theory, Techniques, and New Developments in Psychosynthesis, Vol 1*, Psychosynthesis Books, Kindle edition, 2021.

Hackwood, Keith. "Beyond the Wall of Silence." Psychosynthesis Trust, 2015, accessed 5 May 2023
https://psychosynthesistrust.org.uk/beyond-wall-silence-psychosynthesis-inside/

Hardy, Jean. *A Psychology with a Soul: Psychosynthesis in Evolutionary Context.* Woodgrange Press, 1996.

Hillman, James, and Michael Ventura. *We've Had a Hundred Years of Psychotherapy and the World's Getting Worse*. Harper Collins, 1991.

Hillman, James. *Re-Visioning Psychology*. Harper Perennial, 1992.

Hill, Richard, and Matthew Dahlitz. *The Practitioner's Guide to the Science of Psychotherapy*. W.W. Norton & Company, 2022.

Holloway, Susan. *Hidden Wonders of the Human Heart.* Matador, 2021.

Horowitz, Mark. *The Dance of We: The Mindful Use of Love and Power in Human Systems*. Synthesis Center Press, Kindle edition, 2016.

Jung, Carl. *The First Complete English Edition of the Works of C.G.Jung*. Routledge, 2023.

Kalsched, Donald. *The Inner World of Trauma: Archetypal Defences of the Personal Spirit*. Routledge, 1996.

Levine, Stephen K. *Poiesis: The Language of Psychology and the Speech of the Soul.* Jessica Kingsley Publishers, 1997.

Marks-Tarlow, Terry. *Psyche's Veil: Psychotherapy, Fractals, and Complexity*. Routledge, 2008.

Midgley, Mary. *The Myths We Live By*, Routledge, 2003.

Millichamp, Stacey. *Transpersonal Dynamics: The Relational Field, Depth Work and the Unconscious.* Transpersonal Press, 2018.

Mindell, Arnold. *The Quantum Mind and Healing: How to Listen and Respond to Your Body's Symptoms*, Hampton Roads Publishing Company, Inc., 2004.

Parfitt, Will. *The Elements of Psychosynthesis*. PS Avalon, Kindle edition, 1994.

Romanyshyn, Robert. *Psychological Life: From Science to Metaphor*. University of Texas Press, 1982.

Schuller, Michael. *Psychosynthesis in North America: The Story of the Movement, the People, and the Issues*. Self-published (based on his 1988 doctoral dissertation,"Perspectives on the Development of Psychosynthesis in North America"), 1996.

Shorrock, Andrew. *The Transpersonal in Psychology, Psychotherapy, and Counselling,* Palgrave Macmillan, 2008.

Simpson, Steve, Joan Evans, and Roger Evans (ed). *Essays on the Theory and Practice of a Psychospiritual Psychology: Volume 1*, The Institute of Psychosynthesis, 2013.

Somers, Margaret. "Narrativity, Narrative Identity, and Social Action: Rethinking the English Working-Class Formation." *Social Science History 16, No. 4*, 1992.

Sørensen, Kenneth. *The Soul of Psychosynthesis: The Seven Core Concepts.* Kentaur Forlag, Kindle edition, 2016.

Temple, David J. *First Principles and First Values: Forty-Two Propositions on CosmoErotic Humanism, the Meta-Crisis, and the World to Come*. World Philosophy & Religion Press, 2024.

Totton, Nick. *Wild Therapy: Rewilding Our Inner and Outer Worlds*. PCCS Books, 2021.

Yeomans, Thomas. *Readings in Psychosynthesis: Theory, Process & Practice, Volume 2*. Edited by Weiser and Yeomans. The Department of Applied Psychology/The Ontario Institute for Studies in Education, 1988.

Young Brown, Molly. "Ecopsychosynthesis: Meeting the Crisis of Our Times." Lead article in the 1999 edition of *Conversations in Psychosynthesis*, the journal of the Association for the Advancement of Psychosynthesis (AAP). Accessed 15 April 2023, https://mollyyoungbrown.com/ecopsychosynthesis/

Young Brown, Molly. "Psychosynthesis: A Systems Psychology?" 2003. Accessed 3 March 2024 https://mollyyoungbrown.com/essays-books-on-psychosynthesis-and-ecopsychology/essays/psychosynthesis-systems/

Young Brown, Molly. *Unfolding Self: The Practice of Psychosynthesis*. Allworth Press, 2004.

Young Brown, Molly. *Growing Whole: Self-realization for the Great Turning*, Psychosynthesis Press, 2009.

Vargiu, James (editor). *Synthesis ¾: The Realization of the Self*. Synthesis Press, 1977.

Wallis, James. *The Art of Thought*. Solis Press, 2014.

Watkins, Mary. *Invisible Guests: The Development of Imaginal Dialogues*. Spring Publications, 2000.

Whitmore, Diana. *Psychosynthesis Counselling in Action*. Sage Publications Ltd, 2000.

Acknowledgements

There are many to whom I owe a debt of gratitude for their inspiration and support during the writing of this book. In particular, the teachers and students of the Psychosynthesis Trust, who provided me with a context to discuss and clarify my understanding and practice, with a special mention for Diana Whitmore, who generously supported my early psychosynthesis teaching career, without which this book would probably never have come about.

Many thanks need to go to my team of intrepid readers, especially Guy Fearon and Sonja Rose, for their belief in the book at its early stages and the many helpful comments they gave to help move it along to fruition.

The team at Transpersonal Press also need a special mention: Stacey Millichamp, for championing the development of transpersonal psychotherapy and giving me the opportunity to write a second book; Thierry Bogliolo, for his straightforward guidance and endless patience; and Nicky Leach, for her perceptive and astute edits.

Thanks also to the Rijksmuseum in Amsterdam for granting permission to use the wonderful painting *Portrait of a Young Woman* by Madeleine Françoise Basseporte in my beautiful cover design.

I would also like to thank my wife, Bethany, for helping me through the tricky stages of the writing process (brilliantly saying one day, "You are more than your book!").

And last but not least, thank you, dear reader, for bringing the book to life with your time, energy, and imagination, which means a lot to me.

About the Author

Allan Frater grew up on the edge of a small village near Edinburgh, reading comics and walking his dog Jet in the surrounding countryside. He survived an engineering degree and a very short career as a maths teacher by watching movies and reading novels. Inspired by Jack Kerouac and Herman Hesse, he spent his twenties living and working in Buddhist communities where he came across the east-meets-west fusion of transpersonal psychology and eventually trained to become a psychotherapist. His psychotherapy practice and teaching career at the Psychosynthesis Trust have allowed him to research an image-based approach to therapy, which also featured in his first book *Waking Dreams: Imagination in Psychotherapy & Everyday Life* (2021, Transpersonal Press). Now living in North London, married and middle-aged, he feels fortunate to have kept touch with his original sources of inspiration, continuing to read lots of fiction (including comics!) and spend time outdoors walking his three-legged dog Milly. Further info: www.wildimagination.uk

Index

I

J

L

M

N

O

P

R

U

V

W

Y

By the same author

Sometimes experienced spontaneously — when an awareness of a physical reality (i.e. being in bed) coincides with that of an imagined reality (i.e. being in a dreamscape) — waking dream practice (also known as 'active imagination' and 'guided imagery') stretches out these spontaneous moments, allowing for a sustained exploration.

This book develops new possibilities within waking-dream practice to show:

✓ how the in-between waking/dreaming experience allows us to become aware of not just what we imagine but also the process of how we imagine - a process that reveals the principles and skills of image-based transformation and healing.

✓ how a broad understanding of imagination — as present in all perceptions, actions and relationships (not just 'mental pictures') — allows for an image-based approach to psychotherapy and everyday life as an ongoing 'eyes-wide-open' waking dream.

The result is an experiential and theoretical re-appraisal of imagination - drawing upon fresh perspectives from ecopsychology, transpersonal psychology, complexity theory and fractal geometry — as a creative ability at the heart of human potential.

isbn 978-1-912-618-08-0 (print) / 978-1-912618-09-7 (ebook)

TransPersonal Press

Quoted in this work

Transpersonal Dynamics offers approaches to the therapeutic encounter from the leading edge of quantum physics field theory and integrative psychology.

Transpersonal Dynamics is the culmination of over 20 years of feedback about 'what works', gathered through delivering integrative and transpersonal training to counsellors, coaches, psychologists and psychotherapists who work with organisations, adults, couples, families, young people and children.

Using down-to-earth language in a practical way, this book addresses some of the gritty aspects of the therapeutic relationship, with the aim to inspire and support practitioners to take more risks to bring a collaborative, relational quality to their work.

Stacey Millichamp is a trainer on the Masters Degree in Psychotherapy and the Diploma in Integrative and Transpersonal Clinical Supervision at the Psychosynthesis Trust *in London, and teaches on the Diploma in Supervision with Soul at the* Re-Vision Centre for Integrative Psychosynthesis *in London. She is the Director of* Entrust Associates, *which provides counselling to staff and students of secondary and primary schools in London.*

isbn 978-1-912-618-00-4 (print) / 978-1-912618-00-1 (ebook)

TransPersonal
Press

Also available

To celebrate its 30 years of pioneering work in the fields of counselling and psychotherapy training, the Re-Vision Centre for Transpersonal & Integrative Therapy has brought together a selection of writing by practitioners and teachers who have worked at the heart of the organization.

The chapters address a social and cultural crisis which, at this point in the history of our planet, needs new ways of looking at therapy and how it relates to the world beyond the consulting room. Just as 'the personal is political' was a way of seeing individual issues within the context of a wider political field, so we now need to see that the soul is a different kind of agency from that of the ego – one that is both internal and external, individual and cultural. The world may have lost connection with soul in its obsession with merchandise and control, but soul has not lost connection with us. These chapters offer an integrative perspective that both gives a place to the troubles of the modern world and also develops a well-tuned craft to firstly attend to our painful wounds and ultimately transform their bitterness into the salt of wisdom.

This book is a compelling work for psychotherapists, counsellors, trainees, and anyone interested in how psychotherapy influences and is influenced by the state of the planet, by imagination and by the reality of how politics impact on our daily lives.

isbn 978-1-912-618-02-8 (print) / 978-1-912618-03-5 (ebook)

TransPersonal
Press

Also available

Are you looking to make real and lasting change in your life? *Building Intuitive Consciousness* offers a reliable and effective method to support such change by guiding readers on an inner pilgrimage to awaken to their Intuitive Consciousness.

It has been said that no problem can be solved from the same level of consciousness that created it. We believe that by awakening to the Intuitive Consciousness within ourselves, we are able to transcend old patterns and habitual behaviours that may be limiting us in some way from being able to take our next steps forward.

Using the wisdom of ancient spiritual practice and modern psychology, *Building Intuitive Consciousness* is both a practical and mystical manual to guide you on this journey. By delving deep into our psychology and expanding up into the heights of our numinous or spiritual potential, this unsentimental book offers a roadmap to access our true inner wisdom, free from the restraints and distortions of our ego.

Packed with immediately applicable insights and accessible exercises, this second edition now includes notes that are relevant for professionals, making it the perfect manual for psychologists, therapists, managers or anyone on a journey of self-discovery.

isbn 978-1-912-618-04-2 (print) / 978-1-912618-05-9 (ebook)

TransPersonal
Press

Also available

Eastern Spirituality and Western Psychology offers a practical path to harmony between spirituality and Western psychology, between heart and mind.

This book:

- challenges basic assumptions of Western psychology
- demystifies Vedic psychology
- presents how Eastern spirituality can enhance Western psychology

It guides readers by clarifying the relationship between spirituality and psychological growth, and demonstrates that psychotherapy and spirituality are complementary aspects of human development, with both essential for optimum mental, existential, and spiritual growth. It is up to everyone to take responsibility for making the changes that enable us to contribute to the well-being of the whole.

In this insightful book, the authors reflect on this revolution and consider how it is likely to evolve in the future. It paves the way for those interested in the transpersonal, whether psychologists, psychotherapists, Orientalists, or spiritual practitioners.

isbn 978-1-912-618-06-6 (print) / 978-1-912618-07-3 (ebook)

TransPersonal Press

Also available

Active Mind/Receptive Mind: The Journey of Mindfulness is designed to provide readers with a comprehensive introduction to mindfulness and its relationship to constructive action. It also provides readers with a systematic comparison between Eastern and Western models of mindfulness and in-depth instructions for "holding" and transcending negative psychological states.

The book serves as a resource for academics, psychotherapists, and for those who would like to explore the benefits of mindful self-exploration.

Dr. Monopoli, a licensed psychologist for 33 years, treats individuals using a combination of Mindfulness psychotherapy, meditation, hypnotherapy and Cognitive-Behavioral Therapy. He believes that a clear, focused, relaxed and lucid mind is the best instrument for self-discovery, the resolution of personal difficulties, and the identification of a personal life path. He enjoys working with a wide range of individuals, especially young adults and those seeking answers in their spiritual and philosophical paths. His areas of expertise include the treatment of depression, anxiety, stress and a range of life issues using meditative techniques and guided self-analysis.

isbn 978-1-912-618-02-8 (print) / 978-1-912618-03-5 (ebook)

TransPersonal
Press

Also available

The consciousness sutras are a compilation of principles, describing conscious experience and inner evolution. They are intended as experiential guidelines for psychologists, transformational counselors, life coaches, and anyone on a transformational journey.

These principles clarify and describe the structure and the layers of conscious experience, and their dynamics during inner evolution, while providing various first-person methodologies for their exploration. The text includes multidimensional perspectives and highly experiential descriptions from a first-person perspective; due to this complexity, some phrases may require more than one reading.

You could take short pauses while reading, to reflect on how collective mechanisms generate your personal conscious experience. If some ideas don't make sense at first, please continue reading, and allow your mind to slowly form the puzzle, until a coherent big picture emerges. Some pieces of the puzzle will reveal themselves later, after you understand why all the pieces are related to one another, and how they work together to create the conscious experience.

Please consider this compilation of ideas to be my subjective perspective on how inner evolution could unfold. Good journeys!

isbn 978-1-912-618-10-3 (print) / 978-1-912618-11-0 (ebook)

TransPersonal Press

www.ingramcontent.com/pod-product-compliance
Lightning Source LLC
LaVergne TN
LVHW022156200926
848481LV00006B/1769
* 9 7 8 1 9 1 2 6 9 8 1 4 1 *